The Sacred Hoop

The Sacred Hoop

Recovering the Feminine
in American Indian
Traditions

With a new Preface

Paula Gunn Allen

Beacon Press • Boston

Beacon Press
25 Beacon Street
Boston, Massachusetts 02108-2892

Beacon Press books
are published under the auspices of
the Unitarian Universalist Association of Congregations.

99 98 97 96 95 94   8 7 6 5 4

Poem appearing on page xi reprinted by permission of Luci Tapahonso.

Library of Congress Cataloging-in-Publication Data

Allen, Paula Gunn.
    The sacred hoop: recovering the feminine in American Indian
traditions: with a new preface / Paula Gunn Allen
        p.   cm.
    Originally published: 1986.
    Includes bibliographical references and index.
    ISBN 0-8070-4617-5
    1. Indians of North America—Women. 2. American literature—
Indian authors—History and criticism. 3. American literature—
Women authors—History and criticism. I. Title.
E98.W8A44   1992
970.004'970082—dc20   92-6332
                                                         CIP

For Native people everywhere:
may our voices be strong,
our hearts red and sweet.
May we walk in Beauty. Ahô.

—Shimana
(Paula Gunn Allen)

Contents

Contents

Preface to the 1992 Edition

I completed the work of compiling and revising the essays included in *The Sacred Hoop* in early 1984, though it was not published until early 1986. In the few years since its publication my life has seen a number of changes. I lost a grandmother and a grandchild, the one to death, the other to her mother who took her away. I moved from the Department of Ethnic Studies at the University of California, Berkeley, to the Department of English at the University of California, Los Angeles. And this past year I spent helping my mother bear the ravages of cancer. In the end, just this past month, I helped her die. We sang her over to the other side, and I miss her terribly. I am glad that she lived to see my work, because it helped her, as it has helped many native women, to affirm her identity and her heritage and to make peace with the tortures of an Indian woman's life in the first three quarters of the twentieth century.

The Sacred Hoop includes discussions about writers, histories, events, and spiritual recoveries based on information available to me over the years preceding 1982, by which time most of the essays had been completed. In the decade since, many new voices, directions, and signal events have occurred in Indian Country; as we enter the year that marks five centuries of European-Native contact, the recovery of American Indian culture and tradition proceeds ever more rapidly.

Our cultural restoration includes political issues such as self-determination for tribal communities, federal recognition of tribes considered "extinct" by the United States, identification of numerous clusters of Indian peoples who before remained "hidden" throughout the United States, increased funding for realization of tribal sovereignty, and the reburial of human remains carted away to storage in countless bins in museums and universities. Our recovery also looks to economic issues, such as adequate, Indian-oriented health care, fair employment practices, educational parity, and economic development for rural and urban Indian communities. It encompasses the widespread return of Indian people from every tribe to traditional practices and celebrations, the continuing and increasing publication of literary works by American Indian authors, and exhibitions of American Indian arts—both contemporary and traditional—in Indian-owned and -operated museums and galleries as well as in wealthier venues recognized by peoples around the world. These occurrences, along with a growing number of films, plays, dance performances, and scholarship devoted to themes of American Indian life and thought, constitute a mighty cultural flowering, a truly Native American Renaissance.

Surely this is the time referred to in ancient prophecy: the time when the clans come in and the blue star Kachina dances in the village square, when the Grandmother goddesses return and Native Americans lead the world into a new age of peace, balance, harmony, and respect for all that is. In the last census the numbers of Indian people reported almost doubled. This surge is partly attributable to better canvassing, organized and carried out by native community leaders in urban Indian enclaves under the direction of the U.S. Census Bureau. But even more, the increase can be credited to a new willingness of lost Indians to identify themselves. It seems that the restoration of Indian dignity, culture, and tradition has encouraged these dramatic events. Some respondents to a *New York Times* query said that Kevin Costner's film *Dances with Wolves* provided them with the sense of pride and safety they needed to publicly affirm their Indianness. In West Virginia a movement led by local native women seeks to identify native people who fled white persecution under the vicious Removal Act and settled in the north in the early nineteenth century. In the Virginia and West Virginia hills, these refugees survived by passing as white or black. The activists intend to petition for federal recognition of a northern band of Eastern Cherokee based on a count and history of these hidden Indians.

Our impressive recovery notwithstanding, as the Americas mark the five hundredth anniversary of the landing of Columbus, a variety of educational institutions and art and media groups are involved in "rethinking" the Columbian revolution, exploring the event as a not unmixed blessing. To many, portrayal of Indian people as victims, pure and simple, is the most compelling part of the contact story. There is a widespread belief that we, Native American and nonnative alike, have nothing to celebrate. All too many believe we should give forth with great trills of mourning. But it is of utmost importance to our continuing recovery that we recognize our astonishing survival against all odds; that we congratulate ourselves and are congratulated by our fellow Americans for our amazing ability to endure, recover, restore our ancient values and life ways, and then blossom. Indeed, there are many among us who realize the necessity of celebration of native life this year especially. I heard the Navajo poet Luci Tapahonso read the following during the 1991 Modern Language Association's annual convention:

> I am, I am
> In wisdom I walk
> In beauty may I walk . . .
> In beauty it is restored.
> The light, the dawn.
> It is morning.

As she read, my heart was lifted in recognition of our power, our magnificent life. I am Laguna, woman of the lake, daughter of the dawn, sunrise, *kurena*. I can see the light making the world anew. It is the nature of my blood and heritage to do this. There is surely cause to weep, to grieve; but greater than ugliness, the endurance of tribal beauty is our reason to sing, to greet the coming day and the restored life and hope it brings.

A week or so after the Modern Language Association convention, I saw a CNN report about a powwow in Florida, "the largest gathering of Indians" in recent times, which was attended by Indian people from all over the United States and Canada. The powwow footage was accompanied by a story about bingo parlors on Indian lands and the attempts of various states to block sovereign rights, economic prosperity, and the retribalization that accompanies these events. I was warmed to see familiar faces on the screen: boys and men in traditional dress playing the drum, dancing. The sound of their voices, and of the bells with which they adorned their knees and ankles, are the sounds of home. A woman dressed in traditional southeastern garb steadily demonstrated the making of an Indian pot. She seemed a bit wary of the camera's beady eye, but went on with her pottery-shaping, almost undisturbed.

I attend powwows frequently these days. Like so much of Indian life they have changed dramatically over the years. The costumes are ever more elaborate, the dancers reaching back into tribal histories to develop headdresses, bustles, kilts, dresses, shawls, and accessories that harken back to traditional times. Even at home in New Mexico, the dancers now dress as they did long ago; the women no longer wear "mother hubbard" dresses beneath their traditional black mantas that leave one arm and shoulder bare. They dance barefoot rather than moccasined or in long cotton stockings and tennis shoes. Cheering signs of new life characterize contemporary dances, especially the swelling numbers of participants: drummers and dancers, families happily socializing with neighbors and strangers as they eat fry bread and Indian tacos and drink gallons of soda and Coke. This joyful increase has been spurred by a new willingness among a number of tribes to accept the participation of mixed bloods, heretofore mostly prohibited from on-reservation dancing at the Pueblo.

At urban powwows I have seen two particularly moving events in the past two years. The first was a dance sponsored by Vietnam veterans who, in recovery from alcoholism and drug addiction, became active participants in a Lakota alcohol and substance abuse program called The Good Red Road. The warmth and quiet joy with which their dance and honoring was greeted was deeply moving. We were all very proud of their strength and beauty. The other special event I have enjoyed was an honoring dance for a young man who was about to depart for the Persian Gulf. Among those who received gifts from the youth's family were some mothers of soldiers, who received lovely shawls. At that same powwow I learned that over 12,500 native people were serving in the Gulf. I had long known that more Indians per capita served in World War II than any other group, and I know that thousands served in Korea and Vietnam, though the statues at the Vietnam Veterans Memorial in Washington ignore that fact.

At one powwow I attended, the huge one held in Albuquerque every spring, a Cree man selling some lovely articles from his home reserve showed my mother and me a straw-plaited doll and described her part in an ancient dance ceremony. He reported that the dance underscored and reminded the people of the centrality of women to the tribe. Speaking engagements and seminars have also provided me with accounts of the importance of women in native life across the continent. Often the evidence is offered by Indian men from different tribes and different regions. While their reports might be contemporary or historical, they reinforce the central thesis of *The Sacred Hoop*. It seems that gynocracy is a well-advanced social system among all the tribes, and while it falls ever more into disrepute and ignominy as progressive modernism makes its ugly inroads into native life, it simultaneously takes on new life, appearing in new guise and revealing its uncommon tenacity. Wilma Mankiller, principal chief of the Cherokee, is a case in point, one—albeit the best known—of many. The appearance of this decade's wealth of literature, art, and scholarship by Native American women is another welcome sign of our coming spring.

A further development in Indian country that raises my heart from the ground is the recent concerted effort of Indian judges, lawyers, and social workers to address honestly the issues of child welfare. The Indian Child Welfare Act provides for approval of adopting parents of native children by that child's tribe of origin. This legislation aims to prevent unnecessary diminishment of Indian populations and to help adopted youngsters—who will always remain something of outsiders to white culture as long as they look, think, or act like Indians—to find a place where they will be secure and recognized as part of a group much like themselves. In those cases that have come to public attention, the courts, the adopting parents, and the tribe have usually agreed on a course that will bring the child into frequent contact with on-reservation relatives, even when the adopting family has been non-Indian or from a different tribal community.

The other serious child welfare issue that many Indian community leaders and those in helping professions are determined to address is child abuse. Once a people who would never countenance terrorization, abuse, or neglect of the helpless, many native families have borrowed one of the most horrifying aspects of Anglo-European culture, the abuse of children. Partly as a consequence of enforced poverty and despair, partly because millions of Indian people were educated in boarding schools—run by churches and the U.S. government under the auspices of the Bureau of Indian Affairs—wherein serious sexual and other kinds of physical abuse, neglect, terrorization, starvation, and humiliation were the order of the day, men and women of this century have treated their children as they themselves were treated. The horror has continued into the present, often spanning several generations, causing intense personal suffering and deepening the devastation of tribal life. But we are taking charge of this greatest shame, as the people return to the older ways of gentleness, honor, respect, dignity, and the primary importance of relationship.

What is happening in Indian country as we begin our new life, which dates from late summer 1987 when the Grandmothers returned, is more than recovery, more than restoration; it is nothing less than the affirmation of tribal values, tribal thought, and tribal understandings. Everywhere voices are being raised on behalf of peace, freedom, and dignity; the increasing respect for the rights of our nonhuman relatives, plants and animals alike; the new dedication to restoring the entire planet; and the new findings of the advanced sciences, which resemble more and more the old understandings of the nature of life and the universe; all these bear witness to something sacred happening. Worldwide interest in and attention to the wisdom of the "First Peoples" grows apace, while the walls of tyranny come down and the Goddess of Democracy rules briefly in Tiananmen Square. In a North American harbor, the Lady of Liberty is restored to her pristine condition, and reports of sightings of the Virgin, her Son, Spirits, and Extraterrestrials fill news reports and convention halls.

Something sacred indeed is going on. And may it continue to grow, this new dawn. May the Grandmothers of the Light bring us dawn. May we welcome and aid them in the growing light.

Seal Beach, California
January 1992

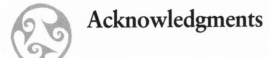 # Acknowledgments

A volume of this sort, compiled from years of study, observation, learning, writing, talking, and thinking, owes much to many.

First honoring must go to my mother, 'Tu'u-we'tsa, whose interest and support of my writings and wanderings have been essential. Her Dial-A-Dictionary service to me has been invaluable, and her willingness to play host to the colleagues I've brought to visit over the years has been unfailing. As my chief archivist—who unlike myself doesn't lose things I've written—her significance in this undertaking has been incalculable. Her life, her cast of mind, and her ways have provided me with the insights and experience of strong women, Indian women, on which these essays are based.

To my father, cowboy, merchant, trader, steadfast friend and benefactor, and Lebanese storyteller supreme, who has spent hours teaching me how to string magic, memory, and observation into tales of life, honoring also goes.

Among the many women whose conversation, support, encouragement, editorial assistance, shared ideas, and willingness to publish, read, respond to, and promote the work that appears in this volume, to share our discoveries, uncoveries, recoveries, the hair-raising adventures of childrearing, career building, and super-

Acknowledgments

womanhood, I want particularly to thank my sister in blood and enterprise Carol Lee Sanchez; my friend Patricia Clark Smith, who as staunch and erudite dissertation chair is responsible for long conversations, editing, and the encouragement that led me to write my first three essays in American Indian studies; Marta Fields, who shared the perils and entertainment of Ph.D. studies; my most gifted and dear student-friend-duenna, Mary TallMountain; the wild and woolly Italian–New Mexican publisher Patricia D'Andrea, whose support, intelligence, and home provided me with a sense of orderliness when such was sorely needed; Elaine Jahner, whose remarkable courage and brilliance often keep me going when I really wanted to quit; LaVonne Ruoff, role model and friend whose ability to function intelligently and professionally in the midst of total chaos and whose mad humor stays intact throughout, is ever comforting and awe inspiring; Dexter Fisher, who insisted I be the project director for the Modern Language Association's Summer Seminar on Native American Literature, thus making it possible for me to meet women and men who have been my friends and comrades in the Great Native American Word Wars ever since and who published my work in *The Third Woman;* Elly Bulkin and Joan Larkin, for careful editing and caring publication of "Beloved Women: The Lesbian in American Indian Cultures." I owe a debt to these women, and to others, such as Henrietta Whiteman, Linda Hogan, Joy Harjo, Wendy Rose, Blanche Cook, Adrienne Rich, Michelle Cliff, Audre Lorde, Marcia Herndon, Melanie Kaye Kantrowitz, Alice Molloy and Carol Wilson, and Kai Hennig and Maureen Farrell. Their personal, public, professional, and spiritual support has made a deep impact on my work and on my life. Each of these women has shared with me her courage, beauty, and delight, and for these and their other, more tangible contributions to this work, I am profoundly grateful.

I also want to honor the midwives at Beacon Press who have given generously of their time, knowledge, and vision and without whom this book would not have entered the world: Marie Cantlon who took the manuscript under her wing, Nancy Lattanzio who watched over it for the entire period of its gestation somewhere in the shadowy womb of the Press, and Joanne Wyckoff who with dispatch and energy is seeing *The Sacred Hoop* into public life.

Honor goes also to those men without whom I would not have begun to study, teach, and write in Native American studies or having started would have had less reason to continue: my younger brother and psychic twin, Lee Francis, for caring, steadfastness, and more help

xvi

than I can ever repay; for my first teaching job in Native American studies I want to thank Dick Wilson. Thanks also to David Remley for my first publication in the field, my first paper at a professional conference, and my early poetry publications; the late John Rouillard, whom I sorely miss, for hiring me to teach and for supporting me in my many endeavors; Kenneth Lincoln, for aid and support in securing my fellowship at UCLA, for recommending me to teach a course while there, for publishing my poetry and my essays, and for being my friend. Thanks also to Geary Hobsen, Joel Jones, Maurice Kenny, Brian Swann, Terry Wilson, Gerald Vizenor, James Welch, James Hirabayashi, Joseph Bruchac, Karl Kroeber, and Robert Stepto, to name only a few of those who have directly or through indirect good offices provided me generously with their faith and time as well as their more tangible financial, intellectual, professional, and personal resources and who have opened their classrooms, positions, information networks, bibliographies, and hearts to me.

I wish also to thank the Regents of the University of California for the generous grant that funded the research and early drafts of three of the essays in this book: "Answering the Deer," "Where I Come from Is Like This," and "When Women Throw Down Bundles."

Most of all, I want to give thanks to the Spirit people who have guided me and taught me all along the way, and the Grandmother Gods, in whose heart-minds are held all things. May they hold this writing in their web, and may it thus go into the world in balance.

The Sacred
Hoop

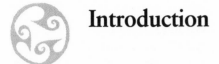 **Introduction**

When I was small, my mother often told me that animals, insects, and plants are to be treated with the kind of respect one customarily accords to high-status adults. "Life is a circle, and everything has its place in it," she would say. That's how I met the sacred hoop, which has been an integral part of my life, though I didn't know to call it that until the early 1970s when I read John G. Neihardt's rendering of the life story of Oglala Lakota Holy Man Black Elk in *Black Elk Speaks*.

I didn't start out to be a Native American scholar. I did my undergraduate work mostly in English, focusing on creative writing where I could, and went on to get a Master of Fine Arts in creative writing. But on my return to Albuquerque from California in late 1970, my friend Dick Wilson asked me to teach in the newly formed Native American Studies Program at the University of New Mexico. My decision to accept his offer signaled a major shift in my focus, one that returned me to my mother's side, to the sacred hoop of my grandmothers' ways.

In the fifteen or so years since I made the shift to American Indian Studies, I've gotten a Ph.D. in the field, taught a number of courses, including literature, history, women's studies, traditional sciences, spirituality, and philosophy, edited a volume of curriculum and criticism for studying and teaching American Indian literature, and published a novel and several books of poetry. During these years I also wrote the essays that appear in this volume.

Over the years I have located the following major themes or issues that pertain to American Indians and that characterize the essays in this volume.

1. Indians and spirits are always found together.

2. Indians endure—both in the sense of living through something so complete in its destructiveness that the mere presence of survivors is a testament to the human will to survive and in the sense of duration or longevity. Tribal systems have been operating in the "new world" for several hundred thousand years. It is unlikely that a few hundred years of colonization will see their undoing.

3. Traditional tribal lifestyles are more often gynocratic than not, and they are never patriarchal. These features make understanding tribal cultures essential to all responsible activists who seek life-affirming social change that can result in a real decrease in human and planetary destruction and in a real increase in quality of life for all inhabitants of planet earth.

American Indians are not merely doomed victims of western imperialism or progress; they are also the carriers of the dream that most activist movements in the Americas claim to be seeking. The major difference between most activist movements and tribal societies is that for millennia American Indians have based their social systems, however diverse, on ritual, spirit-centered, woman-focused worldviews.

Some distinguishing features of a woman-centered social system include free and easy sexuality and wide latitude in personal style. This latitude means that a diversity of people, including gay males and lesbians, are not denied and are in fact likely to be accorded honor. Also likely to be prominent in such systems are nurturing, pacifist, and passive males (as defined by western minds) and self-defining, assertive, decisive women. In many tribes, the nurturing male constitutes the ideal adult model for boys while the decisive, self-directing female is the ideal model to which girls aspire.

The organization of individuals into a wide-ranging field of allowable styles creates the greatest possible social stability because it includes and encourages variety of personal expression for the good of the group.

In tribal gynocratic systems a multitude of personality and character types can function positively within the social order because the systems are focused on social responsibility rather than on privilege and on the realities of the human constitution rather than on denial-based social fictions to which human beings are compelled to conform by powerful individuals within the society.

Tribal gynocracies prominently feature even distribution of goods among all members of the society on the grounds that First Mother enjoined cooperation and sharing on all her children.

One of the major distinguishing characteristics of gynocratic cultures is the absence of punitiveness as a means of social control. Another is the inevitable presence of meaningful concourse with supernatural beings.

Among gynocratic or gynocentric tribal peoples the welfare of the young is paramount, the complementary nature of all life forms is stressed, and the centrality of powerful women to social well-being is unquestioned.

4. The physical and cultural genocide of American Indian tribes is and was mostly about patriarchal fear of gynocracy. The Puritans particularly, but also the Catholic, Quaker, and other Christian missionaries, like their secular counterparts, could not tolerate peoples who allowed women to occupy prominent positions and decision-making capacity at every level of society. Wives telling husbands and brothers whether to buy or sell an item, daughters telling fathers whom they could and could not murder, empresses attending parleys with colonizers and being treated with deference by male leaders did not sit well with the invaders.

The colonizers saw (and rightly) that as long as women held unquestioned power of such magnitude, attempts at total conquest of the continents were bound to fail. In the centuries since the first attempts at colonization in the early 1500s, the invaders have exerted every effort to remove Indian women from every position of authority, to obliterate all records pertaining to gynocratic social systems, and to ensure that no American and few American Indians would remember that gynocracy was the primary social order of Indian America prior to 1800.

But colonial attempts at cultural gynocide notwithstanding, there were and are gynocracies—that is, woman-centered tribal societies in which matrilocality, matrifocality, matrilinearity, maternal control of household goods and resources, and female deities of the magnitude of the Christian God were and are present and active features of traditional tribal life.

5. There is such a thing as American Indian literature, and it can be divided into several interlocking categories. The major divisions are traditional literature and genre literature of the present. Traditional literature can be further divided into ceremonial and popular varieties—that is, into canonical works and those that derive from the canon but that are widely told and appeal to audiences gathered on social occasions. Contemporary works, or genre literature, can be divided into the classic western categories of poetry, short fiction, the novel, and drama, with the addition of autobiography, as-told-to narrative, and mixed genre works. Structural and thematic elements from the oral tradition, usually from the writer's own tribe, always show up in contemporary works by American Indians, and elements from contemporary, non-Indian works sometimes show up in contemporaneous tribal social literature.

Native American literature should be important to Americans not as a curio, an artifact of the American past that has little pertinence to an American present or future, but rather as a major tradition that informs American writers ranging from Cotton Mather and Nathaniel Hawthorne through Walt Whitman, William Carlos Williams, and William Faulkner to Adrienne Rich, Toni Cade Bambara, and Judy Grahn.

The whole body of American Indian literature, from its traditional, ceremonial aspects to its formal literary aspects, forms a field, or, we might say, a hoop dance, and as such is a dynamic, vital whole whose different expressions refer to a tradition that is unified and coherent on its own terms. It is a literary tradition that is breathtaking in its aesthetic realization and fundamental to coherent understanding of non-Indian varieties of American literature.

6. Western studies of American Indian tribal systems are erroneous at base because they view tribalism from the cultural bias of patriarchy and thus either discount, degrade, or conceal gynocratic features or recontextualize those features so that they will appear patriarchal.

Americans divide Indians into two categories: the noble savage and the howling savage. The noble savage is seen as the appealing but doomed victim of the inevitable evolution of humanity from primitive to postindustrial social orders. The American belief in progress and evolution makes this a particularly difficult idea to dislodge, even though it is a root cause of the genocide practiced against American Indians since the colonial period. This attitude, which I characterize as the Progressive Fallacy, allows American Indians victim status only. And while its adherents suffer some anguish when encountering the brutal facts of exterminationist policies, they inevitably shrug resignedly and say—quite directly—that Indians have to assimilate or perish. So while the Progressives allow the noble savage to be the guardian of the wilds and on occasion the conscience of ecological responsibility, the end result of their view for Indians is the same as its counterpart view of American Indians as howling denizens of a terrifying wilderness.

The view of Indians as hostile savages who capture white ladies and torture them, obstruct the westward movement of peaceable white settlers, and engage in bloodthirsty uprisings in which they glory in the massacre of innocent colonists and pioneers is dear to the hearts of producers of bad films and even worse television. However, it is this view that is most deeply embedded in the American unconscious, where it forms the basis for much of the social oppression of other people of color and of women.

In contemporary times those who view Indians as hostile savages paint modern Indian people as worthless, alcoholic, and lazy, unwilling to join in the general progressiveness and prosperity that is the final index of the righteousness of the American dream. Allied with the view of the Indian as hostile savage is the common practice (I should say obsession) of proving that Indians mistreat their women brutally, at every level and in every way—the implication being that civilized people revere women, and savages, who don't revere them, deserve extermination. This unstated but compelling rationale for genocide is at the bottom of the academic, political, and popular attempts to paint Native American cultures as patriarchal when they are not.

7. The sacred, ritual ways of the American Indian peoples are similar in many respects to other sacred cultures on the planet, such as the Tibetan and trans-Caucasus cultures (including those of the Mediterranean and their descendents in the western lands of Brittany, Normandy, England, Wales, Ireland, and Scotland). Tribal societies of Native America incorporate many of the same features characteristic of tribal people in Southeast Asia, Melanesia, Micronesia, Polynesia, and Africa. That is, we share in a worldwide culture that predates western systems derived from the "civilization" model, and, as such,

5

Indians are only some of the tribespeople compelled to suffer the outrages of patriarchal industrial conquest and genocide.

The wide diversity of tribal systems on the North American continent notwithstanding—and they are as diverse as Paris and Peking on the Asian continent (yes, they're both on the Asian continent despite the European delusion that Europe occupies a separate landmass), tribal world-views are more similar to one another than any of them are to the patriarchal world-view, and they have a better record of survival.

The methods used in American Indian Studies are various because it is an interdisciplinary field. So while I employ variously the methodologies of anthropology, literary studies, folklore, psychology, sociology, historiography, philosophy, culture studies, and women's studies in these essays, my method of choice is my own understanding of American Indian life and thought. For although I am a somewhat nontraditional Indian, I grew up in the homes of Indians and have spent my adult life in the company of traditionals, urbanites, and all the shades of Indian in between.

Because I am thus personally involved in my discipline, because I study and write out of a Laguna Indian woman's perspective, these essays present a picture of American Indian life and literature unfiltered through the minds of western patriarchal colonizers. The essays in this volume are framed by neither the anthropological nor the missionary mind, and they do not particularly reflect a white mind-set. As a consequence, much of what they contain might feel strange to readers who are well versed in books about Indians, even to those who have had occasion to visit Indian country. In a way, I *am* "Kochinnenako in Academe," and my essays are subject to the same vicissitudes of interpretation as are her stories when they appear in a western context. However, I know from experience that the American Indian way of being is both highly idiosyncratic and deeply persistent, so I trust that the fact that you can take the Indian out of Indian country but you can't take the Indian out of the Indian will inform these essays and their reading as it informs contemporary American Indian life.

Whatever I read about Indians I check out with my inner self. Most of what I have read—and some things I have said based on that reading—is upside-down and backward. But my inner self, the self who knows what is true of American Indians because it *is* one, always warns me when something deceptive is going on. And with that warning, I am moved to do a great deal of reflecting, some more reading, and a lot of questioning and observing of real live human beings who are Indian in order to discover the source of my unease. Sometimes that confirmation comes about in miraculous ways; that's when I know guidance from the nonphysicals and the supernaturals, and that the Grandmothers have taken pity on me in my dilemma.

So you see, my method is somewhat western and somewhat Indian. I draw from each, and in the end I often wind up with a reasonably accurate picture of truth. And in that context I would caution readers and students of American Indian life and culture to remember that Indian America does not in any sense function in the same ways or from the same assumptions that western systems do. Unless and until that fact is clearly acknowledged, it is virtually impossible to make much sense out of the voluminous materials available concerning American Indians.

I am fortunate in that I have had excellent training for the work I do, training I received primarily at home, but also gained in a more formal sense. I am especially fortunate because the wind and the sky, the trees and the rocks, and the sticks and the stars are usually in a teaching mood; so when I need an answer to some dilemma, I can generally get one. For which I must say thank you to them all.

The Ways of
Our Grandmothers

In the beginning was thought, and her name was Woman. The Mother, the Grandmother, recognized from earliest times into the present among those peoples of the Americas who kept to the eldest traditions, is celebrated in social structures, architecture, law, custom, and the oral tradition. To her we owe our lives, and from her comes our ability to endure, regardless of the concerted assaults on our, on Her, being, for the past five hundred years of colonization. She is the Old Woman who tends the fires of life. She is the Old Woman Spider who weaves us together in a fabric of interconnection. She is the Eldest God, the one who Remembers and Re-members; and though the history of the past five hundred years has taught us bitterness and helpless rage, we endure into the present, alive, certain of our significance, certain of her centrality, her identity as the Sacred Hoop of Be-ing.

The essays in this section chronicle Her presence among us in our rituals and traditions (they are usually one and the same thing), in the history of the gynocidal assaults we have endured, and in our present American and Indian lives. The first essay, "Grandmother of the Sun," is concerned with female gods in Native American traditions. While it is not exhaustive in scope, based as it is on the Keres Pueblos of the American Southwest, who are among the last surviving Mother-Right peoples on the planet, it conveys a clear sense of what gynocratic culture is about.

The second essay, "When Women Throw Down Bundles," chronicles some of the history of American Indian women in North America since white contact, a period that extends from 1492 in the Caribbean to the late eighteenth or early nineteenth century for some tribes. That history is seldom mentioned in popular or scholarly books but is essential to an accurate understanding both of American Indian life and history and of American patriarchy in the past few hundred years. Modern feminists sometimes theorize about the shift from matriarchies to patriarchy in the Old World, but a more complete and accurate retelling of history and of the contemporary manifestations of that shift among American Indian peoples would make such theorizing unnecessary. This essay is one of a few that concerns itself with the subject. I trust that it will soon be one of a multitude.

The last essay in this section, "Where I Come from Is Like This," is a personal chronicle of an Indian woman's life during and after colonization. It is about me and mine. About our resistance, and our survival, and our meaning to each other and to ourselves. It is a testimony, a pictograph, of a contemporary woman's life which says that while we change as Indian women, as Indian women we endure.

Grandmother of the Sun:
Ritual Gynocracy in
Native America

I

There is a spirit that pervades everything, that is capable of
powerful song and radiant movement, and that moves in and out of the
mind. The colors of this spirit are multitudinous, a glowing, pulsing
rainbow. Old Spider Woman is one name for this quintessential spirit,
and Serpent Woman is another. Corn Woman is one aspect of her, and
Earth Woman is another, and what they together have made is called
Creation, Earth, creatures, plants, and light.

At the center of all is Woman, and no thing is sacred (cooked, ripe,
as the Keres Indians of Laguna Pueblo say it) without her blessing, her
thinking.

> . . . In the beginning Tse che nako, Thought Woman finished
> everything, thoughts, and the names of all things. She finished also
> all the languages. And then our mothers, Uretsete and Naotsete
> said they would make names and they would make thoughts. Thus
> they said. Thus they did.[1]

This spirit, this power of intelligence, has many names and many
emblems. She appears on the plains, in the forests, in the great canyons,
on the mesas, beneath the seas. To her we owe our very breath, and to

her our prayers are sent blown on pollen, on corn meal, planted into the earth on feather-sticks, spit onto the water, burned and sent to her on the wind. Her variety and multiplicity testify to her complexity: she is the true creatrix for she is thought itself, from which all else is born. She is the necessary precondition for material creation, and she, like all of her creation, is fundamentally female—potential and primary.

She is also the spirit that informs right balance, right harmony, and these in turn order all relationships in conformity with her law.

To assign to this great being the position of "fertility goddess" is exceedingly demeaning: it trivializes the tribes and it trivializes the power of woman. Woman bears, that is true. She also destroys. That is true. She also wars and hexes and mends and breaks. She creates the power of the seeds, and she plants them. As Anthony Purley, a Laguna writer, has translated a Keres ceremonial prayer, "She is mother of us all, after Her, mother earth follows, in fertility, in holding, and taking again us back to her breast."[2]

The Hopi account of their genatrix, Hard Beings Woman, gives the most articulate rendering of the difference between simple fertility cultism and the creative prowess of the Creatrix. Hard Beings Woman (Huruing Wuhti) is of the earth. But she lives in the worlds above where she "owns" (empowers) the moon and stars. Hard Beings Woman has solidity and hardness as her major aspects. She, like Thought Woman, does not give birth to creation or to human beings but breathes life into male and female effigies that become the parents of the Hopi—in this way she "creates" them. The male is Muingwu, the god of crops, and his sister-consort is Sand Altar Woman who is also known as Child-birth Water Woman. In Sand Altar Woman the mystical relationship between water, worship, and woman is established; she is also said to be the mother of the katsinas, those powerful messengers who relate the spirit world to the world of humankind and vice versa.[3]

Like Thought Woman, Hard Beings Woman lived in the beginning on an island which was the only land there was. In this regard she resembles a number of Spirit Woman Beings; the Spirit genatrix of the Iroquois, Sky Woman, also lived on an island in the void which only later became the earth. On this island, Hard Beings Woman is identified with or, as they say, "owns" all hard substances—moon, stars, beads, coral, shell, and so forth. She is a sea goddess as well, the single inhabitant of the earth, that island that floats alone in the waters of space. From this meeting of woman and water, earth and her creatures were born.[4]

The waters of space are also crucial in the Sky Woman story of the Seneca. Sky Woman is catapulted into the void by her angry, jealous, and fearful husband, who tricks her into peering into the abyss he has revealed by uprooting the tree of light (which embodies the power of woman) that grows near his lodge. Her terrible fall is broken by the Water Fowl who live in that watery void, and they safely deposit Sky Woman on the back of Grandmother Turtle, who also inhabits the void. On the body of Grandmother Turtle earth-island is formed.[5] Interestingly, the shell of the turtle is one of the Hard Substances connected to Hard Beings Woman.[6]

Contemporary Indian tales suggest that the creatures are born from the mating of sky father and earth mother, but that seems to be a recent interpolation of the original sacred texts. The revision may have occurred since the Christianizing influence on even the arcane traditions, or it may have predated Christianity. But the older, more secret texts suggest that it is a revision. It may be that the revision appears only in popular versions of the old mythic cycles on which ceremony and ritual are based; this would accord with the penchant in the old oral tradition for shaping tales to reflect present social realities, making the rearing and education of children possible even within the divergent worlds of the United States of America and the tribes.

According to the older texts (which are sacred, that is, power-engendering), Thought Woman is not a passive personage: her potentiality is dynamic and unimaginably powerful. She brought corn and agriculture, potting, weaving, social systems, religion, ceremony, ritual, building, memory, intuition, and their expressions in language, creativity, dance, human-to-animal relations, and she gave these offerings power and authority and blessed the people with the ability to provide for themselves and their progeny.

Thought Woman is not limited to a female role in the total theology of the Keres people. Since she is the supreme Spirit, she is both Mother and Father to all people and to all creatures. She is the only creator of thought, and thought precedes creation.[7]

Central to Keres theology is the basic idea of the Creatrix as She Who Thinks rather than She Who Bears, of woman as creation thinker and female thought as origin of material and nonmaterial reality. In this epistemology, the perception of female power as confined to maternity is a limit on the power inherent in femininity. But "she is the supreme Spirit, . . . both Mother and Father to all people and to all creatures."[8]

In the nineteenth century, Fr. Noël Dumarest reported from another Keres Pueblo, Cochiti, on Spider Woman (Thought Woman, although he does not mention her by this name). In his account, when the "Indian sister" made stars, she could not get them to shine, so "she consulted Spider, the creator." He characterized the goddess-sisteಃs as living "with Spider Woman, their mother, at *shipapu*, under the waters of the lake, in the second world." It should be mentioned that while she is here characterized as the sisters' mother, the Cochiti, like the other Keres, are not so much referring to biological birth as to sacred or ritual birth. To address a person as "mother" is to pay the highest ritual respect.[9]

In Keres theology the creation does not take place through copulation. In the beginning existed Thought Woman and her dormant sisters, and Thought Woman thinks creation and sings her two sisters into life. After they are vital she instructs them to sing over the items in their baskets (medicine bundles) in such a way that those items will have life. After that crucial task is accomplished, the creatures thus vitalized take on the power to regenerate themselves—that is, they can reproduce others of their kind. But they are not in and of themselves self-sufficient; they depend for their being on the medicine power of the three great Witch creatrixes, Thought Woman, Uretsete, and Naotsete. The sisters are not related by virtue of having parents in common; that is, they are not alive because anyone bore them. Thought Woman turns up, so to speak, first as Creatrix and then as a personage who is acting out someone else's "dream." But there is no time when she did not exist. She has two bundles in her power, and these bundles contain Uretsete and Naotsete, who are not viewed as her daughters but as her sisters, her coequals who possess the medicine power to vitalize the creatures that will inhabit the earth. They also have the power to create the firmament, the skies, the galaxies, and the seas, which they do through the use of ritual magic.

The idea that Woman is possessed of great medicine power is elaborated in the Lakota myth of White Buffalo Woman. She brought the Sacred Pipe to the Lakota, and it is through the agency of this pipe that the ceremonies and rituals of the Lakota are empowered.[10] Without the pipe, no ritual magic can occur. According to one story about White Buffalo Woman, she lives in a cave where she presides over the Four Winds.[11] In Lakota ceremonies, the four wind directions are always acknowledged, usually by offering a pipe to them. The pipe is ceremonial, modeled after the Sacred Pipe given the people by the

Sacred Woman. The Four Winds are very powerful beings themselves, but they can function only at the bidding of White Buffalo Woman. The Lakota are connected to her still, partly because some still keep to the ways she taught them and partly because her pipe still resides with them.

The pipe of the Sacred Woman is analogous in function to the ear of corn left with the people by Iyatiku, Corn Woman, the mother goddess of the Keres. Iyatiku, who is called the mother of the people, is in a ceremonial sense another aspect of Thought Woman. She presently resides in Shipap from whence she sends counsel to the people and greets them when they enter the spirit world of the dead. Her representative, Irriaku (Corn Mother), maintains the connection between individuals in the tribe as well as the connection between the nonhuman supernaturals and the tribe. It is through the agency of the Irriaku that the religious leaders of the tribe, called Yaya and Hotchin, or hochin in some spellings of the word, (Mother and leader or chief), are empowered to govern.

The Irriaku, like the Sacred Pipe, is the heart of the people as it is the heart of Iyatiku. In the form of the perfect ear of corn, Naiya Iyatiku (Mother, Chief) is present at every ceremony. Without the presence of her power, no ceremony can produce the power it is designed to create or release.[12] These uses of the feminine testify that primary power—the power to make and to relate—belongs to the preponderantly feminine powers of the universe.

According to one story my great-grandmother told me, in time immemorial when the people lived in the White Village or Kush Katret, Iyatiku lived with them. There came a drought, and since many normal activities had to be suspended and since the people were hungry and worried because of the scarcity of food from the drought, Iyatiku gave them a gambling game to while away the time. It was meant to distract them from their troubles. But the men became obsessed and began to gamble everything away. When the women scolded them and demanded that they stop gambling and act responsibly toward their families, the men got mad and went into the kivas.

Now, since the kivas were the men's space, the women didn't go there except for ritual reasons. The men continued to gamble, neglecting their ritual duties and losing all their possessions of value. Because they didn't do the dances or make the offerings as they were supposed to, the drought continued and serious famine ensued. Finally one old man who was also a priest, or cheani, became very concerned. He sought the advice of a shaman nearby, but it was too late. Iyatiku had left Kush Katret in anger at her foolish people. She went back to Shipap where she lives now and keeps an eye on the people. The people were forced to abandon the village, which was inundated by floods brought on by the angry lake spirits. So the beautiful village was destroyed and the people were forced to build a new one elsewhere and to live without the Mother of Corn. But she left with them her power, Irriaku, and told them that it was her heart she left in their keeping. She charged them always to share the fruits of her body with one another, for they were all related, and she told them that they must ever remain at peace in their hearts and their relationships.

The rains come only to peaceful people, or so the Keres say. As a result of this belief, the Keres abhor violence or hostility. They are very careful to contain their emotions and to put a smooth face on things, for rain is essential to the very life of their villages. Without it the crops can't grow, the livestock will starve, there will be no water for drinking or bathing—in short, all life, physical and ceremonial, will come to a halt. For ceremonies depend on corn and corn pollen and birds and water; without these they are not likely to be efficacious, if they can be held at all.

II

There is an old tradition among numerous tribes of a two-sided, complementary social structure. In the American Southeast this tradition was worked out in terms of the red chief and the white chief, positions held by women and by men and corresponding to internal affairs and external affairs. They were both spiritual and ritualistic, but the white chief or internal chief functioned in harmony-effective ways. This chief maintained peace and harmony among the people of the band, village, or tribe and administered domestic affairs. The red chief, also known as the war chief, presided over relations with other tribes and officiated over events that took people away from the village. Among the Pueblo of the American Southwest are two notable traditional offices: that of the cacique (a Spanish term for the Tiamuni Hotchin or traditional leader), who was charged with maintaining internal harmony, and that of the hotchin or "war captain," whose office was concerned with mediating between the tribe and outsiders, implementing foreign policy, and, if necessary, calling for defensive or retaliatory forays. This hotchin, whose title is usually translated "country chief" or "outside chief," was first authorized by Iyatiku when she still lived among the people.[13] At that time there was no "inside" chief other than the Mother herself and the clan mothers whom she instructed in the proper ritual ways as each clan came into being. Since Iyatiku was in residence, an inside chief or cacique was unnecessary. The present-day caciques continue even now to act as her representatives and gain their power directly from her.[14]

Thus the Pueblos are organized—as are most gynocratic tribes—into a moiety system (as anthropologists dub it) that reflects their understanding of ritual empowerment as dialogic. This dyadic structure, which emphasizes complementarity rather than opposition, is analogous to the external fire/internal fire relationship of sun and earth. That is, the core/womb of the earth is inward fire as the heart of heaven, the sun, is external fire. The Cherokee and their northern cousins the Iroquois acknowledge the femaleness of both fires: the sun is female to them both, as is the earth. Among the Keres, Shipap, which is in the earth, is white, as was the isolated house Iyatiku dwelt in before she left the mortal plane entirely for Shipap. The color of Shipap is white. The Hopi see Spider Woman as Grandmother of the sun and as the great Medicine Power who sang the people into this fourth world we live in now.

The understanding of universal functioning as relationship between the inner and the outer is reflected in the social systems of those tribal groups that are based on clan systems. It is reflected in ritual systems, as seen in the widespread incidence of legends about the Little War Twins among the Pueblos or the Sacred Twins among other tribes and Nations. The Sacred Twins embody the power of dual creative forces. The potency of their relationship is as strong as that of the negative and positive charges on magnetic fields. It is on their complementariness and their relationship that both destructive and creative ritual power rests.

Among the western Keres, the war captains are the analogues of the Little War Twins, Ma'sewe and O'yo'yo'we. Their prototype appears to be those puzzling twin sisters of the Keres pantheon, Uretsete and Naotsete, who were sung into life by Thought Woman before the creation of the world. These sisters appear and reappear in Pueblo stories in various guises and various names. One of them, Uretsete, becomes male at some point in the creation story of the Keres. Transformation of this kind is common in American Indian lore, and the transformation processes embedded in the tales about the spirit beings and their alternative aspects point to the regenerative powers embodied in their diversity.[15]

When the whites came, the tribes who were organized matrifocally resorted to their accustomed modes of dealing with outsiders; they relied on the red chief (or whatever that personage might be called) and on their tribal groups whose responsibility was external affairs. The Iroquois of the northern regions, the Five "Civilized" Tribes of the southern regions, and the Pueblo of the American Southwest—all among those earliest contacted by Anglo-European invaders—had some dual structure enabling them to maintain internal harmony while engaging in hostilities with invading or adversary groups. The Aztecs also had such complementary deities: the internal or domestic god was a goddess, Cihuacoatl, Coatlique, or some similar supernatural woman-being; their external god was Quetzalcoatl, the winged serpent, who was a god of amalgamation or expansion.[16]

Indian stories indicate that a dialogic construct based on complementary powers (an interpretation of polarity that focuses on the ritual uses of magnetism) was current among the Pueblos, particularly the Keres. To the Keres Naotsete was the figure associated with internal affairs, and Uretsete was concerned with maintaining tribal psychic and political boundaries.[17]

Essentially, the Keres story goes something like this (allowing for variations created by the informant, the collector-translator, or differences in clan-based variations): Naotsete and Uretsete were sung into life by Ts'its'tsi'nako Thought Woman. They carried bundles from which all the creatures came. The goddess Uretsete gave birth to twin boys, and one of these boys was raised by the other sister, who later married him. Of this union the Pueblo race was born. Some tales (probably of fairly recent origin) make Uretsete the alien sister and Naotsete the Indian sister. Other stories, as noted earlier, make Uretsete male at some undetermined point (but "he" always starts as female). The Indian sister Uretsete is later known as Iyatiku, or Ic'city, and is seen as essentially the same as her. But it is reasonable to conjecture that Uretsete is the prototype for the hotchin, while the cacique (town chief) is derived from the figure of Naotsete. Certainly the office of hotchin is authorized by Iyatiku, who counsels the Tiamuni hotchin, Chief Remembering Prayer Sticks, to keep the people ever in peace and harmony and to remember that they are all her children and thus are all entitled to the harvest of her body/thought.[18] She in turn is empowered by Thought Woman, who sits on her shoulder and advises her.

While the tribal heads are known as cacique and hotchin—or town chief and country chief, respectively—the Keres do not like fighting. War is so distasteful to them that they long ago devised ritual institutions to deal with antagonism between persons and groups such as medicine societies. They also developed rituals that would purify those who had participated in warfare. If a person had actually killed someone, the ritual purification was doubly imperative, for without it a sickness would come among the people and would infect the land and the animals and prevent the rainfall. The Warrior Priest was and is responsible for seeing to the orderly running of Pueblo life, and to some extent he mediates between strangers and the people. In this sense he functions as the outside chief. The inside chief maintains an internal conscious awareness of Shipap and the Mother, and he advises, counsels, and exhorts the people to the ways of peace.

Traditional war was not practiced as a matter of conquest or opposition to enemies in the same way it has been practiced by western peoples; it is not a matter of battling enemies into a defeat in which they surrender and come to terms dictated by the conqueror. Warfare among most traditional American Indian tribes who practiced it (went on the war path) was a ritual, an exercise in the practice of shamanism, and it is still practiced that way by the few "longhairs" left. Its outcome was the seizure of a certain sacred power, and that outcome could be as the result of defeat as well as of victory. The point was to gain the attention of supernatural powers, who would then be prevailed upon to give certain powers to the hero.

The Navajo have a ceremonial and an accompanying myth that commemorate the gain of such a gift as the result of a battle with some Pueblos. The hero in that tale is a woman who journeys to the spirit world with Snake Man, where she is initiated by Snake Man's mother. After she has passed the tests provided for her learning, she is given particular rites to take back to her people. Along with this ceremonial, which is called Beautyway, is a companion ceremonial, Mountainway. Its hero is a woman who accompanies Bear Man into the spirit world and is also taught and tested. Like the Beautyway hero, she returns with a chantway or healing ceremony to give her people. In a more contemporary version of these tales, the battle is World War II, and an even later tale might be about Vietnam. The exact war is not important. What is important is that from warfare comes certain powers that benefit the people and that are gained by a hero who encounters and transcends mortal danger.

So the hotchin is a medium for the regulation of external ritual events, and the cacique is the medium through whom Iyatiku guides, guards, and empowers her people and keeps them whole. Each is responsible for maintaining the harmonious working of the energies on which the entire existence of the people depends, and they are necessarily men who must be careful how they use the energies at their disposal.

III

As the power of woman is the center of the universe and is both heart (womb) and thought (creativity), the power of the Keres people is the corn that holds the thought of the All Power (deity) and connects the people to that power through the heart of Earth Woman, Iyatiku. She is the breath of life to the Keres because for them corn holds the essence of earth and conveys the power of earth to the people. Corn connects us to the heart of power, and that heart is Iyatiku, who under the guidance of Thought Woman directs the people in their affairs.

It is likely that the power embodied in the Irriaku (Corn Mother) is the power of dream, for dream connections play an important part in the ritual of life of the Pueblos as of other tribes of the Americas. As the frightening katsina, K'oo'ko, can haunt the dreams of uncleansed warriors and thus endanger everything, the power that moves between the material and nonmaterial worlds often does so in dreams. The place when certain dreams or ceremonies occur is said to be in "time immemorial." And the point where the two meet is Shipap, where Earth Woman lives. Corn, like many of its power counterparts is responsible for maintaining linkage between the worlds, and Corn Mother, Irriaku, is the most powerful element in that link. John Gunn describes the Irriaku as "an ear of corn perfect in every grain, the plume is a feather from every known bird."[19]

This representative of Iyatiku is an individual's link and the ceremonial link to medicine power. Of similar power is the Sacred Pipe that White Buffalo Woman brought to the Lakota. This pipe is called wakan, which means "sacred" or possessing power.

The concept of power among tribal people is related to their understanding of the relationships that occur between the human and nonhuman worlds. They believe that all are linked within one vast, living sphere, that the linkage is not material but spiritual, and that its essence is the power that enables magical things to happen. Among these magical things are transformation of objects from one form to another, the movement of objects from one place to another by tele-portation, the curing of the sick (and conversely creating sickness in people, animals, or plants), communication with animals, plants, and nonphysical beings (spirits, katsinas, goddesses, and gods), the com-pelling of the will of another, and the stealing or storing of souls. Mythical accounts from a number of sources illustrate the variety of forms the uses of ritual power can take.

According to the Abanaki, First Woman, who came to live with a spirit being named Kloskurbeh and his disciple, offered to share her strength and comfort with them. Her offer was accepted and she and the disciple of Kloskurbeh had many children. All was well until a famine came. Then the children were starving and First Woman was very sad. She went to her husband and asked him to kill her so she could be happy again. When he agreed, she instructed him to let two men lay hold of her corpse after she was dead and drag her body through a nearby field until all the flesh was worn away. Then, she said, they should bury her bones in the middle of the field and leave the field alone for seven months. After that time, they should return to the field and gather the food they would find there and eat all of it except for a portion that they should plant. The bones, she said, would not be edible; they should burn them, and the smoke would bring peace to them and their descendants.

As the tale is recorded in one source, the narrator continues.

Now have the first words of the first mother come to pass, for she said she was born of the leaf of the beautiful plant and that her power should be felt over the whole world, and that all should love her. And now that she is gone into this substance, take care that this, the second seed of the first mother, be always with you, for it is her flesh. Her bones also have been given for your good; burn them, and the smoke will bring freshness to the mind, and since these things came from the goodness of a woman's heart, see that you hold her always in memory; remember her when you eat, remem-ber her when the smoke of her bones rises before you. And because you are all [related], divide among you her flesh and her bones—let all shares be alike—for so will the love of the first mother have been fulfilled.[20]

Worth noting in this passage are the ideas of kinship that requires peacefulness and cooperation among people and of the centrality of the woman's power, which is her gift to the disciple. Because she is sacred, her flesh and bones are capable of generating life; because she is embued with power, she can share it with human beings. When she came among them the first time, First Woman told Kloskurbeh and his disciple that she was "born of the beautiful plant of the earth; for the dew fell on the leaf, and the sun warmed the dew, and the warmth was life," and she was that life.[21]

Another important point is that the love of the first mother carries several significances. The love of a mother is not, as is presently supposed, a reference to a sentimental attachment. Rather, it is a way of saying that a mother is bonded to her offspring through her womb. *Heart* often means "womb," except when it means "vulva." In its aspect of vulva, it signifies sexual connection or bonding. But this cannot be understood to mean sex as sex; rather, sexual connection with woman means connection with the womb, which is the container of power that women carry within their bodies. So when the teacher Kloskurbeh says that "these things come from the goodness of a woman's heart,"[22] he is saying that the seeds of her power are good— that is, they are alive, bearing, nourishing, and cooperative with the well-being of the people.

The tobacco that she leaves to them is connected also with her power, for it is the "beautiful plant" that was her own mother, and its property is clear thought. She was born of clear (harmonious) thought (for beauty and harmony are synonymous among Indians) that was empowered by water (dew) and heat (sun). (Dew is a reference to vaginal secretions during tumescence.) Tobacco smoke is connected to water, for it imitates clouds in appearance and behavior. It is used to evoke spirits as well as a sense of well-being and clearheadedness and is often a feature of religious ceremonies. That First Woman is connected to water is made clear in another passage of the same account: First Woman (who had referred to both Kloskurbeh the teacher and his nephew the disciple as "my children") had said that she was born of the beautiful plant. The famine had made her very sad, and every day she left home and was gone for long periods. One day the disciple followed her and saw her wade into the river, singing. "And as long as her feet were in the water, she seemed glad, and the man saw something that trailed behind her right foot, like a long green blade."[23]

Among medicine people it is well known that immersing oneself in water will enable one to ward off dissolution. Bodies of apprentices, sorcerers, and witches are subject to changes, including transformation from corporeal to spirit. Immersion also helps one resist the pull of supernatural forces unleashed by another sorcerer, though this does not seem to be what occurs in this story. But the connection of First Woman with water is clear: in the water she is happy, centered, powerful, for she is deeply connected to water, as is implied by her birth story. If she was born of the beautiful plant, then she is in some basic sense a vegetation spirit who has taken a human body (or something like it) to further the story of creation. Her "sacrifice" is the culmination of her earthly sojourn: by transferring the power she possesses to the corn and tobacco (her flesh and her bones), she makes certain that the life forms she has vitalized will remain vital. Thus, one aspect of her power is embodied in the children, while another aspect is embodied in the corn and tobacco. In their mutuality of energy transfer, all will live.

In Zia Pueblo version of the Supernatural Woman, Anazia Pueblo, Utset wanted to make certain that the people would have food when they came up from the lower world (previous world and underworld). As their mother (chief), Utset was responsible for their well-being, so she made fields north, west, south, and east of the village and planted in it bits of her heart (power). She made words over the seeds she had planted: "This corn is my heart and it shall be to my people as milk from my breasts."[24] In a Cherokee version of how food was given to the people to guarantee their provision and their connection to the goddess, Selu (Corn Woman) similarly made the first food from her own body-seed, as does Grandmother Spider in a Kiowa version.

According to Goetz and Morley's rendering of the *Popul Vuh*, the sacred myth of the Quiché Mayans, the heart is related to the power of creation. In the beginning the makers (grandparents) were in the water (void) hidden under green and blue feathers. They were by nature great thinkers or sages. "In this manner the sky existed and also the Heart of Heaven, which is the name of God (the All Power)."[25] The grandparents, called feathered beings (Gucumatz), meditated, and it became clear that creation of the earth that human beings inhabit was imminent. "Thus it was arranged in the darkness and in the night by the Heart of Heaven who is called Huracán."[26] The Gucumatz or Bird Grandparents were so called because the flashes of light around their thinking-place resembled the bright wings of the bird now known as quetzal but known to the ancient Mayans as gucumatz. In their appearance they resemble the Irriaku, and in their characterization as Water Winged Beings they resemble the Water Fowl who saved the Iroquois Sky Woman from her fall through the void (designated as water in some versions of that myth). They also resemble representations of Iyatiku as a bird being, as she appears on a Fire Society altar. In a drawing an informant made of her, Iyatiku appears as a bird woman, with the body of a bird and the head of a woman. Her body is spotted yellow "to represent the earth," and centered on her breast is "a red, arrow-shaped heart" which "is the center of herself and the world. Around her is a blue circle to represent the sky, while an inner arc represents the milky way; above it are symbols for sun, moon and the stars."[27]

One of the interesting features of this depiction of Earth Woman is her resemblance of Tinotzin, the goddess who appeared to the Indian Juan Diego in 1659 and who is known as Our Lady of Guadalupe today. The Virgin Morena (the dark virgin), as she is also called, wears a salmon-colored gown that is spotted yellow to represent the stars. She wears a cloak of blue, and her image is surrounded by fiery tongues—lightning or flames, presumably.

Certainly the Keres Fire Society's goddess was made to represent, that is, to produce, medicine power, and the arrow-shaped heart she exhibited spoke to the relationship between the ideas of "heart" and "strength," or power.

A Mayan prayer connected with Huracán, or the Heart of Heaven, that refers to her as "grandmother of the sun, grandmother of the light":

> Look at us, hear us! . . . Heart of Heaven, Heart of Earth! Give us our descendants, our succession, as long as the sun shall move . . . Let it dawn, let the day come! . . . May the people have peace . . . may they be happy . . . give us good life . . . grandmother of the sun, grandmother of the light, let there be dawn . . . let the light come![28]

Certainly, there is reason to believe that many American Indian tribes thought that the primary potency in the universe was female, and that understanding authorizes all tribal activities, religious or social. That power inevitably carries with it the requirement that the people live in cooperative harmony with each other and with the beings and powers that surround them. For without peacefulness and harmony, which are the powers of a woman's heart, the power of the light and of the corn, of generativity and of ritual magic, cannot function. Thus, when Corn Woman, Iyatiku, was about to leave the people and return to Shipap, she told the cacique how to guide and counsel the people:

I will soon leave you. I will return to the home whence I came. You will be to my people as myself; you will pass with them over the straight road; I will remain in my house below and will hear all that you say to me. I give you all my wisdom, my thoughts, my heart, and all. I fill your head with my mind.[29]

The goddess Ixchel whose shrine was in the Yucatán on Cozumel Island, twenty miles offshore, was goddess of the moon, water childbirth, weaving, and love. The combination of attributes signifies the importance of childbirth, and women go to Ixchel's shrine to gain or increase their share of these powers as well as to reinforce their sense of them.

Ixchel possesses the power of fruitfulness, a power associated with both water and weaving and concerned with bringing to life or vitalization. Also connected with Ixchel is the power to end life or to take life away, an aspect of female ritual power that is not as often discussed as birth and nurturing powers are.[30] These twin powers of primacy, life and death, are aspects of Ixchel as moon-woman in which she waxes and wanes, sometimes visible and sometimes invisible. Similarly, her power to weave includes the power to unravel, so the weaver, like the moon, signifies the power of patterning and its converse, the power of disruption. It is no small matter to worship the goddess Ixchel, as it is no small matter to venerate Iyatiku, Thought Woman, or White Buffalo Woman. Their connection with death and with life makes them the preponderant powers of the universe, and this connection is made through the agency of water.

Pre-Conquest American Indian women valued their role as vitalizers. Through their own bodies they could bring vital beings into the world—a miraculous power whose potency does not diminish with industrial sophistication or time. They were mothers, and that word did not imply slaves, drudges, drones who are required to live only for others rather than for themselves as it does so tragically for many modern women. The ancient ones were empowered by their certain knowledge that the power to make life is the source of all power and that no other power can gainsay it. Nor is that power simply of biology, as modernists tendentiously believe. When Thought Woman brought to life the twin sisters, she did not give birth to them in the biological sense. She sang over the medicine bundles that contained their potentials. With her singing and shaking she infused them with vitality. She gathered the power that she controlled and focused it on those bundles, and thus they were "born." Similarly, when the sister goddesses Naotsete and Uretsete wished to bring forth some plant or creature they reached into the basket (bundle) that Thought Woman had given them, took out the effigy of the creature, and thought it into life. Usually they then instructed it in its proper role. They also meted out consequences to creatures (this included plants, spirits, and katsinas) who disobeyed them.

The water of life, menstrual or postpartum blood, was held sacred. Sacred often means taboo; that is, what is empowered in a ritual sense is not to be touched or approached by any who are weaker than the power itself, lest they suffer negative consequences from contact. The blood of woman was in and of itself infused with the power of Supreme Mind, and so women were held in awe and respect. The term *sacred*, which is connected with power, is similar in meaning to the term *sacrifice*, which means "to make sacred." What is made sacred is empowered. Thus, in the old way, sacrificing meant empowering, which is exactly what it still means to American Indians who adhere to traditional practice. Blood was and is used in sacrifice because it possesses the power to make something else powerful or, conversely, to weaken or kill it.

Pre-contact American Indian women valued their role as vitalizers because they understood that bearing, like bleeding, was a transformative ritual act. Through their own bodies they could bring vital beings into the world—a miraculous power unrivaled by mere shamanic displays. They were mothers, and that word implied the highest degree of status in ritual cultures. The status of mother was so high, in fact, that in some cultures Mother or its analogue, Matron, was the highest office to which a man or woman could aspire.

The old ones were empowered by their certain knowledge that the power to make life is the source and model for all ritual magic and that no other power can gainsay it. Nor is that power really biological at base; it is the power of ritual magic, the power of Thought, of Mind, that gives rise to biological organisms as it gives rise to social organizations, material culture, and transformations of all kinds—including hunting, war, healing, spirit communication, rain-making, and all the rest.

At Laguna, all entities, human or supernatural, who are functioning in a ritual manner at a high level are called Mother. The story "Arrow Youth, the Witches and the K'a·'ts'ina" is filled with addresses of this sort.[31]

The cacique is addressed as mother by the war captain as well as by Arrow Youth. The Turkey-Buzzard Spirit is greeted as mother by the shaman who goes to consult him. When the cacique goes to consult with the k'apina shamans, he greets them saying, "How are things, mothers of everyone, chiefs of everyone." After he has made his ritual offering of corn pollen to them, he says, "Enough . . . mothers, chiefs."[32] He greets them this way to acknowledge their power, a power that includes everything: long life, growth, old age, and life during the daytime. Not all the entities involved in the story are addressed in this fashion. Only those who command great respect are so titled. Yellow Woman herself is acknowledged "the mother of all of us" by the katsina chief or spokesman when he pledges the katsina's aid in her rescue.[33] Many more examples of the practice exist among tribes, and all underscore that motherness is a highly valued characteristic.

But its value signifies something other than the kind of sentimental respect for motherhood that is reflected in Americans' Mother's Day observances. It is ritually powerful, a condition of being that confers the highest adeptship on whoever bears the title. So central to ritual activities is it in Indian cultures that men are honored by the name mother, recognizing and paying respect to their spiritual and occult competence. That competence derives entirely from Mother Iyatiku, and, through her, from Thought Woman herself.

A strong attitude integrally connects the power of Original Thinking or Creation Thinking to the power of mothering. That power is not so much the power to give birth, as we have noted, but the power to make, to create, to transform. Ritual, as noted elsewhere, means transforming something from one state or condition to another, and that ability is inherent in the action of mothering. It is the ability that is sought and treasured by adepts, and it is the ability that male seekers devote years of study and discipline to acquire. Without it, no practice of the sacred is possible, at least not within the Great Mother societies.

And as the cultures that are woman-centered and Mother-ritual based are also cultures that value peacefulness, harmony, cooperation, health, and general prosperity, they are systems of thought and practice that would bear deeper study in our troubled, conflict-ridden time.

When Women Throw Down Bundles: Strong Women Make Strong Nations

Not until recently have American Indian women chosen to define themselves politically as Indian *women*—a category that retains American Indian women's basic racial and cultural identity but distinguishes women as a separate political force in a tribal, racial, and cultural context—but only recently has this political insistence been necessary. In other times, in other circumstances more congenial to womanhood and more cognizant of the proper place of Woman as creatrix and shaper of existence in the tribe and on the earth, everyone knew that women played a separate and significant role in tribal reality.

This self-redefinition among Indian women who intend that their former stature be restored has resulted from several political factors. The status of tribal women has seriously declined over the centuries of white dominance, as they have been all but voiceless in tribal decision-making bodies since reconstitution of the tribes through colonial fiat and U.S. law. But over the last thirty years women's sense of ourselves as a group with a stake in the distribution of power on the reservations, in jobs, and within the intertribal urban Indian communities has grown.

As writer Stan Steiner observes in *The New Indians*, the breakdown of women's status in tribal communities as a result of colonization led to their migration in large numbers into the cities, where they regained the self-sufficiency and positions of influence they had held in earlier centuries. He writes, "In the cities the power of women has been recognized by the extra-tribal communities. Election of tribal women to the leadership of these urban Indian centers has been a phenomenon in modern Indian life."[1]

Since the 1960s when Steiner wrote, the number of women in tribal leadership has grown immensely. Women function as council members and tribal chairs for at least one-fourth of the federally recognized tribes. In February 1981, the Albuquerque *Journal* reported that sixty-seven American Indian tribes had women heads of state. In large measure, the urbanization of large numbers of American Indians has resulted in their reclaiming their traditions (though it was meant to work the other way when in the 1950s the Eisenhower administration developed "Relocation" and "Termination" policies for Indians).

The coming of the white man created chaos in all the old systems, which were for the most part superbly healthy, simultaneously cooperative and autonomous, peace-centered, and ritual-oriented. The success of their systems depended on complementary institutions and organized relationships among all sectors of their world. The significance of each part was seen as necessary to the balanced and harmonious functioning of the whole, and both private and public aspects of life were viewed as valuable and necessary components of society. The private ("inside") was shared by all, though certain rites and knowledge were shared only by clan members or by initiates into ritual societies, some of which were gender-specific and some of which were open to members of both sexes. Most were male-dominated or female-dominated with helping roles assigned to members of the opposite gender. One category of inside societies was exclusive to "berdaches"—males only—and "berdaches"*—female only. All categories of ritual societies function in present-day American Indian communities, though the exclusively male societies are best recorded in ethnographic literature.

The "outside" was characterized by various social institutions, all of which had bearing on the external welfare of the group. Hunting,

---

*The term *berdache* is applied (or rather misapplied) to both lesbians and gay males. It is originally an Arabic word meaning sex-slave boy, or a male child used sexually by adult males. As such it has no relevance to American Indian men or women.

gathering, building, ditch cleaning, horticulture, seasonal and permanent moves, intertribal relationships, law and policy decisions affecting the whole, crafts, and childrearing are some of the areas governed
by outside institutions. These were most directly affected by white
government policies; the inside institutions were most directly affected
by Christianization. Destruction of the institutions rested on the overthrow or subversion of the gynocratic nature of the tribal system, as
documents and offhand comments by white interveners attest.

Consider, for example, John Adair's remark about the Cherokee,
as reported by Carolyn Foreman: "The Cherokee had been for a
considerable while under petticoat government and they were just
emerging, like all of the Iroquoian Indians from the matriarchal
period."[2] Adair's idea of "petticoat government" included the power
of the Women's Council of the Cherokee. The head of the Council was
the Beloved Woman of the Nation, "whose voice was considered that
of the Great Spirit, speaking through her."[3] The Iroquoian peoples,
including the Cherokee, had another custom that bespoke the existence of their "petticoat government," their gynocracy. They set the
penalty for killing a woman of the tribe at double that for killing a man.
This regulation was in force at least among the Susquehanna, the
Hurons, and the Iroquois; but given the high regard in which the tribes
held women and given that in killing a woman one killed the children
she might have borne, I imagine the practice of doubling the penalty
was widespread.[4]

The Iroquois story is currently one of the best chronicles of the
overthrow of the gynocracy. Material about the status of women in
North American groups such as the Montagnais-Naskapi, Keres,
Navajo, Crow, Hopi, Pomo, Turok, Kiowa, and Natchez and in South
American groups such as the Bari and Mapuche, to name just a few, is
lacking. Any original documentation that exists is buried under the
flood of readily available, published material written from the colonizer's patriarchal perspective, almost all of which is based on the white
man's belief in universal male dominance. Male dominance may have
characterized a number of tribes, but it was by no means as universal
(or even as preponderant) as colonialist propaganda has led us to
believe.

The Seneca prophet Handsome Lake did not appreciate "petticoat
government" any more than did John Adair. When his code became
the standard for Iroquoian practice in the early nineteenth century,

power shifted from the hands of the "meddling old women," as he characterized them, to men. Under the old laws, the Iroquois were a mother-centered, mother-right people whose political organization was based on the central authority of the Matrons, the Mothers of the Longhouses (clans). Handsome Lake advocated that young women cleave to their husbands rather than to their mothers and abandon the clan-mother–controlled longhouse in favor of a patriarchal, nuclear family arrangement. Until Handsome Lake's time, the sachems were chosen from certain families by the Matrons of their clans and were subject to impeachment by the Matrons should they prove inadequate or derelict in carrying out their duties as envisioned by the Matrons and set forth in the Law of the Great Peace of the Iroquois Confederacy. By provision in the Law, the women were to be considered the progenitors of the nation, owning the land and the soil.[5]

At the end of the Revolutionary War, the Americans declared the Iroquois living on the American side of the United States–Canadian border defeated. Pressed from all sides, their fields burned and salted, their daily life disrupted, and the traditional power of the Matrons under assault from the missionaries who flocked to Iroquois country to "civilize" them, the recently powerful Iroquois became a subject, captive people. Into this chaos stepped Handsome Lake who, with the help of devoted followers and the exigencies of social disruption in the aftermath of the war, encouraged the shift from woman-centered society to patriarchal society. While that shift was never complete, it was sufficient. Under the Code of Handsome Lake, which was the tribal version of the white man's way, the Longhouse declined in importance, and eventually Iroquois women were firmly under the thumb of Christian patriarchy.

The Iroquois were not the only Nation to fall under patriarchal-ization. No tribe escaped that fate, though some western groups retained their gynecentric egalitarianism[6] until well into the latter half of the twentieth century. Among the hundreds of tribes forced into patriarchal modes, the experiences of the Montagnais-Naskapi, the Mid-Atlantic Coastal Algonkians, and the Bari of Colombia,[7] among others, round out the hemisphere-wide picture.

Among the Narragansett of the area now identified as Rhode Island was a woman chief, one of the six sachems of that tribe. Her name was Magnus, and when the Narragansetts were invaded by Major Talcot and defeated in battle, the Sunksquaw Magnus was executed along with ninety others. Her fate was a result of her position; in contrast, the wife and child of the sachem known as King Philip among the English colonizers were simply sold into slavery in the West Indies.[8]

This sunksquaw, or queen (hereditary female head of state), was one of scores in the Mid-Atlantic region. One researcher, Robert Grumet, identifies a number of women chiefs who held office during the seventeenth and eighteenth centuries. Grumet begins his account by detailing the nonauthoritarian character of the Mid-Atlantic Coastal Algonkians and describes their political system, which included inheritance of rank by the eldest child through the maternal line. He concludes with the observation that important historians ignore documented information concerning the high-status position of women in the leadership structure of the Coastal Algonkians:

> Both Heckewelder (1876) and Zeisberger (1910) failed to mention women in their lengthy descriptions of Delawaran leadership during the westward exile. Eight out of the eleven sources listed in Kinietz (1946) noted that women could not be chiefs. The remaining three citations made no mention of women leaders. These same sources stated that "women had no voice in council and were only admitted at certain times." Roger Williams translated the Narragansett term *saunks* as "the Queen, or Sachims Wife," with the plural "Queenes" translating out as *sauncksquuaog* (1866). He nowhere indicated that these *sauncksquuaog* were anything more than wives.
>
> The ethnographic record has indicated otherwise. Even a cursory scanning of the widely available primary documentation clearly shows the considerable role played by Coastal Algonkian women throughout the historic contact period. Many sources state that women were able to inherit chiefly office. Others note that women sachems were often the sisters of wives of male leaders who succeeded them upon their decease. This does not mean that every "sunksquaw's" husband or brother was a leader. Many women sachems were married to men who made no pretension to leadership.[9]

The first sunksquaw Grumet mentions was noted in John Smith's journal as "Queene of Appamatuck." She was present during the council that decided on his death—a decision that Pocahontas, daughter of one of the sachems, overturned.[10] The Wampanoag Confederacy's loss of control over the Chesapeake Bay area did not cause an end to the rule of sunksquaws or of the empress: George Fox, founder of the Quaker religion, recorded that "the old Empress [of Accomack] ... sat in council" when he was visiting in March 1673.[11] In 1705, Robert Beverley mentioned two towns governed by queens: Pungoteque and Nanduye. Pungoteque, he said, was a small Nation, even though governed by a Queen, and he listed Nanduye as "a seat of the Empress." He seemed impressed. For while Nanduye was a small settlement of "not above 20 families," the old Empress had "all the Nations of this shore under Tribute."[12]

From before 1620 until her death in 1617, a squaw-sachem known as the "Massachusetts Queen" by the Virginia colonizers governed the Massachusetts Confederacy.[13] It was her fortune to preside over the Confederacy's destruction as the people were decimated by disease, war, and colonial manipulations. Magnus, the Narragansett sunksquaw whose name was recorded by whites, is mentioned above. Others include the Pocasset sunksquaw Weetamoo, who was King Philip's ally and "served as war chief commanding over 300 warriors" during his war with the British.[14] Queen Weetamoo was given the white woman Mary Rowlandson, who wrote descriptions of the sunksquaw in her captivity narrative.

Awashonks, another queen in the Mid-Atlantic region, was squaw-sachem of the Sakonnet, a tribe allied with the Wampanoag Confederacy. She reigned in the latter part of the seventeenth century. After fighting for a time against the British during King Philip's War, she was forced to surrender. Because she then convinced her warriors to fight with the British, she was able to save them from enslavement in the West Indies.[15]

The last sunksquaw Grumet mentions was named Mamanuchqua. An Esopus and one of the five sachems of the Esopus Confederacy, Mamanuchqua is said to be only one name that she used. The others include Mamareoktwe, Mamaroch, and Mamaprocht,[16] unless they were the names of other Esopus sunksquaws who used the same or a similar mark beside the written designation. Grumet wisely comments on the presence of women chiefs and the lack of notice of them in secondary documents—that is, in books about the region during those centuries.

> Ethnohistorians have traditionally assigned male gender to native figures in the documentary record unless otherwise identified. They have also tended to not identify native individuals as leaders unless so identified in the specific source. This policy, while prop-

erly cautious, has fostered the notion that all native persons mentioned in the documentation were both male and commoners unless otherwise identified. This practice has successfully masked the identities of a substantial number of Coastal Algonkian leaders of both sexes.[17]

And that's not all it successfully achieves. It falsifies the record of people who are not able to set it straight; it reinforces patriarchal socialization among all Americans, who are thus led to believe that there have never been any alternative structures; it gives Anglo-Europeans the idea that Indian societies were beneath the level of organization of western nations, justifying colonization by presumption of lower stature; it masks the genocide attendant on the falsification of evidence, as it masks the gynocidal motive behind the genocide. Political actions coupled with economic and physical disaster in the forms of land theft and infection of native populations caused the Mid-Atlantic Algonkians to be overwhelmed by white invaders.

Politics played an even greater role in the destruction of the Cherokee gynocracy, of a region that included parts of Georgia, Mississippi, and North Carolina. Cherokee women had the power to decide the fate of captives, decisions that were made by vote of the Women's Council and relayed to the district at large by the War Woman or Pretty Woman. The decisions had to be made by female clan heads because a captive who was to live would be adopted into one of the families whose affairs were directed by the clan-mothers. The clan-mothers also had the right to wage war, and as Henry Timberlake wrote, the stories about Amazon warriors were not so farfetched considering how many Indian women were famous warriors and powerful voices in the councils.[18]

The war women carried the title Beloved Women, and their power was so great "that they can, by the wave of a swan's wing, deliver a wretch condemned by the council, and already tied to the stake," Lieutenant Timberlake reports.[19] A mixed-blood Cherokee man who was born in the early nineteenth century reported knowing an old woman named Da'nawa-gasta, or Sharp War, which meant a fierce warrior.[20]

The Women's Council, as distinguished from the District, village, or Confederacy councils, was powerful in a number of political and socio-spiritual ways, and may have had the deciding voice on what males would serve on the Councils, as its northern sisters had. Certainly the Women's Council was influential in tribal decisions, and its spokeswomen served as War Women and as Peace Women, presumably holding those offices in the towns designated red towns and white towns, respectively. Their other powers included the right to speak in men's Council, the right to inclusion in public policy decisions, the right to choose whom and whether to marry, the right to bear arms, and the right to choose their extramarital occupations.

During the longtime colonization of the Cherokee along the Atlantic seaboard, the British worked hard to lessen the power of women in Cherokee affairs. They took Cherokee men to England and educated them in English ways. These men returned to Cherokee country and exerted great influence on behalf of the British in the region. By the time the Removal Act was under consideration by Congress in the early 1800s, many of these British-educated men and men with little Cherokee blood wielded considerable power over the Nation's policies.

In the ensuing struggle women endured rape and murder, but they had no voice in the future direction of the Cherokee Nation. The Cherokee were by this time highly stratified, though they had been much less so before this period, and many were Christianized. The male leadership bought and sold not only black men and women but also men and women of neighboring tribes, the women of the leadership class retreated to Bible classes, sewing circles, and petticoats that rivaled those worn by their white sisters. Many of these upper-strata Cherokee women married white ministers and other opportunists, as the men of their class married white women, often the daughters of white ministers. The traditional strata of Cherokee society became rigid and modeled on Christian white social organization of upper, middle, and impoverished classes usually composed of very traditional clans.

In an effort to stave off removal, the Cherokee in the early 1800s, under the leadership of men such as Elias Boudinot, Major Ridge, and John Ross (later Principal Chief of the Cherokee in Oklahoma Territory), and others, drafted a constitution that disenfranchised women and blacks. Modeled after the Constitution of the United States, whose favor they were attempting to curry, and in conjunction with Christian sympathizers to the Cherokee cause, the new Cherokee constitution relegated women to the position of chattel. No longer possessing a voice in the Nation's business, women became pawns in the struggle between white and Cherokee for possession of Cherokee lands.

The Cherokee, like their northern cousins, were entirely represented by men in the white courts, in the U.S. Congress, and in gatherings where lobbying of white officials was carried on. The great organ of Cherokee resistance, the *Cherokee Phoenix*, was staffed by men. The last Beloved Woman, Nancy Ward, resigned her office in 1817 sending her cane and her vote on important questions to the Cherokee Council, and "thus renounced her high office of Beloved Woman, in favor of written constitutional law."[21]

In spite of their frantic attempts to prevent their removal to Indian Territory by aping the white man in patriarchal particulars, the Cherokee were removed, as were the other tribes of the region and those living north and west of them, whom the Cherokee thought of as "uncivilized." Politics does make strange bedfellows, as the degynocratization of the Cherokee Nation shows. Boudinot and Ridge were condemned as traitors by the newly reconstituted Cherokee government in Indian Territory and were executed (assassinated, some say). The Cherokee got out from under the petticoats in time to be buried under the weight of class hierarchies, male dominance, war, and loss of their homeland.

While the cases cited above might be explained as a general conquest over male Indian systems that happened to have some powerful women functioning within them rather than as a deliberate attempt to wipe out female leadership, the case of the Montagnais women clarifies an otherwise obscure issue. The Montagnais-Naskapi of the St. Lawrence Valley was contacted early in the fifteenth century by fur traders and explorers and fell under the sway of Jesuit missionizing in the mid-sixteenth century. The Jesuits, under the leadership of Fr. Paul Le Jeune (whose name, appropriately, means The Little or The Young One), determined to convert the Montagnais to Christianity, resocialize them, and transform them into peasant-serfs as were the Indians' counterparts in France centuries earlier.

To accomplish this task, the good fathers had to loosen the hold of Montagnais women on tribal policies and to convince both men and women that a woman's proper place was under the authority of her husband and that a man's proper place was under the authority of the priests. The system of vassalage with which the Frenchmen were most familiar required this arrangement.

In pursuit of this end, the priests had to undermine the status of the women, who, according to one of Le Jeune's reports, had "great power . . . A man may promise you something and if he does not keep his promise, he thinks he is sufficiently excused when he tells you that his wife did not wish him to do it."[22] Further, the Jesuit noted the equable relations between husbands and wives among the Montagnais. He commented that "men leave the arrangement of the household to the women, without interfering with them; they cut and decide to give away as they please without making the husband angry. I have never seen my host ask a giddy young woman that he had with him what became of the provisions, although they were disappearing very fast."[23]

Undaunted, Paul Le Jeune composed a plan whereby this state of affairs could be put aright. His plan had four parts, which, he was certain, would turn the Montagnais into proper, civilized people. He figured that the first requirement was the establishment of permanent settlements and the placement of officially constituted authority in the hands of one person. "Alas!" he mourned. "If someone could stop the wanderings of the Savages, and give authority to one of them to rule the others, we would see them converted and civilized in a short time."[24] More ominously, he believed that the institution of punishment was essential in Montagnais social relations. How could they understand tyranny and respect it unless they wielded it upon each other and experienced it at each other's hands? He was most distressed that the "Savages," as he termed them, thought physical abuse a terrible crime.

He commented on this "savage" aberration in a number of his reports, emphasizing his position that its cure rested only in the abduction or seduction of the children into attendance at Jesuit-run schools located a good distance from their homes. "The Savages prevent their [children's] instruction; they will not tolerate the chastisement of their children, whatever they may do, they permit only a simple reprimand," he complains.[25]

What he had in mind was more along the lines of torture, imprisonment, battering, neglect, and psychological torment—the educational methods to which Indian children in government and mission schools would be subjected for some time after Conquest was accomplished. Doubtless these methods were required, or few would have traded the Montagnais way for the European one. Thus his third goal was subsumed under the "education" of the young.

Last, Le Jeune wished to implement a new social system whereby the Montagnais would live within the European family structure with its twin patriarchal institutions of male authority and female fidelity. These would be enforced by the simple expediency of forbidding divorce. He informed the men that in France women do not rule their husbands, information that had been conveyed by various means, including Jesuit education, to other tribes such as the Iroquois and the Cherokee.

Le Jeune had his work cut out for him: working with people who did not punish children, encouraged women in independence and decision making, and had a horror of authority imposed from without—who, in Le Jeune's words could not "endure in the least those who seem desirous of assuming superiority over the others, and place all virtue in a certain gentleness or apathy,"[26] who

> ... imagine that they ought by right of birth, to enjoy the liberty of wild ass colts, rendering no homage to anyone whomsoever, except when they like. They have reproached me a hundred times because we fear our Captains, while they laugh at and make sport of theirs. All the authority of their chief is in his tongue's end, for he is powerful insofar as he is eloquent; and even if he kills himself talking and haranguing, he will not be obeyed unless he pleases the Savages.[27]

The wily Le Jeune did not succeed entirely in transforming these gentle and humorous people into bastard Europeans, but he did succeed in some measure. While the ease of relationships between men and women remains and while the Montagnais retain their love of gentleness and nurturing, they are rather more male-centered than not.[28] Positions of formal power such as political leadership, shamanhood, and matrilocality, which placed the economic dependence of a woman with children in the hands of her mother's family, had shifted. Shamans were male, leaders were male, and matrilocality had become patrilocality. This is not so strange given the economics of the situation and the fact that over the years the Montagnais became entirely Catholicized.

With the rate of assimilation increasing and with the national political and economic situation of Indians in Canada, which is different in details but identical in intent and disastrous effect to that of Indians in the United States, the Montagnais will likely be fully patriarchal before the turn of the next century.

As this brief survey indicates, the shift from gynecentric-egalitarian and ritual-based systems to phallocentric, hierarchical systems is not accomplished in only one dimension. As Le Jeune understood, the assault on the system of woman power requires the replacing of a peaceful, nonpunitive, nonauthoritarian social system wherein women wield power by making social life easy and gentle with one based on child terrorization, male dominance, and submission of women to male authority.

Montagnais men who would not subscribe to the Jesuit program (and there were many) were not given authority backed up by the patriarchy's churchly or political institutions. Under patriarchy men are given power only if they use it in ways that are congruent with the authoritarian, punitive model. The records attest, in contrast, that gynecentric systems distribute power evenly among men, women, and berdaches as well as among all age groups. Economic distribution follows a similar pattern; reciprocal exchange of goods and services among individuals and between groups is ensured because women are in charge at all points along the distribution network.

Effecting the social transformation from egalitarian, gynecentric systems to hierarchical, patriarchal systems requires meeting four objectives. The first is accomplished when the primacy of female as creator is displaced and replaced by male-gendered creators (generally generic, as the Great Spirit concept overtakes the multiplicitous tribal designation of deity). This objective has largely been met across North America. The Hopi goddess Spider Woman has become the masculine Maseo or Tawa, referred to in the masculine, and the Zuñi goddess is on her way to malehood. Changing Woman of the Navajo has contenders for her position, while the Keres Thought Woman trembles on the brink of displacement by her sister-goddess-cum-god Utset. Among the Cherokee, the goddess of the river foam is easily replaced by Thunder in many tales, and the Iroquois divinity Sky Woman now gets her ideas and powers from her dead father or her monstrous grandson.

The second objective is achieved when tribal governing institutions and the philosophies that are their foundation are destroyed, as they were among the Iroquois and the Cherokee, to mention just two. The conqueror has demanded that the tribes that wish federal recognition and protection institute "democracy," in which powerful officials are elected by majority vote. Until recently, these powerful officials were inevitably male and were elected mainly by nontraditionals, the traditionals being until recently unwilling to participate in a form of governance imposed on them by right of conquest. Democracy by coercion is hardly democracy, in any language, and to some Indians recognizing that fact, the threat of extinction is preferable to the ignominy of enslavement in their own land.

The third objective is accomplished when the people are pushed off their lands, deprived of their economic livelihood, and forced to curtail or end altogether pursuits on which their ritual system, philosophy, and subsistence depend. Now dependent on white institutions for survival, tribal systems can ill afford gynocracy when patriarchy—that is, survival—requires male dominance. Not that submission to white laws and customs results in economic prosperity; the unemployment rates on most reservations is about 50 to 60 percent, and the situation for urban Indians who are undereducated (as many are) is almost as bad.

The fourth objective requires that the clan structure be replaced, in fact if not in theory, by the nuclear family. By this ploy, the women clan heads are replaced by elected male officials and the psychic net that is formed and maintained by the nature of nonauthoritarian gynecentricity grounded in respect for diversity of gods and people is thoroughly rent. Decimation of populations through starvation, disease, and disruption of all social, spiritual, and economic structures along with abduction and enforced brainwashing of the young serve well in meeting this goal.

Along the way, each of these parts of the overall program of degynocraticization is subject to image control and information control. Recasting archaic tribal versions of tribal history, customs, institutions, and the oral tradition increases the likelihood that the patriarchal revisionist versions of tribal life, skewed or simply made up by patriarchal non-Indians and patriarchalized Indians, will be incorporated into the spiritual and popular traditions of the tribes. This is reinforced by the loss of rituals, medicine societies, and entire clans through assimilation and a dying off of tribal members familiar with the elder rituals and practices. Consequently, Indian control of the image-making and information-disseminating process is crucial, and the contemporary prose and poetry of American Indian writers, particularly of woman-centered writers, is a major part of Indian resistance to cultural and spiritual genocide.

Where I Come from Is Like This

I

Modern American Indian women, like their non-Indian sisters, are deeply engaged in the struggle to redefine themselves. In their struggle they must reconcile traditional tribal definitions of women with industrial and postindustrial non-Indian definitions. Yet while these definitions seem to be more or less mutually exclusive, Indian women must somehow harmonize and integrate both in their own lives.

An American Indian woman is primarily defined by her tribal identity. In her eyes, her destiny is necessarily that of her people, and her sense of herself as a woman is first and foremost prescribed by her tribe. The definitions of woman's roles are as diverse as tribal cultures in the Americas. In some she is devalued, in others she wields considerable power. In some she is a familial/clan adjunct, in some she is as close to autonomous as her economic circumstances and psychological traits permit. But in no tribal definitions is she perceived in the same way as are women in western industrial and postindustrial cultures.

In the west, few images of women form part of the cultural mythos, and these are largely sexually charged. Among Christians, the madonna is the female prototype, and she is portrayed as essentially passive: her contribution is simply that of birthing. Little else is attributed to her and she certainly possesses few of the characteristics that are attributed to mythic figures among Indian tribes. This image is countered (rather than balanced) by the witch-goddess/whore characteristics designed to reinforce cultural beliefs about women, as well as western adversarial and dualistic perceptions of reality.

The tribes see women variously, but they do not question the power of femininity. Sometimes they see women as fearful, sometimes peaceful, sometimes omnipotent and omniscient, but they never portray women as mindless, helpless, simple, or oppressed. And while the women in a given tribe, clan, or band may be all these things, the individual woman is provided with a variety of images of women from the interconnected supernatural, natural, and social worlds she lives in.

As a half-breed American Indian woman, I cast about in my mind for negative images of Indian women, and I find none that are directed to Indian women alone. The negative images I do have are of Indians in general and in fact are more often of males than of females. All these images come to me from non-Indian sources, and they are always balanced by a positive image. My ideas of womanhood, passed on largely by my mother and grandmothers, Laguna Pueblo women, are about practicality, strength, reasonableness, intelligence, wit, and competence. I also remember vividly the women who came to my father's store, the women who held me and sang to me, the women at Feast Day, at Grab Days, the women in the kitchen of my Cubero home, the women I grew up with; none of them appeared weak or helpless, none of them presented herself tentatively. I remember a certain reserve on those lovely brown faces; I remember the direct gaze of eyes framed by bright-colored shawls draped over their heads and cascading down their backs. I remember the clean cotton dresses and carefully pressed hand-embroidered aprons they always wore; I remember laughter and good food, especially the sweet bread and the oven bread they gave us. Nowhere in my mind is there a foolish woman, a dumb woman, a vain woman, or a plastic woman, though the Indian women I have known have shown a wide range of personal style and demeanor.

My memory includes the Navajo woman who was badly beaten by her Sioux husband; but I also remember that my grandmother abandoned her Sioux husband long ago. I recall the stories about the Laguna woman beaten regularly by her husband in the presence of her children so that the children would not believe in the strength and power of femininity. And I remember the women who drank, who got into fights with other women and with the men, and who often won those battles. I have memories of tired women, partying women, stubborn women, sullen women, amicable women, selfish women, shy women, and aggressive women. Most of all I remember the women who laugh and scold and sit uncomplaining in the long sun on feast days and who cook wonderful food on wood stoves, in beehive mud ovens, and over open fires outdoors.

Among the images of women that come to me from various tribes as well as my own are White Buffalo Woman, who came to the Lakota long ago and brought them the religion of the Sacred Pipe which they still practice; Tinotzin the goddess who came to Juan Diego to remind him that she still walked the hills of her people and sent him with her message, her demand and her proof to the Catholic bishop in the city nearby. And from Laguna I take the images of Yellow Woman, Coyote Woman, Grandmother Spider (Spider Old Woman), who brought the light, who gave us weaving and medicine, who gave us life. Among the Keres she is known as Thought Woman who created us all and who keeps us in creation even now. I remember Iyatiku, Earth Woman, Corn Woman, who guides and counsels the people to peace and who welcomes us home when we cast off this coil of flesh as huskers cast off the leaves that wrap the corn. I remember Iyatiku's sister, Sun Woman, who held metals and cattle, pigs and sheep, highways and engines and so many things in her bundle, who went away to the east saying that one day she would return.

II

Since the coming of the Anglo-Europeans beginning in the fifteenth century, the fragile web of identity that long held tribal people secure has gradually been weakened and torn. But the oral tradition has prevented the complete destruction of the web, the ultimate disruption of tribal ways. The oral tradition is vital; it heals itself and the tribal web by adapting to the flow of the present while never relinquishing its connection to the past. Its adaptability has always been required, as many generations have experienced. Certainly the modern American Indian woman bears slight resemblance to her forebears—at least on superficial examination—but she is still a tribal woman in her deepest being. Her tribal sense of relationship to all that is continues to flourish. And though she is at times beset by her knowledge of the

45

enormous gap between the life she lives and the life she was raised to live, and while she adapts her mind and being to the circumstances of her present life, she does so in tribal ways, mending the tears in the web of being from which she takes her existence as she goes.

My mother told me stories all the time, though I often did not recognize them as that. My mother told me stories about cooking and childbearing; she told me stories about menstruation and pregnancy; she told me stories about gods and heroes, about fairies and elves, about goddesses and spirits; she told me stories about the land and the sky, about cats and dogs, about snakes and spiders; she told me stories about climbing trees and exploring the mesas; she told me stories about going to dances and getting married; she told me stories about dressing and undressing, about sleeping and waking; she told me stories about herself, about her mother, about her grandmother. She told me stories about grieving and laughing, about thinking and doing; she told me stories about school and about people; about darning and mending; she told me stories about turquoise and about gold; she told me European stories and Laguna stories; she told me Catholic stories and Presbyterian stories; she told me city stories and country stories; she told me political stories and religious stories. She told me stories about living and stories about dying. And in all of those stories she told me who I was, who I was supposed to be, whom I came from, and who would follow me. In this way she taught me the meaning of the words she said, that all life is a circle and everything has a place within it. That's what she said and what she showed me in the things she did and the way she lives.

Of course, through my formal, white, Christian education, I dis-covered that other people had stories of their own—about women, about Indians, about fact, about reality—and I was amazed by a number of startling suppositions that others made about tribal cus-toms and beliefs. According to the un-Indian, non-Indian view, for instance, Indians barred menstruating women from ceremonies and indeed segregated them from the rest of the people, consigning them to some space specially designed for them. This showed that Indians considered menstruating women unclean and not fit to enjoy the company of decent (nonmenstruating) people, that is, men. I was surprised and confused to hear this because my mother had taught me that white people had strange attitudes toward menstruation: they thought something was bad about it, that it meant you were sick, cursed, sinful, and weak and that you had to be very careful during that time. She taught me that menstruation was a normal occurrence, that I could go swimming or hiking or whatever else I wanted to do during my period. She actively scorned women who took to their beds, who were incapacitated by cramps, who "got the blues."

As I struggled to reconcile these very contradictory interpretations of American Indians' traditional beliefs concerning menstruation, I realized that the menstrual taboos were about power, not about sin or filth. My conclusion was later borne out by some tribes' own explanations, which, as you may well imagine, came as quite a relief to me.

The truth of the matter as many Indians see it is that women who are at the peak of their fecundity are believed to possess power that throws male power totally out of kilter. They emit such force that, in their presence, any male-owned or -dominated ritual or sacred object cannot do its usual task. For instance, the Lakota say that a menstruating woman anywhere near a yuwipi man, who is a special sort of psychic, spirit-empowered healer, for a day or so before he is to do his ceremony will effectively disempower him. Conversely, among many if not most tribes, important ceremonies cannot be held without the presence of women. Sometimes the ritual woman who empowers the ceremony must be unmarried and virginal so that the power she channels is unalloyed, unweakened by sexual arousal and penetration by a male. Other ceremonies require tumescent women, others the presence of mature women who have borne children, and still others depend for empowerment on postmenopausal women. Women may be segregated from the company of the whole band or village on certain occasions, but on certain occasions men are also segregated. In short, each ritual depends on a certain balance of power, and the positions of women within the phases of womanhood are used by tribal people to empower certain rites. This does not derive from a male-dominant view; it is not a ritual observance imposed on women by men. It derives from a tribal view of reality that distinguishes tribal people from feudal and industrial people.

Among the tribes, the occult power of women, inextricably bound to our hormonal life, is thought to be very great; many hold that we possess innately the blood-given power to kill—with a glance, with a step, or with a judicious mixing of menstrual blood into somebody's soup. Medicine women among the Pomo of California cannot practice until they are sufficiently mature; when they are immature, their power is diffuse and is likely to interfere with their practice until time and experience have it under control. So women of the tribes are not

47

especially inclined to see themselves as poor helpless victims of male domination. Even in those tribes where something akin to male domination was present, women are perceived as powerful, socially, physically, and metaphysically. In times past, as in times present, women carried enormous burdens with aplomb. We were far indeed from the "weaker sex," the designation that white aristocratic sisters unhappily earned for us all.

I remember my mother moving furniture all over the house when she wanted it changed. She didn't wait for my father to come home and help—she just went ahead and moved the piano, a huge upright from the old days, the couch, the refrigerator. Nobody had told her she was too weak to do such things. In imitation of her, I would delight in loading trucks at my father's store with cases of pop or fifty-pound sacks of flour. Even when I was quite small I could do it, and it gave me a belief in my own physical strength that advancing middle age can't quite erase. My mother used to tell me about the Acoma Pueblo women she had seen as a child carrying huge ollas (water pots) on their heads as they wound their way up the tortuous stairwell carved into the face of the "Sky City" mesa, a feat I tried to imitate with books and tin buckets. ("Sky City" is the term used by the Chamber of Commerce for the mother village of Acoma, which is situated atop a high sandstone table mountain.) I was never very successful, but even the attempt reminded me that I was supposed to be strong and balanced to be a proper girl.

Of course, my mother's Laguna people are Keres Indian, reputed to be the last extreme mother-right people on earth. So it is no wonder that I got notably nonwhite notions about the natural strength and prowess of women. Indeed, it is only when I am trying to get non-Indian approval, recognition, or acknowledgment that my "weak sister" emotional and intellectual ploys get the better of my tribal woman's good sense. At such times I forget that I just moved the piano or just wrote a competent paper or just completed a financial transaction satisfactorily or have supported myself and my children for most of my adult life.

Nor is my contradictory behavior atypical. Most Indian women I know are in the same bicultural bind: we vacillate between being dependent and strong, self-reliant and powerless, strongly motivated and hopelessly insecure. We resolve the dilemma in various ways: some of us party all the time; some of us drink to excess; some of us travel and move around a lot; some of us land good jobs and then quit them;

some of us engage in violent exchanges; some of us blow our brains out. We act in these destructive ways because we suffer from the societal conflicts caused by having to identify with two hopelessly opposed cultural definitions of women. Through this destructive dissonance we are unhappy prey to the self-disparagement common to, indeed demanded of, Indians living in the United States today. Our situation is caused by the exigencies of a history of invasion, conquest, and colonization whose searing marks are probably ineradicable. A popular bumper sticker on many Indian cars proclaims: "If You're Indian You're In," to which I always find myself adding under my breath, "Trouble."

III

No Indian can grow to any age without being informed that her people were "savages" who interfered with the march of progress pursued by respectable, loving, civilized white people. We are the villains of the scenario when we are mentioned at all. We are absent from much of white history except when we are calmly, rationally, succinctly, and systematically dehumanized. On the few occasions we are noticed in any way other than as howling, bloodthirsty beings, we are acclaimed for our noble quaintness. In this definition, we are exotic curios. Our ancient arts and customs are used to draw tourist money to state coffers, into the pocketbooks and bank accounts of scholars, and into support of the American-in-Disneyland promoters' dream.

As a Roman Catholic child I was treated to bloody tales of how the savage Indians martyred the hapless priests and missionaries who went among them in an attempt to lead them to the one true path. By the time I was through high school I had the idea that Indians were people who had benefited mightily from the advanced knowledge and superior morality of the Anglo-Europeans. At least I had, perforce, that idea to lay beside the other one that derived from my daily experience of Indian life, an idea less dehumanizing and more accurate because it came from my mother and the other Indian people who raised me. That idea was that Indians are a people who don't tell lies, who care for their children and their old people. You never see an Indian orphan, they said. You always know when you're old that someone will take care of you—one of your children will. Then they'd list the old folks who were being taken care of by this child or that. No child is ever considered illegitimate among the Indians, they said. If a girl gets pregnant, the

49

baby is still part of the family, and the mother is too. That's what they said, and they showed me real people who lived according to those principles.

Of course the ravages of colonization have taken their toll; there are orphans in Indian country now, and abandoned, brutalized old folks; there are even illegitimate children, though the very concept still strikes me as absurd. There are battered children and neglected children, and there are battered wives and women who have been raped by Indian men. Proximity to the "civilizing" effects of white Christians has not improved the moral quality of life in Indian country, though each group, Indian and white, explains the situation differently. Nor is there much yet in the oral tradition that can enable us to adapt to these inhuman changes. But a force is growing in that direction, and it is helping Indian women reclaim their lives. Their power, their sense of direction and of self will soon be visible. It is the force of the women who speak and work and write, and it is formidable.

Through all the centuries of war and death and cultural and psychic destruction have endured the women who raise the children and tend the fires, who pass along the tales and the traditions, who weep and bury the dead, who are the dead, and who never forget. There are always the women, who make pots and weave baskets, who fashion clothes and cheer their children on at powwow, who make fry bread and piki bread, and corn soup and chili stew, who dance and sing and remember and hold within their hearts the dream of their ancient peoples—that one day the woman who thinks will speak to us again, and everywhere there will be peace. Meanwhile we tell the stories and write the books and trade tales of anger and woe and stories of fun and scandal and laugh over all manner of things that happen every day. We watch and we wait.

My great-grandmother told my mother: Never forget you are Indian. And my mother told me the same thing. This, then, is how I have gone about remembering, so that my children will remember too.

The Word
Warriors

The acts of aggression committed against every aspect of American Indian life and society over the centuries—what the Aztecs foresaw as Nine Hells or Nine Descents—have left indelible, searing scars on the minds and spirits of the native peoples on this continent. But voices of the spirits that inform Native America are being heard in every region.

This section is devoted to a number of studies of traditional and contemporary American Indian literature. The oral tradition, from which the contemporary poetry and fiction take their significance and authenticity, has, since contact with white people, been a major force in Indian resistance. It has kept the people conscious of their tribal identity, their spiritual traditions, and their connection to the land and her creatures. Contemporary poets and writers take their cue from the oral tradition, to which they return continuously for theme, symbol, structure, and motivating impulse as well as for the philosophic bias that animates our work.

The Sacred Hoop:
A Contemporary Perspective

Literature is one facet of a culture. The significance of a literature can be best understood in terms of the culture from which it springs, and the purpose of literature is clear only when the reader understands and accepts the assumptions on which the literature is based. A person who was raised in a given culture has no problem seeing the relevance, the level of complexity, or the symbolic significance of that culture's literature. We are all from early childhood familiar with the assumptions that underlie our own culture and its literature and art. Intelligent analysis becomes a matter of identifying smaller assumptions peculiar to the locale, idiom, and psyche of the writer.

The study of non-Western literature poses a problem for Western readers, who naturally tend to see alien literature in terms that are familiar to them, however irrelevant those terms may be to the literature under consideration. Because of this, students of traditional American Indian literatures have applied the terms "primitive," "savage," "childlike," and "pagan" to these literatures. Perceiving only the most superficial aspects of American Indian literary traditions, western scholars have labeled the whole body of these literatures "folklore," even though the term specifically applies only to those parts of the literatures that are the province of the general populace.

The great mythic[1] and ceremonial cycles of the American Indian peoples are neither primitive, in any meaningful sense of the word, nor necessarily the province of the folk; much of the literature, in fact, is known only to educated, specialized persons who are privy to the philosophical, mystical, and literary wealth of their own tribe.

Much of the literature that was in the keeping of such persons, engraved perfectly and completely in their memories, was not known to most other men and women. Because of this, much literature has been lost as the last initiates of particular tribes and societies within the tribes died, leaving no successors.

Most important, traditional American Indian literature is not similar to western literature because the basic assumptions about the universe and, therefore, the basic reality experienced by tribal peoples and by Western peoples are not the same, even at the level of folklore. This difference has confused non-Indian students for centuries. They have been unable or unwilling to accept this difference and to develop critical procedures to illuminate the materials without trivializing or otherwise invalidating them.

For example, American Indian and Western literary traditions differ greatly in the assumed purposes they serve. The purpose of traditional American Indian literature is never simply pure self-expression. The "private soul at any public wall" is a concept alien to American Indian thought. The tribes do not celebrate the individual's ability to feel emotion, for they assume that all people are able to do so. One's emotions are one's own; to suggest that others should imitate them is to impose on the personal integrity of others. The tribes seek—through song, ceremony, legend, sacred stories (myths), and tales—to embody, articulate, and share reality, to bring the isolated, private self into harmony and balance with this reality, to verbalize the sense of the majesty and reverent mystery of all things, and to actualize, in language, those truths that give to humanity its greatest significance and dignity. To a large extent, ceremonial literature serves to redirect private emotion and integrate the energy generated by emotion within a cosmic framework. The artistry of the tribes is married to the essence of language itself, for through language one can share one's singular being with that of the community and know within oneself the communal knowledge of the tribe. In this art, the greater self and all-that-is are blended into a balanced whole, and in this way the concept of being that is the fundamental and sacred spring of life is given voice and being for all. American Indian people do not content themselves with simple

55

preachments of this truth, but through the sacred power of utterance they seek to shape and mold, to direct and determine, the forces that surround and govern human life and the related lives of all things.

An old Keres song says:

> I add my breath to your breath
> That our days may be long on the Earth
> That the days of our people may be long
> That we may be one person
> That we may finish our roads together
> May our mother bless you with life
> May our Life Paths be fulfilled.

In this way one learns how to view oneself and one's tradition so as to approach both rightly. Breath is life, and the intermingling of breaths is the purpose of good living. This is in essence the great principle on which all productive living must rest, for relationships among all the beings of the universe must be fulfilled; in this way each individual life may also be fulfilled.

This idea is apparent in the Plains tribes' idea of a medicine wheel[2] or sacred hoop.[3] The concept is one of singular unity that is dynamic and encompassing, including all that is contained in its most essential aspect, that of life. In his introduction to Geronimo's autobiography, Frederick Turner III incorrectly characterizes the American Indian cultures as static.[4] Stasis is not characteristic of the American Indians' view of things. As any American Indian knows, all of life is living—that is, dynamic and aware, partaking as it does in the life of the All Spirit and contributing as it does to the continuing life of that same Great Mystery. The tribal systems are static in that all movement is related to all other movement—that is, harmonious and balanced or unified; they are not static in the sense that they do not allow or accept change. Even a cursory examination of tribal systems will show that all have undergone massive changes while retaining those characteristics of outlook and experience that are the bedrock of tribal life.[5] So the primary assumptions tribespeople make can be seen as static only in that these people acknowledge the essential harmony of all things and see all things as being of equal value in the scheme of things, denying the opposition, dualism, and isolation (separateness) that characterize non-Indian thought. Christians believe that God is separate from humanity and does as he wishes without the creative assistance of any of his creatures, while the non-Christian tribal person assumes a place in creation that is dynamic, creative, and responsive. Further, tribal people allow all animals, vegetables, and minerals (the entire biota, in short) the same or even greater privileges than humans. The Indian participates in destiny on all levels, including that of creation. Thus this passage from a Cheyenne tale in which Maheo, the All Spirit, creates out of the void four things—the water, the light, the sky-air, and the peoples of the water:

> "How beautiful their wings are in the light," Maheo said to his Power, as the birds wheeled and turned, and became living patterns against the sky.
> The loon was the first to drop back to the surface of the lake. "Maheo," he said, looking around, for he knew that Maheo was all about him, "You have made us sky and light to fly in, and you have made us water to swim in. It sounds ungrateful to want something else, yet still we do. When we are tired of swimming and tired of flying, we should like a dry solid place where we could walk and rest. Give us a place to build our nests, please, Maheo."
> "So be it," answered Maheo, "but to make such a place I must have your help, all of you. By myself, I have made four things . . . Now I must have help if I am to create more, for my Power will only let me make four things by myself."[6]

In this passage we see that even the All Spirit, whose "being was a Universe,"[7] has limited power as well as a sense of proportion and respect for the powers of the creatures. Contrast this spirit with the Judeo-Christian God, who makes everything and tells everything how it may and may not function if it is to gain his respect and blessing and whose commandments make no allowance for change or circumstance. The American Indian universe is based on dynamic self-esteem, while the Christian universe is based primarily on a sense of separation and loss. For the American Indian, the ability of all creatures to share in the process of ongoing creation makes all things sacred.

In Paradise, God created a perfect environment for his creatures. He arranged it to their benefit, asking only that they forbear from eating the fruit of one particular tree. In essence, they were left with only one means of exercising their creative capacities and their ability to make their own decisions and choices. Essentially, they were thus prevented from exercising their intelligence while remaining loyal to the creator. To act in a way that was congruent with their natural

57

curiosity and love of exploration and discovery, they were forced to disobey God and thus be exiled from the perfect place he had made for them. They were severely punished for exercising what we might call liberty—Eve more than Adam, for hers was the greater sin (or so the story goes):

> And the Lord God commanded the man, saying, Of every tree of the garden thou mayest freely eat:
> But of the tree of the knowledge of good and evil, thou shalt not eat: for in the day that thou eatest thereof thou shalt surely die. (Gen. 2:16–17)

The Cheyennes' creator is somewhat wiser. He gives his creatures needs so that they can exert their intelligence and knowledge to satisfy those needs by working together to solve common problems or attain common goals. Together Maheo, the creator, and the water beings create the earth, and with the aid of these beings, Maheo creates first man and first woman and the creatures and environment they will need to live good and satisfying lives. These creation stories demonstrate the basic ordering principles of two different cultures. The Judeo-Christian view is hierarchical. God commands first; within the limits of those commands, man rules; woman is subject to man, as are all the creatures, for God has brought them to Adam for him to name (Gen. 2:18–24, 3:16). In this scheme, the one who is higher has the power to impose penalties or even to deny life to those who are lower:

> And the Lord God said, Behold, the man is become as one of us, to know good and evil; and now, lest he put forth his hand, and take also of the tree of life, and eat, and live for ever;
> Therefore, the Lord God sent him forth from the garden of Eden to till the ground from whence he was taken. (Gen. 3:22–23)

The sin Adam and Eve committed in the Garden of Eden was attempting to become knowledgeable. Their attempt opened the further possibility that, with knowledge, they might become immortal. This, apparently, was not acceptable, not because knowledge and immortality were sinful but because the possession of them by human beings would reorder the hierarchical principles on which the Judeo-Christian universe is posited. Those reared in a Christian society are inclined to perceive social relationships—and literary works—in this context; they order events and phenomena in hierarchical and dualistic terms. Those reared in traditional American Indian societies are inclined to relate events and experiences to one another. They do not organize perceptions or external events in terms of dualities or priorities. This egalitarianism is reflected in the structure of American Indian literature, which does not rely on conflict, crisis, and resolution for organization, nor does its merit depend on the parentage, education, or connections of the author. Rather, its significance is determined by its relation to creative empowerment, its reflection of tribal understandings, and its relation to the unitary nature of reality.

The way the loon prays in the Cheyenne creation story is indicative of that difference. The loon looks around him as he addresses Maheo, "for he knew that Maheo was all about him," just as earlier in the story the snowgoose addressed Maheo in these words: "I do not know where you are, but I know you must be everywhere."[8]

Another difference between these two ways of perceiving reality lies in the tendency of the American Indian to view space as spherical and time as cyclical, whereas the non-Indian tends to view space as linear and time as sequential. The circular concept requires all "points" that make up the sphere of being to have a significant identity and function, while the linear model assumes that some "points" are more significant than others. In the one, significance is a necessary factor of being in itself, whereas in the other, significance is a function of placement on an absolute scale that is fixed in time and space. In essence, what we have is a direct contradiction of Turner's notion about the American Indian universe versus that of the West: the Indian universe moves and breathes continuously, and the Western universe is fixed and static. The Christian attitude toward salvation reflects this basic stance: one can be "saved" only if one believes in a Savior who appeared once and will not come again until "the end of time." The idea "once a saint, always a saint" is another expression of the same underlying perception and experience.

The notion that nature is somewhere over there while humanity is over here or that a great hierarchical ladder of being exists on which ground and trees occupy a very low rung, animals a slightly higher one, and man (never woman)—especially "civilized" man—a very high one indeed is antithetical to tribal thought. The American Indian sees all creatures as relatives (and in tribal systems relationship is central), as offspring of the Great Mystery, as cocreators, as children of our mother, and as necessary parts of an ordered, balanced, and living whole. This concept applies to what non-Indian Americans think of as the supernatural, and it applies as well to the more tangible (phenomenal) aspects of the universe. American Indian thought makes no such dualistic division, nor does it draw a hard and fast line between what is material and what is spiritual, for it regards the two as different expressions of the same reality, as though life has twin manifestations that are mutually interchangeable and, in many instances, virtually identical aspects of a reality that is essentially more spirit than matter or, more correctly, that manifests its spirit in a tangible way. The closest analogy in Western thought is the Einsteinian understanding of matter as a special state or condition of energy. Yet even this concept falls short of the American Indian understanding, for Einsteinian energy is believed to be unintelligent, while energy according to the Indian view is intelligence manifested in yet another way.

Many non-Indians believe that human beings possess the only intelligence in phenomenal existence (often in any form of existence). The more abstractionist and less intellectually vain Indian sees human intelligence as rising out of the very nature of being, which is of necessity intelligent in and of itself, as an attribute of being. Again, this idea probably stems from the Indian concept of a circular, dynamic universe in which all things are related and are of one family. It follows that those attributes possessed by human beings are natural attributes of *all* being. The Indian does not regard awareness of being as an abnormality peculiar to one species, but, because of a sense of relatedness to (instead of isolation from) what exists, the Indian assumes that this awareness is a natural by-product of existence itself.

In English, one can divide the universe into two parts: the natural and the supernatural. Humanity has no real part in either, being neither animal nor spirit—that is, the supernatural is discussed as though it were apart from people, and the natural as though people were apart from it. This necessarily forces English-speaking people into a position of alienation from the world they live in. Such isolation is entirely foreign to American Indian thought. At base, every story, every song, every ceremony tells the Indian that each creature is part of a living whole and that all parts of that whole are related to one another by virtue of their participation in the whole of being.

In American Indian thought, God is known as the All Spirit, and other beings are also spirit—more spirit than body, more spirit than intellect, more spirit than mind. The natural state of existence is whole. Thus healing chants and ceremonies emphasize restoration of wholeness, for disease is a condition of division and separation from the harmony of the whole. Beauty is wholeness. Health is wholeness.

Goodness is wholeness. The Hopi refer to a witch—a person who uses the powers of the universe in a perverse or inharmonious way—as a two-hearts, one who is not whole but is split in two at the center of being. The circle of being is not physical, but it is dynamic and alive. It is what lives and moves and knows, and all the life forms we recognize—animals, plants, rocks, winds—partake of this greater life. Acknowledgment of this dynamic unity allows healing chants such as this from the Night Chant to heal (make a person whole again):

> Happily I recover.
> Happily my interior becomes cool.
> Happily I go forth.
> My interior feeling cool, may I walk.
> No longer sore, may I walk.
> As it used to be long ago, may I walk.
> Happily, with abundant dark clouds, may I walk.
> Happily, with abundant showers, may I walk.
> Happily, with abundant plants, may I walk.
> Happily, on a trail of pollen, may I walk.
> Happily, may I walk.[9]

Because of the basic assumption of the wholeness or unity of the universe, our natural and necessary relationship to all life is evident; all phenomena we witness within or "outside" ourselves are, like us, intelligent manifestations of the intelligent universe from which they arise, as do all things of earth and the cosmos beyond. Thunder and rain are specialized aspects of this universe, as is the human race. Consequently, the unity of the whole is preserved and reflected in language, literature, and thought, and arbitrary divisions of the universe into "divine" and "worldly" or "natural" and "unnatural" beings do not occur.

Literature takes on more meaning when considered in terms of some relevant whole (like life itself), so let us consider some relationships between specific American Indian literary forms and the symbols usually found in them. The two forms basic to American Indian literature are the ceremony and the myth. The ceremony is the ritual enactment of a specialized perception of a cosmic relationship, while the myth is a prose record of that relationship. Thus, the wiwanyag wachipi (sun dance) is the ritual enactment of the relationship the Plains people see between consecration of the human spirit and Wakan Tanka as manifested as Sun, or Light, and Life-Bestower.

Through purification, participation, sacrifice, and supplication, the participants act as instruments or transmitters of increased power and wholeness, which bestows health and prosperity, from Wakan Tanka.

The formal structure of a ceremony is as holistic as the universe it purports to reflect and respond to, for the ceremony contains other forms such as incantation, song (dance), and prayer, and it is itself the central mode of literary expression from which all allied songs and stories derive. The Lakota view all the ceremonies as related to one another in various explicit and implicit ways, as though each were one face of a multifaceted prism. This interlocking of the basic forms has led to much confusion among non-Indian collectors and commentators, and this complexity makes all simplistic treatments of American Indian literature more confusing than helpful. Indeed, the non-Indian tendency to separate things from one another—be they literary forms, species, or persons—causes a great deal of unnecessary difficulty with and misinterpretation of American Indian life and culture. It is reasonable, from an Indian point of view, that all literary forms should be interrelated, given the basic idea of the unity and relatedness of all the phenomena of life. Separation of parts into this or that category is not agreeable to American Indians, and the attempt to separate essentially unified phenomena results in distortion.

For example, to say that a ceremony contains songs and prayers is misleading, for prayers are one form of address and songs are another. It is more appropriate to say that songs, prayers, dances, drums, ritual movements, and dramatic address are compositional elements of a ceremony. It is equally misleading to single out the wiwanyag wachipi and treat it as an isolated ceremony, for it must of necessity include the inipi (rite of purification) and did at one time contain the hanblecheyapi (vision quest), which was how the Lakota learned about it in the first place.[10] Actually, it might best be seen as a communal vision quest.

The purpose of a ceremony is to integrate: to fuse the individual with his or her fellows, the community of people with that of the other kingdoms, and this larger communal group with the worlds beyond this one. A raising or expansion of individual consciousness naturally accompanies this process. The person sheds the isolated, individual personality and is restored to conscious harmony with the universe. In addition to this general purpose, each ceremony has its own specific purpose. This purpose usually varies from tribe to tribe and may be culture-specific. For example, the rain dances of the Southwest are peculiar to certain groups, such as the Pueblos, and are not found among some other tribes, while war ceremonies, which make up a large part of certain Plains tribes' ceremonial life, are unknown among many tribes in California.[11] But all ceremonies, whether for war or healing, create and support the sense of community that is the bedrock of tribal life. This community is not made up only of members of the tribe but necessarily includes all beings that inhabit the tribe's universe.

Within this context the dynamic characteristics of American Indian literature can best be understood. The structures that embody expressed and implied relationships between human and nonhuman beings, as well as the symbols that signify and articulate them, are designed to integrate the various orders of consciousness. Entities other than the human participants are present at ceremonial enactments, and the ceremony is composed for their participation as well as for that of the human beings who are there. Some tribes understand that the human participants include members of the tribe who are not physically present and that the community as a community, not simply the separate persons in attendance, enact the ceremony.

Thus devices such as repetition and lengthy passages of "meaningless" syllables take on significance within the context of the dance. Repetition has an entrancing effect. Its regular recurrence creates a state of consciousness best described as "oceanic," but without the hypersentimental side effects implied by that term. It is hypnotic, and a hypnotic state of consciousness is the aim of the ceremony. The participants' attention must become diffused. The distractions of ordinary life must be put to rest and emotions redirected and integrated into a ceremonial context so that the greater awareness can come into full consciousness and functioning. In this way the participants become literally one with the universe, for they lose consciousness of mere individuality and share the consciousness that characterizes most orders of being.

In some sense repetition operates like the chorus in Western drama, serving to reinforce the theme and to focus the participants' attention on central concerns while intensifying their involvement with the enactment. One suits one's words and movements (if one is a dancer) to the repetitive pattern. Soon breath, heartbeat, thought, emotion, and word are one. The repetition integrates or fuses, allowing thought and word to coalesce into one rhythmic whole, which is not as jarring to the ear as rhyme.

Margot Astrov suggests that this characteristic device stems from two sources, one psychic and one magical:

> . . . this drive that forces man to express himself in rhythmic patterns has its ultimate source in psychic needs, for example the need of spiritual ingestion and proper organization of all the multiform perceptions and impressions rushing forever upon the individual from without and within . . . Furthermore, repetition, verbal and otherwise, means accumulation of power.[12]

Astrov finds evidence that the first, the need to organize perception, predominates in the ceremonies of some tribes, such as the Apaches, and that the second, a "magically creative quality," is more characteristic of others, such as the Navajo. In other words, some tribes appear to stress form while others stress content, but either way a tribe will make its selection in terms of which emphasis is most likely to bring about fusion with the cosmic whole in its group and environment. This fusion depends on the emphasis that is most congenial to the aesthetic and psychic sense of the tribe.

One should remember, when considering rhythmic aspects of American Indian poetic forms, that all ceremony is chanted, drummed, and danced. American Indians often refer to a piece of music as a dance instead of a song because song without dance is very rare, as is song without the use of a drum or other percussion instrument. One must also note that the drum does not "accompany" the song, for that implies separation between instrument and voice where no separation is recognized. Words, structure, music, movement, and drum combine to form an integral whole, and accompaniment per se is foreign to the ceremony, though it is common in western music. The ceremony may be enacted before people who are neither singing nor dancing, but their participation is nevertheless assumed. Participation is a matter of attention and attunement, not of activity.

Repetition is of two kinds, incremental and simple. In the first, variations will occur. A stanza may be repeated in its entirety four times—once for each of the directions—or six times—once for each lateral direction plus above and below—or seven times—once for each direction plus the center "where we stand." Alternatively, the repetition may be of a phrase only, as in the Yei be chi, or of a phrase repeated four times with one word—the ceremonial name for each of four mountains, say, or the names of significant colors, animals, or powers—inserted in the appropriate place at each repetition, as in this Navajo Mountain Chant:

Seated at home behold me,
Seated amid the rainbow;
Seated at home behold me,
Lo, here, the Holy Place!
    Yea, seated at home behold me.
At Sisnajinni, and beyond it,
    Yea, seated at home behold me;
The Chief of Mountains, and beyond it,
    Yea, seated at home behold me;
In Life Unending, and beyond it,
    Yea, seated at home behold me;
In Joy Unchanging, and beyond it,
    Yea, seated at home behold me.

Seated at home behold me,
Seated amid the rainbow;
Seated at home behold me,
Lo, here, the Holy Place!
    Yea, seated at home behold me.
At Tsodschl, and beyond it,
    Yea, seated at home behold me;
The Chief of Mountains, and beyond it,
    Yea, seated at home behold me;
In Life Unending, and beyond it,
    Yea, seated at home behold me;
In Joy Unchanging, and beyond it,
    Yea, seated at home behold me.

Seated at home behold me,
Seated amid the rainbow;
Seated at home behold me,
Lo, here, the Holy Place!
    Yea, seated at home behold me.
At Doko-oslid, and beyond it,
    Yea, seated at home behold me;
The Chief of Mountains, and beyond it,
    Yea, seated at home behold me;
In Life Unending, and beyond it,
    Yea, seated at home behold me;
In Joy Unchanging, and beyond it,
    Yea, seated at home behold me.

> Seated at home behold me,
> Seated amid the rainbow;
> Seated at home behold me,
> Lo, here, the Holy Place!
> Yea, seated at home behold me.
> At Depenitsa, and beyond it,
> Yea, seated at home behold me;
> The Chief of Mountains, and beyond it,
> Yea, seated at home behold me;
> In Life Unending, and beyond it,
> Yea, seated at home behold me;
> In Joy Unchanging, and beyond it,
> Yea, seated at home behold me.[13]

Some critics have said that this device results from the oral nature of American Indian literature, that repetition ensures attention and makes the works easy to remember. If this is a factor at all, however, it is a peripheral one, for nonliterate people have more finely developed memories than do literate people. The child learns early to remember complicated instructions, long stories—often verbatim—multitudes of details about plants, animals, kinship and other social relationships, privileges, and responsibilities, all "by heart." For a person who can't run to a bookshelf or a notebook to look up either vital or trivial information, reliance on memory becomes very important in everyday life. This highly developed everyday memory is not likely to fail on ceremonial occasions, so the use of repetition for ease of memorization is not significant.

Astrov, in her discussion of the "psychic" basis of the device, touches on another reason folklorists give for the widespread use of repetition in oral ceremonial literature:

> A child repeats a statement over and over for two reasons. First, in order to make himself familiar with something that appears to him to be threateningly unknown and thus to organize it into his system of familiar phenomena; and, second, to get something he wants badly.[14]

Astrov implies that repetition is childish on two counts: that it (rather than rational thought) familiarizes and defuses threat and that the person, irrationally, believes that oral repetition of a desire will ensure its gratification. Let us ignore the obvious fact that shamans, dancers, and other adult participants in the ceremony are not children and concentrate on actual ceremonies to see whether they contain factors that are or might appear "threatening" to the tribe or whether they simply repeat wishes over and over. Nothing in the passages quoted so far could be construed as threatening, unless beauty, harmony, health, strength, rain, breath, life unending, or sacred mountains can be so seen. Nor are any threatening unknowns mentioned in the songs and chants Astrov includes in her collection; there are threats implicit in death or great powers, but while these constitute unknowns to many civilized people, they are familiar to the tribes. And, by Astrov's own admission, the works approach death or severe illness in positive ways, as in this death song:

> From the middle
> Of the great water
> I am called by the spirits.[15]

"Light as the last breath of the dying," she comments, "these words flutter out and seem to mingle with the soft fumes and mists that rise from the river in the morning"—hardly a threatening description. She continues:

> It is as though the song, with the lightness of a bird's feather, will carry the departing soul up to where the stars are glittering and yonder where the rainbow touches the dome of the sky.[16]

Nowhere in her discussion of Indian songs does Astrov indicate that the singers feel threatened by the chants. Instead, she points out that they express serenity and even joy in the face of what might seem frightening to a child. Nor do there appear any passages, in her extensive collection, that are the equivalent of "Lord, Won't You Buy Me a Color TV," and the absence of such material weakens the childhood-magic theory of repetition. In fact, the usual American Indian perception of humanity (collectively, not individually) as cocreator discourages the people from perceiving the deity as a sort of cosmic bellhop who alone is responsible for their personal well-being. This perception simultaneously discourages people from setting themselves up as potentates, tyrants, dictators, or leaders of any other kind.

The failure of folklorists to comprehend the true metaphysical and psychic nature of structural devices such as ceremonial repetition is a result of the projection of one set of cultural assumptions onto another culture's customs and literatures. People of the Western cultures, particularly those in professions noted for their "objectivity" and intellectual commitment to Freudian tenets, are likely not to interpret psychic components of ceremonial literature in its extramundane sense but rather in its more familiar psychological sense. The twin assumptions that repetition serves to quiet childish psychological needs and to assure participants in a ceremony that they are exerting control over external phenomena—getting something they want badly—are projections. The participants do indeed believe that they can exert control over natural phenomena, but not because they have childishly repeated some syllables. Rather, they assume that all reality is internal in some sense, that the dichotomy of the isolate individual versus the "out there" only appears to exist, and that ceremonial observance can help them transcend this delusion and achieve union with the All Spirit. From a position of unity within this larger Self, the ceremony can bring about certain results, such as healing one who is ill, ensuring that natural events move in their accustomed way, or bringing prosperity to the tribe.

The westerner's bias against nonordinary states of consciousness is as unthinking as the Indian's belief in them is said to be. The westerner's bias is the result of an intellectual climate that has been carefully fostered in the west for centuries, that has reached its culmination in Freudian and Darwinian theories, and that only now is beginning to yield to the masses of data that contradict it. This cultural bias has had many unfortunate side effects, only one of which is deep misunderstanding of tribal literatures that has for so long marked the learned and popular periodicals that deal with tribal culture.

In his four-volume treatise on nonordinary reality, Carlos Castaneda has described what living in the universe as a shaman is like. Unfortunately, he does not indicate that this experience is rather more common to ordinary than to extraordinary people, that the state of consciousness created through ceremony and ritual and detailed in mythic cycles is exactly that of the "man of knowledge," or sage. He makes the whole thing sound exotic, strange, beyond the reach of most persons, yet the great body of American Indian literature suggests quite a different conclusion. This literature can best be approached as a psychic journey. Only in the context of the consciousness of the universe can it be understood.

American Indian thought is essentially mystical and psychic in nature. Its distinguishing characteristic is a kind of magicalness—not the childish sort described by Astrov but rather an enduring sense of the fluidity and malleability, or creative flux, of things. This is a reasonable attitude in its own context, derived quite logically from the central assumptions that characterize tribal thought. The tribal person perceives things not as inert but as viable and alive, and he or she knows that living things are subject to processes of growth and change as a necessary component of their aliveness. Since all that exists is alive and since all that is alive must grow and change, all existence can be manipulated under certain conditions and according to certain laws. These conditions and laws, called "ritual" or "magic" in the West, are known to American Indians variously. The Sioux refer to them as "walking in a sacred manner," the Navajo as "standing in the center of the world," and the Pomo as "having a tradition." There are as many ways of referring to this phenomenon as there are tribes.

The symbolism in American Indian ceremonial literature, then, is not symbolic in the usual sense; that is, the four mountains in the Mountain Chant do not stand for something else. They are those exact mountains perceived psychically, as it were, or mystically. The color red, as used by the Lakota, doesn't stand for sacred or earth, but it is the quality of a being, the color of it, when perceived "in a sacred manner" or from the point of view of the earth itself. That is, red is a psychic quality, not a material one, though it has a material dimension, of course. But its material aspect is not its essential one. As the great metaphysician Madame Blavatsky put it, the physical is not a principle; or, as Lame Deer the Lakota shaman suggests, the physical aspect of existence is only representative of what is real:

> The meat stands for the four-legged creatures, our animal brothers, who gave of themselves so that we should live. The steam [from the stewpot] is living breath. It was water; now it goes up to the sky, becomes a cloud again . . .
>
> We Sioux spend a lot of time thinking about everyday things, which in our mind are mixed up with the spiritual. We see in the world around us many symbols that teach us the meaning of life. We have a saying that the white man sees so little, he must see with only one eye. We see a lot that you no longer notice. You could notice if you wanted too, but you are usually too busy. We Indians live in a world of symbols and images where the spiritual and the commonplace are one. To you symbols are just words, spoken or written in a book. To us they are part of nature, part of ourselves, even little insects like ants and grasshoppers. We try to understand them not with the head but with the heart, and we need no more than a hint to give us the meaning.[17]

Not only are the "symbols" statements of perceived reality rather than metaphorical or poetic statements but the formulations that are characterized by brevity and repetition are also expressions of that perception. One sees life as part of oneself; a hint as to which particular part is all that is needed to convey meaning. This accounts for the "purity" and "simplicity" that apparently characterize traditional American Indian literatures. The works are simple in that they concern themselves with what is known and familiar, not in that they are childlike or unsophisticated.

In a sense, the American Indian perceives all that exists as symbolic. This outlook has given currency to the concept of the Indian as one who is close to the earth, but the closeness is actual, not a quaint result of savagism or childlike naiveté. An Indian, at the deepest level of being, assumes that the earth is alive in the same sense that human beings are alive. This aliveness is seen in nonphysical terms, in terms that are perhaps familiar to the mystic or the psychic, and this view gives rise to a metaphysical sense of reality that is an ineradicable part of Indian awareness. In brief, we can say that the sun or the earth or a tree is a symbol of an extraordinary truth.

This attitude is not anthropomorphic. No Indian would regard personal perception as the basic, or only, unit of universal consciousness. Indians believe that the basic unit of consciousness is the All Spirit, the living fact of intelligence from which all other perceptions arise and derive their power:

> I live, but I will not live forever.
> Mysterious moon, you only remain,
> Powerful sun, you alone remain,
> Wonderful earth, you remain forever.
> All of us soldiers must die.[18]

This attitude is not superstitious, though it can degenerate into superstition when the culture disintegrates. It is based very solidly on experience, and most members of the tribe share that experience to some degree. The experience is verified by hundreds and thousands of years of experience and is a result of actual perception—sight, taste, hearing, smell—as well as more indirect social and natural phenomena. In the West, if a person points to a building and says, "There is a building," and if other people looking in the direction indicated agree, and if that building can be entered, walked through, touched, then the building is said to be really there.

In the same way, traditional American Indians encounter and verify metaphysical reality. No one's experience is idiosyncratic. The singer who tells of journeying to the west and climbing under the sky speaks of a journey that many have taken in the past and will take in the future. Every traveler will describe the same sights and sounds and will enter and return in like fashion.

Generations of Western observers have noticed this peculiarity of psychic travel, and many attempt to explain it in psychoanalytic terms, referring to Jung's "collective unconscious," for example, or to Freud's notion of the projection of repressed conflict. Nevertheless, the evidence, however one interprets it, suggests that the psychic life of all humanity is the same. Western sophisticates presume that the experiences—sights, sounds, and beings encountered on psychic journeys—are imaginary and hallucinatory; they are equally inclined to presume that thoughts are idiosyncratic events of no real consequence. Nowhere in the literature on ceremonialism have I encountered a Western writer willing to suggest that the "spiritual and the commonplace are one."[19] Many argue that these "hallucinations" are good, others that they are the product of diseased minds,[20] but none suggests that one may *actually* be "seated amid the rainbow."

Symbols in American Indian systems are not symbolic in the usual sense of the word. The words articulate reality—not "psychological" or imagined reality, not emotive reality captured metaphorically in an attempt to fuse thought and feeling, but that reality where thought and feeling are one, where objective and subjective are one, where speaker and listener are one, where sound and sense are one.

The many kinds of American Indian literature can be categorized in various ways, but, given the assumptions behind the creation and performance of the literature, a useful division might be along functional lines rather than along more mechanical ones.

It might be said that the basic purpose of any culture is to maintain the ideal status quo. What creates differences among cultures and literatures is the way in which the people go about this task, and this in turn depends on, and simultaneously maintains, basic assumptions about the nature of life and humanity's place in it. The ideal status quo is generally expressed in terms of peace, prosperity, good health, and stability. Western cultures lean more and more heavily on technological and scientific methods of maintenance, while traditional cultures such as those of American Indian tribes tend toward mystical and philosophical methods. Because of this tendency, literature plays a central role in the traditional cultures that it is unable to play in technological ones. Thus, the purpose of a given work is of central importance to understanding its deeper significance.

We can divide traditional literature into two basic genres: ceremonial and popular, as opposed to the Western prose and poetry distinction. Ceremonial literature includes all literature that is accompanied by ritual actions and music and that produces mythic (metaphysical) states of consciousness and/or conditions. This literature may appear to the westerner as either prose or poetry, but its distinguishing characteristic is that it is to some degree sacred. The word *sacred*, like the words *power* and *medicine*, has a very different meaning to tribal people than to members of technological societies. It does not signify something of religious significance and therefore believed in with emotional fervor—"venerable, consecrated, or sacrosanct," as the Random House dictionary has it—but something that it is filled with an intangible but very real power or force, for good or bad. Lame Deer says in his discussion of symbolism:

> *Four* is the number that is most wakan, most sacred. Four stands for Tatuye Tope—the four quarters of the earth. One of its chief symbols is Umane, which looks like this:

> It represents the unused earth force. By this I mean that the Great Spirit pours a great unimaginable amount of force into all things— pebbles, ants, leaves, whirlwinds—whatever you will . . .
>
> This force is symbolized by the Umane. In the old days men used to have an Umane altar made of raised earth in their tipis on certain special occasions. It was so *wakan* you couldn't touch it or even hold your hand over it.[21]

Lame Deer is not saying that one was forbidden to touch the altar; he is saying that one *could not* touch it. The Umane does not represent the power; it *is* the power. *Sacred, power,* and *medicine* are related terms. Having power means being able to use this extra force without being harmed by it. This is a particular talent that human beings possess to greater or lesser degree, and *medicine* is a term used for the personal force through which one possesses power. Medicine is powerful in itself, but its power can be used only by certain persons, under certain conditions, and for certain purposes.

Ceremonial literature is sacred; it has power. It frequently uses language of its own: archaisms, "meaningless" words, or special words that are not used in everyday conversation. It can be divided into several subcategories, some of which appear in some tribes but not in others, and others that can be found throughout Indian America. Ceremonial literature includes songs for many occasions: healing; initiation; planting, harvesting, and other agricultural pursuits; hunting; blessing new houses, journeys, and undertakings. There are also dream-related songs; war songs; personal power songs; songs for food preparation, purification, and vision seeking. The subjects of the major ceremonial cycles include origin and creation, migration, celebration of new laws, and commemoration of legendary or mythic occurrences. Each serves to hold the society together, create harmony, restore balance, ensure prosperity and unity, and establish right relations within the social and natural world. At base the ceremonials restore the psychic unity of the people, reaffirm the terms of their existence in the universe, and validate their sense of reality, order, and propriety. The most central of these perform this function at levels that are far more intense than others, and these great ceremonies, more than any single phenomenon, distinguish one tribe from another.

Every tribe has a responsibility to the workings of the universe; today as yesterday, human beings play an intrinsic role in the ongoing creation. This role is largely determined by the place where the tribe lives, and the role changes when the tribe moves. In the Southwest, for example, the Zuñi dance Shalako every winter at the solstice so that the sun will turn in its course and move once again toward summer. Cosmic cycles such as Shalako or Wúwuchim relate to life processes on earth and, by virtue of natural relationship, within the universe. They aim toward forces far bigger than the community or the individual, though each is inescapably dependent on the other—"circles within circles," as Lame Deer says, "with no beginning and no end."[22]

The greater and lesser symbols incorporated into the ceremonies take their meaning from the context of the ceremony—its purpose and its meaning. Attempts to understand ceremonial literature without knowledge of this purpose often have ludicrous results. The symbols cannot be understood in terms of another culture, whether it be that of Maya or of England, because those other cultures have different imperatives and have grown on different soil, under a different sky within

73

the nexus of different spirits, and within a different traditional context. "Owl" in one situation will have a very different significance from "owl" in another, and a given color—white or blue—will vary from place to place and from ceremony to ceremony in its significance, intensity, and power. In other words, the rules that govern traditional American Indian literatures are very different from those that govern western literature, though the enormity of the difference is, I think, a fairly recent development. Literature must, of necessity, express and articulate the deepest perceptions, relationships, and attitudes of a culture, whether it does so deliberately or accidentally. Tribal literature does this with a luminosity and clarity that are largely free of pretension, stylized "elegance," or show. Experiences that are held to be the most meaningful—from those that completely transcend ordinary experience to those that are commonplace—are celebrated in the songs and ceremonial cycles of the people.

The more commonplace experiences are celebrated in popular tales and songs, which may be humorous, soothing, pedagogical, or entertaining. In this category are lullabies, corn-grinding and ditch-digging songs, jokes, pourquoi tales, "little" stories, and stories with contemporary settings. Included here, too, are those delightful dances called '49s.[23] All but the '49s appear in collections of Indian lore, sometimes masquerading as true myths or simple songs. This masquerade, of course, does little to clear up misunderstandings regarding American Indian literature, for frequently those "myths" that seem childlike are forms developed for children and bear only a slight resemblance to the true mythic chants from which they derive.

Between the trivial, popular forms and the ceremonial works are songs and stories such as various games; incantations and other simple forms of magic; prose cycles such as the Trickster tales recorded by Paul Radin; and some journey and food-related songs and legends.

Individual songs may be difficult to classify, though the level of symbolism they contain and the amount of prescribed ritual and associated ceremony, the number and special qualifications of the celebrants, and the physical setting and costume can help distinguish one kind from another. To classify any given song, though, one needs more than a nodding acquaintance with the locality and the tribe whose song or story is under consideration.

Another important factor to consider in classification of a song is the relative secrecy of parts or all of the ceremony, especially when tourists, cameras, or tape recorders are present. The amount of secrecy will vary to some extent from tribe to tribe, some being more open than others, but some secrecy is nearly always the rule.

Another such indicator, particularly valuable for classroom work, is the source of the song or story. Only very erudite tomes are likely to have much that is really sacred, and even those have usually been altered in some way. Popular books are likely to carry mainly popular literature, with a few selections from the next more powerful category. It would be well to mention, in this connection, that the use of really sacred materials by ordinary mortals and publishers is generally forbidden. Also, these works do not make good classroom materials for a variety of reasons: they are arcane; they are usually taboo; they tend to confuse non-Indian students; they may cause resentment among Indian students; and they create questions and digressions that are usually beyond the competence of the teacher or of the academic setting. Frequently they lead to ridicule, disrespect, and belittlement; non-Indian students are not inclined by training or culture to view the sacred as that which has power beyond that of economics, history, or politics.

Underlying all their complexity, traditional American Indian literatures possess a unity and harmony of symbol, structure, and articulation that is peculiar to the American Indian world. This harmony is based on the perceived harmony of the universe and on thousands of years of refinement. This essential sense of unity among all things flows like a clear stream through the songs and stories of the peoples of the western hemisphere. This sense is embodied in the words of an old man:

> There are birds of many colors—red, blue, green, yellow—yet it is all one bird. There are horses of many colors—brown, black, yellow, white—yet it is all one horse. So cattle, so all living things—animals, flowers, trees. So men: in this land where once were only Indians are now men of every color—white, black, yellow, red—yet all one people. That this should come to pass was in the heart of the Great Mystery. It is right thus. And everywhere there shall be peace.[24]

So Hiamove said, more than fifty years ago. It remains for scholars of American Indian literature to look at this literature from the point of view of its people. Only from this vantage can we understand fully the richness, complexity, and true meaning of a people's life; only in this way can we all learn the lessons of the past on this continent and the essential lesson of respect for all that is.

Whose Dream Is This Anyway?
Remythologizing and
Self-definition in Contemporary
American Indian Fiction

Indian narrative, old and new, portrays living
history, an angle of truth, a belief in people telling their lives directly, with pride and beauty.
To tell a story the Indian way, no less to write,
means not so much to fictionalize as to inflect
the truth of the old ways still with us . . . The
Indian storyteller enters the narrative less a
point-of-view, detached on the crosshairs of art,
more as a human presence, attended by an audience taking part in the narrative.
—Kenneth Lincoln,
Native American Renaissance

There are various kinds of American Indian novels. Some of them,
though written by American Indians, have little or nothing to say about
Indian life. The first novel published by a Native American, the Cherokee breed John Rollin Ridge's *Joaquin Murieta: The Celebrated
California Bandit* (1854), and the three novels written in the 1920s by
another Cherokee breed John Milton Oskison are largely of this category, though each in its way takes up themes that pervade later Native
American fiction proper. Ridge's novel, while not about Indians, is
about native response to invasion and conquest. Joaquin Murieta is a
California Mexican who avenges the murders of his people that occur
as a result of the gold rush, the Mexican-American War, and the
takeover of California by the United States. The novel contributed to
Chicano/Latino protest lore more than a hundred years after its writing. Oskison's three novels do not treat identifiably Indian themes, but

they are each set in Indian Territory and include Indians as minor characters. In his last novel, *Brothers Three,* Indians (breeds like himself) appear as major characters, and the futile struggle to function in the white world is that book's major theme. In *Brothers Three,* Oskison is the first Native American writer to take as a theme the prejudice experienced by breeds. In various guises, that theme would pervade Native American novels throughout the twentieth century.

Some Indian novels, such as James Fenimore Cooper's Leatherstocking series, James Rafferty's *Okla Hannali,* Frank Waters's *The Man Who Killed the Deer,* and Oliver LaFarge's *Laughing Boy,* are about Native Americans but are written by non-Indians. Many novels by white, Black, and Hispanic novelists have Indian characters or themes. These treatments are generally historic, centering around cultural conflict. Some, such as Lynn Andrews's or Carlos Castaneda's mystic series, incorporate ritual themes as a basis of their plot, but by far the most favored theme in novels about Indians by non-Indians is the plight of the noble Indian who is the hapless victim of civilized forces beyond his control. In a way, these are novels that underscore General Sherman's observation that "the only good Indians are dead" or that reflect America's view of the Indian "as a noble red man, either safely dead or dying as fast as could reasonably be expected," as A. LaVonne Ruoff succinctly summarizes it.[1]

The dying savage is the major theme of Oliver LaFarge's *Laughing Boy,* Frank Waters's *The Man Who Killed the Deer,* and James Fenimore Cooper's *The Last of the Mohicans.* Basically, the plot line is that a tribal person, usually a traditional, tries to adopt or adapt to white ways or values and comes to grief as a result. It is about the impact of conflicting cultures on an Indian. These writers view that impact as necessarily destructive to the protagonists and any others caught between two worlds with them. Similar to the morality tales of an older tradition in western literature and perhaps in an attempt to make contemporary the myth of the dying god, these novels tell of the innocent victim who must be sacrificed for reasons that are putatively historical and political but that are tightly allied with ancient western ritual literature at its source.

These novels seem to warn Indians against trying to make it in the white man's world. They often reinforce the belief common among both Indians and whites that Indians who attempt to adapt to white ways in any sense are doomed to death. Novels that portray the Indian as primitive, earth-loving guru and those that portray the Indian as

77

cosmic victim are written out of a white consciousness, and by and large they reflect white understanding of tribal culture and the impact of white culture on it. Essentially, they play on American notions about American Indian life and history, and where they are centrally concerned with the devastation wreaked on Indians by white people or white society, they highlight white guilt, rage, or grief at the supposed disappearance (always about to happen) of American Indians. Written for a white readership, these are white novels that take on Indians and Indian history, politics, cultures, and individuals as characters and themes in a white drama that descends from the ancient ritual and literary traditions of the west. They focus on culture conflict and its devastating impact on human life, largely because conflict is as basic to contemporary white fiction as ritual is to tribal Indian narrative. In this way, they are novels of colonization and treat its impacts, effects, and disasters as part of a novelistic plot.

Early novels by American Indian novelists leaned heavily on the same theme of the dying savage partly because it was most acceptable to potential publishers. In addition, popular and scholarly images of Indians as conquered, dying people had deeply affected American Indian self-perception, leading even Indian novelists to focus their works on that stereotype. But Indians used the colonization theme coupled with the western plot structure of conflict-crisis-resolution to tell their own stories largely because these structures appeared to explain tribal life and its chaotic disorganization since invasion and colonization. In such westernized Indian novels the Indians are portrayed as tragic heroes, beset by an unjust but inexorable fate. In a sense they become a race of dying kings. In all of the novels that use the story of conquest, devastation, and genocide as their major theme, white civilization plays the antagonist and becomes imbued with demonic power reserved in classic literature to fate and the gods.

The experience and the traditions of American Indians are complex and diverse rather than simple and unitary. We are much more than victims of white invasion and colonization, though that is a part of our common experience. But the ritual life of the tribes, the "religion" of the tribes, is also a common factor. For although our traditions are as diverse as the tribes who practice and live within them, they are all earth-based and wilderness-centered; all are "animistic," polytheistic, concerned with sacred or nonpolitical power, and all incorporate patterns that many in the western world identify as profane.

Indians have ever been polymorphous. Although commonly tribal in outlook and culture, Indians and their traditions are multitudinous, and so are the themes of their novels. But more and more, American Indian novels by Native American writers are concerned with tribal and urban life and have taken up themes that characterize and define that life in Native American terms. Most of these contemporary novels are ritualistic in approach, structure, theme, symbol, and significance, even though they use an overlay of western narrative plotting. They are the novels most properly termed American Indian novels because they rely on native rather than non-Indian forms, themes, and symbols and so are not colonial or exploitative. Rather, they carry on the oral tradition at many levels, furthering and nourishing it and being furthered and nourished by it.

American Indian novelists use cultural conflict as a major theme, but their work shows an increasing tendency to bind that theme to its analogues in whatever tribal oral tradition they write from. So while the protagonists in Native American novels are in some sense bicultural and must deal with the effects of colonization and an attendant sense of loss of self, each is also a participant in a ritual tradition that gives their individual lives shape and significance.

American Indians are tribal people who define themselves and are defined by ritual understandings, that is, by spiritual or sacred ceremonial shapings. What they choose of the options offered to or forced on them and how they shape those options and integrate them into their lives are determined by the form those choices can take within the ritual context of their tribal and personal life. Ritual rather than politics or language forms the basis of the tribal world and contemporary novels by American Indian writers reflect this grounding. This is not to say that the novels are rituals; rather, they derive many of their structural and symbolic elements from certain rituals and the myths that are allied with those rituals.[2]

Traditional tribal narratives possess a circular structure, incorporating event within event, piling meaning upon meaning, until the accretion finally results in a story. The structure of tribal narratives, at least in their native language forms, is quite unlike that of western fiction; it is not tied to any particular time line, main character, or event. It is tied to a particular point of view—that of the tribe's tradition—and to a specific idea—that of the ritual tradition and accompanying perspective that inform the narrative. Ritual provides coherence and significance to traditional narrative as it does to traditional life.

Ritual can be defined as a procedure whose purpose is to transform someone or something from one condition or state to another. While most rituals are related in some way to communitas, not all have social relationship and communication as their purpose. Their communitarian aspect derives simply from the nature of the tribal community, which is assumed to be intact as long as the ritual or sacred center of the community is intact. These centers vary from tribe to tribe: for the Lakota the ritual center of the people is the Sacred Pipe brought to them long ago by White Buffalo Woman. For the Kiowa that center is the ten Grandmother bundles. For the Cherokee it is the ceremonial fire. For many Pueblos it is the plaza, the "middle place," as N. Scott Momaday terms it in *House Made of Dawn*. It is not so much an idea of community as it is a tangible object seen as possessing nonrational powers to unite or bind diverse elements into a community, a psychic and spiritual whole. Thus a healing ritual changes a person from an isolated (diseased) state to one of incorporation (health); a solstice ritual turns the sun's path from a northerly direction to a southerly one or vice versa; a hunting ritual turns the hunted animal's thoughts away from the individual consciousness of physical life to total immersion in collective consciousness. In tribal traditions beings such as certain people and beasts, the sun, the earth, and sacred plants like corn are in a constant state of transformation, and that transformative process engenders the ritual cycle of dying, birth, growth, ripening, dying, and rebirth. In the transformation from one state to another, the prior state or condition must cease to exist. It must die.

Ritual-based cultures are founded on the primary assumption that the universe is alive and that it is supernaturally ordered. That is, they do not perceive economic, social, or political elements as central; rather, they organize their lives around a sacred, metaphysical principle. If they see a cause-and-effect relationship between events, they would ascribe the cause to the operation of nonmaterial energies or forces. They perceive the universe not as blind or mechanical, but as aware and organic. Thus ritual—organized activity that strives to manipulate or direct nonmaterial energies toward some larger goal— forms the foundation of tribal culture. It is also the basis of cultural artifacts such as crafts, agriculture, hunting, architecture, art, music, and literature. These all take shape and authority from the ritual tradition. Literature, which includes ceremony, myth, tale, and song, is the primary mode of the ritual tradition. The tribal rituals necessarily include a verbal element, and contemporary novelists draw from that verbal aspect in their work.

Western fiction, in contrast, is based on nonsacred aesthetic and intellectual precepts such as the importance of the unities of time, place, and action, and it is structured to create the illusion of change in the characters occurring over a period of time as a result of conflict and crisis. Myth criticism to the contrary, western novels are not ritual-based; that is, although they might incorporate elements drawn from ritual-based cultures such as those of pre-Christian England or ancient Greece, those borrowings are intellectual, aesthetic, or allusive. Indeed, critics of the 1970s and 1980s question whether rituals on which certain plots, such as that of the dying king, are based ever in fact existed.[3] Such questions are not germane to Native American novelists' use of ritual traditions; the Night Chant, from which Momaday draws heavily, does indeed exist and is practiced in Navajo country. The vision quest or "crying for pity" ritual from which James Welch draws for the structure and significance of both of his novels is currently practiced in much the same way it was practiced centuries ago.

Postmodern and experimental fiction writers often appear to disregard classic Western literary conventions, but they implicitly recognize them all the same. Native Americans reared in the oral tribal tradition, however, are not ignoring or "experimenting" with accepted conventions when they do not follow western structural conventions. Indeed, when they write within the conventions of the (Western) tradition from which James Joyce departs, they are being as experimental as he was when he wrote *Finnegans Wake*.

American Indian novelists who write more or less chronological narratives centered on Indian themes and adapt ritual narrative structures to the western convention of conflict resolution based on the unities of location, time, and action are very daring indeed. Those who follow western theme and plot conventions find themselves restricted to stories that center on loss of identity, loss of cultural self-determination, genocide or deicide, and culture clash. Perhaps as a result of following western literary imperatives, most writers of Indian novels create mixed-blood or half-breed protagonists, treating the theme of cultural conflict by incorporating it into the psychological and social being of the characters.

But at least since the publication of *Cogewea, the Half-Blood* by Okanogan/Coleville writer Mourning Dove (Humishuma) in 1927, this acquiescence to western publishing tastes is offset by a counterdevice. The protagonists are also participants in a ritual tradition, symbolizing the essential unity of a human being's psyche in spite of conflict. This development implies integration in the midst of conflict, fragmentation, and destruction and provides literary shapings of the process of nativistic renewal, a process that characterizes American Indian public life in the last quarter of the twentieth century.

Western novels of protest are aesthetic responses to oppression and cultural dissolution and generally focus on the oppressor rather than on the oppressed, a focus different from that taken by American Indians in this century. American Indians in general have more often than not refused to engage in protest in their politics as in their fiction and poetry. They have chosen rather to focus on their own customs and traditions and to ignore the white man as much as possible. As a result they have been able to resist effectively both colonization and genocide.

Since Mourning Dove, American Indian novelists have increasingly opted to focus on tribal consciousness in their work, a choice that results in more positive (because more actual) images of Indians. The ritual tradition is adaptive, and its adaptations are often strikingly dynamic. One of its recent major adaptations has been the merging of western and tribal literary forms by tribal story writers, including N. Scott Momaday (Kiowa), James Welch (Blackfeet/Gros Ventre), Leslie Marmon Silko (Laguna Pueblo), Gerald Vizenor (Anishinabe), and myself (Laguna Pueblo/Sioux). These American Indian novelists, published since 1967, have written particularly tribal novels: *House Made of Dawn* (Momaday), *Ceremony* (Silko), *Winter in the Blood* and *The Death of Jim Loney* (Welch), *The Darkness in Saint Louis Bearheart* (Vizenor), and *The Woman Who Owned the Shadows* (Allen).

These works reflect the complementary traditions of women and men, which have always been separate but interdependent in ritual traditions. Every part of the oral tradition expresses the idea that ritual is gender-based, but rather than acting as a purely divisive structure, the separation by gender emphasizes complementarity. The women's traditions are largely about continuity, and men's traditions are largely about transitoriness or change. Thus, women's rituals and lore center on birth, death, food, householding, and medicine (in the medical rather than the magical sense of the term)—that is, all that goes into the maintenance of life over the long term. Man's rituals are concerned with risk, death, and transformation—that is, all that helps regulate and control change. As long as conflict is not the primary requirement of fiction, these twin traditions can be incorporated into contemporary novels because their ideas are universal.

Mourning Dove and D'Arcy McNickle: Engulfment and Endurance

... We despised *breeds* are in a zone of our own and when we break from the corral erected about us, we meet up with trouble.
—Mourning Dove, *Cogewea, the Half-Blood*

It's too damn bad you people never learn that you can't run away. It's pathetic . . .
—D'Arcy McNickle, *The Surrounded*

Reflecting the female and male traditions, respectively, Mourning Dove focuses on survival as the recovery of tradition and D'Arcy McNickle focuses on the extinction of tradition.

Published in 1927, Mourning Dove's *Cogewea, the Half-Blood* is one of the early attempts at reconciliation of western and tribal narrative approaches.[4] The novel's heroine, the half-breed woman Cogewea, longs for a place in white society and views the Indian ways of her Okanogan grandmother (the Stemteema) with scorn. Uninterested in the advances of the half-breed cowboy Jim, she becomes infatuated instead with a white easterner on the make for money and position who courts Cogewea because the ranch hands lead him to believe that she is wealthy. Predictably, the white man betrays Cogewea and nearly murders her. Recovering from her loss of trust and self-confidence by reconnecting with tribal traditions and the spirit world, Cogewea heals and marries the faithful Jim.

Mourning Dove herself was caught between the contradictory imperatives of her editor's desires and tastes and her knowledge of how an Okonagon story should go. Her lack of formal schooling increased her dependence on her editor's tastes and opinions about novel writing. Her attempt to satisfy both white and tribal literary requirements resulted in a maimed—I should say martyred—book. *Cogewea, the Half-Blood* is far from being great literature. Rather, it is a melodramatic dime-novel western, but in focus on the anguish of a half-breed it "introduces a theme which dominates Native American fiction of the 30's and of the last decade."[5] It also incorporates myth and tribal history, political viewpoint, and spirit-based, ritual understanding and uses them to further plot. The resolution of Cogewea's dilemma rests on her acceptance of spirit and ritual approaches as having real significance in her life. For all its "cowboy" English, contrived plot, and polemical pronouncements, it integrates ritual symbolic, thematic, and structural elements and as such is one of the first Indian books of its kind.

Like Mourning Dove, D'Arcy McNickle (Salish) was born and raised in the Northwest. In addition to publications on American Indian history and ethnography and one children's novel, McNickle published two adult novels, *The Surrounded* (1936) and *Wind from an Enemy Sky* (1978).[6] From invasion, which stretches from 1492 in the Caribbean to the 1880s in the United States (and is still occurring in parts of Central and South America), onward as far as the colonizers, particularly Americans, were concerned, Native Americans were faced with a choice between assimilation and extinction. This choice, forced on them through wars and policies that made other options such as resistance appear untenable, was eventually accepted as inevitable by many Native Americans. McNickle explores the Indian view of their dilemma in his novels, writing within the constraints of western literary forms. He focuses on tribal perspectives, pitting traditional values and customs against those of the alien invaders. Although this approach makes him the first Native American novelist to successfully use the novel to present a tribal point of view, he does not rely on ritual tradition to inform his work in any intrinsic way. Consequently, his novels treat the Indian as tragic victim as do the novels of non-Indian American writers. Like Mourning Dove, McNickle uses references to tribal beliefs as a way of furthering the plot, illuminating the terms of the conflict the Indian characters face, and providing the basis for resolution. The resolution for both his novels is the colonial solution to the Indian dilemma: resignation to inevitable extinction.

Like Cogewea, the protagonist in *The Surrounded* is a half-breed, Archilde Leon. Leon, inextricably caught in the conflict between Indian and white worlds, is largely an innocent victim of that clash, helpless to alter his fate or that of his Salish people. *Wind from an Enemy Sky* has full-bloods as main characters and more fully and more significantly uses ritual to advance the plot. *Wind from an Enemy Sky* begins with the completion of a dam, which in the traditionals' view kills the water, and the book ends with the murder of the traditional leader of the longhair band that had held out against accepting white ways. Long before, the same white man whose company built the dam bought the Feather Boy medicine bundle, which was sold him by a local cleric. The bundle is the ritual heart of the people, and their loss of it affects them deeply. They hope throughout the book that the bundle will be returned, but they discover, at the white man's admission, that he has somehow lost it. Thus with the death of the water comes the tribe's knowledge of the death of its ritual center.

The foregrounding of ritual in *Wind from an Enemy Sky* reflects changes in Native American self-images in the years between 1936, when *The Surrounded* was written, and 1976, when *Wind from an Enemy Sky* was written. But the late book does not depart significantly from the earlier work in the way it uses ritual structures. As a result it presents an even more anguished view of the ultimate fate of traditional Indians. In both novels the primary conflict is between Indian and white, and both are mainly concerned with cultural extinction as the inexorable fate of the Indians, whether they are half-breed or full-blood, traditional or assimilated.

McNickle's novels effectively demonstrate an interesting feature of novels about Indians written out of a western literary tradition: conflict-based plots require a tragic outcome if the relationships between Indian and white are represented with historical accuracy. When Indian is pitted against white, ritual against technology, and spirit-based value systems against materialistic philosophies, there can be no resolution other than the destruction of the tribal, that is, the ritual life of the colonized. In *The Surrounded* McNickle succinctly sums up the terms of the conflict in the words of the Indian agent who stalks the Indians: "It's too damn bad you people never learn that you can't run away. It's pathetic" (pp. 296–297).

Whereas *The Surrounded* is brutally fatalistic, *Wind from an Enemy Sky* is profoundly tragic, concerned as it is with deicide. It is about the conflict between traditionals and whites and between traditional Indians and those Indians who "came in," that is, accepted the whites' peace terms and left their traditional life, becoming ranchers or farmhands. Mostly it is concerned with the loss of the ritual center of the people, the Feather Boy medicine bundle that is their source of psychic and spiritual identity. The ultimate fate of the Indians is left to the imagination of the reader, but McNickle gives little doubt as to what that fate will be. In the words of Two Sleeps, an old man whose visions have guided the traditionals for some time, "This is where we end. All our days are here together at last" (p. 256).

N. Scott Momaday and James Welch: Transition and Transcendence

> *Dypolah.* There was a house made of dawn. It was made of pollen and of rain, and the land was very old and everlasting. There were many colors on the hills, and the plain was bright with different-colored clays and sands. Red and blue and spotted horses grazed in the plain, and there was a dark wilderness on the mountains beyond. The land was still and strong. It was beautiful all around.
>
> —N. Scott Momaday, *House Made of Dawn*

> Scattered in the wind
> Earthboy calls me from my dreams:
> Dirt is where the dreams must end.
>
> —James Welch, *Winter in the Blood*

American Indian novels can easily be read as novels of protest. Such a reading is of course heavily influenced by contemporary social attitudes toward all colonized people in the United States—black and Chicano as well as Native American. Male Indian novelists further the impression of protest because their heroes are beset by difficulties, many directly attributable to white presence. The hero is unable to overcome the deadly onslaught of forces inimical to his survival, and the result is often the hero's death or the destruction of his accustomed life.

But the male novelist's preoccupation with the theme of the inexorability of death may be as much a function of male ritual life as of recent Native American history. As far as I know, the male tradition across the Americas centers on encounters with death that lead to transformation. For tribes that follow the ritual path of war, the warrior is able to face death with courage, honor, and dignity. The warrior path requires that a man look at death and face it down. Hunting rituals, when all is said and done, are death rituals, and rituals initiating a male into manhood, medicine societies, or shamanism are generally formulated in terms of physical death followed by a transformed life that is not the same as physical life but that in some characteristics, especially bodily ones, resembles it.[7] Often the novice experiences ritual death, and only when his "death" has been accomplished can he enter into the ritual life he is being readied for, transformed by his experience into a quasi-supernatural. In this way tribal men's rituals enable them to participate directly in the process of transformation, a participation that women, by virtue of their ability to bleed menstrually and to give birth, are naturally privy to. Initiation into a medicine society or into shamanhood requires a transformation analogous to that experienced by the hunted deer or other creature. Men's rituals often center on transformation as an entity in itself.

In keeping with the ritual bias that informs American Indian novels, the male writers' focus on personal, cultural, or ritual death reflects traditional tribal male understandings. Of the Indian men who have published major novels, N. Scott Momaday is the clearest in denying that cultural conflict must result in either genocide or deicide. Although he does not in the end spare Abel, the protagonist of *House Made of Dawn* (1968), pain and mutilation, he weaves the suffering into the context of both a Walotowa (Jemez Pueblo) and Navajo ritual framework in which they are comprehensible and necessary in the life of the tribal hero.[8] In this way Momaday makes male ritual traditions the basis of a plot that transforms Abel from a fragmented, isolated human being into a member of a supernatural brotherhood and from an alienated man into a spiritual participant in the cosmic being of the tribe. Abel, the mixed-blood (Walotowa and probably Navajo) grandson of a Walotowa named Francisco, is so alienated from his people that he cannot speak to his grandfather in any of the three languages they speak. Although he has exhibited symptoms of alienation throughout his youth, Abel's alienation, intensified by alcoholism, has reached nearly psychotic proportions by the time he returns from his stint in the U.S. Army during World War II. Shortly after his return, he engages in a sexual affair with a pregnant, wealthy white woman from Los Angeles, Angela St. John, who is taking the baths at Los Ojos near Walotowa. The relationship only heightens his alienation and adds to his inarticulate rage. At the Feast of Santiago during the rooster pull, he is savagely beaten with the dead rooster by the winner, an albino tribesman. That night he kills the albino because he believes (rightly, it seems) that the albino, who is usually referred to in the text as the white man, is a witch and that "a man kills such an enemy if he can" (95).[9] But it is not the fact of his witchery that makes the albino a victim of Abel's murderous rage; Abel murders the witch because, for personal and historical reasons that become apparent as the plot develops, he believes that paganism is evil and that it must be destroyed. His dilemma is one that Native Americans have faced since white contact: how does one remain whole while accepting the supernatural and ritual practices of the tribe and simultaneously assimilating white Christian attitudes required by white presence and white colonization? Abel's personality, his alcoholism, and his rejection of tribal ways lead him to violence as a response to the dilemma, a response that characterizes him as psychologically disturbed among a people who do not condone interpersonal violence as a means of resolving difficulties, however arcane those difficulties might be.

Charged in the white courts with murder, Abel is sent to federal prison. On his release, he is relocated by the parole board to Los Angeles, where he tries unsuccessfully to hold a job and find companionship among the Indians there. This is impossible, partly because of Abel's intransigent traditionalism and partly because that traditionalism arouses the scorn of the community's leader, a highly assimilated Kiowa named Tosamah. Abel reverts to drinking and is beaten nearly fatally by a Mexican-American police officer named Martinez. Lying on the Los Angeles beach where he crawled after the beating, he understands, finally, his own place in the universe. After he is released from the hospital, he returns to Walotowa, still wounded and mutilated, in time to watch over his grandfather's death. When the old man is dead, Abel smears himself with ashes and joins the ritual runners. So marked, he participates in the ancient "race of the dead" (195) and takes his place behind his grandfather in the long line of "hombres negros" (175) in their eternity-long run that keeps evil in its place. He runs behind them into clear seeing and into the ritual song of healing that Benally, Abel's Navajo friend in Los Angeles, sang for him so often: "House made of pollen, House made of dawn" (191).

From the beginning to the end of the novel, Momaday focuses on rituals and traditions of the Walotowa, Navajo, and Kiowa. The plot loosely follows a conflict-crisis-resolution pattern, but the novel is more deeply structured to match the Navajo ceremonials known as chantways. The primary purpose of these rituals is healing, based on the Navajo understanding that health depends on an integrated psyche. In the Navajo system, an isolated or alienated individual is a sick one, so the healing practice centers on reintegrating the isolated individual into the matrix of the universe. Because it is structured after ritual patterns, the resolution of *House Made of Dawn* lies not in the death of Abel or that of Francisco but in their willing and knowledgeable participation in the ritual pattern that informs their tribal life. That is, not only do they engage in ritual practice but they understand its proper role in the scheme of things, a role that continues beyond the grave and that thus makes death only another kind of ritual trans-formation.

The narrative that accompanies the Navajo Night Chant, one of the many chantways used among the Navajo for healing, is about Crippled Boy and Blind Boy, who are abandoned when the tribe moves. Thus condemned to certain death, Blind Boy carries Crippled Boy on his shoulders, and so teamed they make their way. They come to a high cliff and climb it. At the top they encounter some Holy People who teach them the Night Chant. Momaday has reformulated the overt elements of the narrative: Abel is not blind, but dumb. He is not crippled, though his grandfather Francisco walks with a limp, and Abel himself is seriously maimed in the beating from the Mexican cop. The main way in which Abel resembles the heroes of the traditional tale is in his ostracism and the seeming inevitability of his death in isolation and despair. The Holy People do not appear directly as characters in the novel until the final episode, but they are present throughout in a number of indirect ways. They are most like themselves in the story Abel's white lover Angela tells to her son about the bear and the maiden (169–171). The story told by the assimilated Tosamah about the Taime tree of the Kiowa gives a Kiowa version of the supernaturals (89–90), and they are at least referred to in the Peyote ceremony in Los Angeles (104–106), and in the Bull and Horse ceremony at the pueblo (80). They are most present in the superb descriptions of the land, in which Momaday expresses the reverence for the land and its creatures that is the hallmark of American Indian consciousness and of tribal literature.

The question of witchcraft enters powerfully into the tale Moma-day weaves. Nicolas teah-whau, as the children called the Bahkyush witch, cursed Abel when he was young (15–16). It seems that years before, Francisco had engaged in sexual relations with Porcingula, Nicolas's daughter, who was also considered a witch and whose in-volvement with dark powers was made clear when the child she carried as a result of her affair with Francisco was stillborn. Momaday sug-gests that Nicolas holds Francisco responsible for that event, cursing not only Abel but his mother and his brother, both of whom died when Abel was young.

As a youth, Francisco was chosen by the supernaturals, an honor that was signaled when he ran a perfect race, winning against his rival, Mariano. On that day he did everything perfectly, and "from then on had a voice in the clan and the next year he healed a child who had been sick from birth." It is clear that Francisco has bear power, for he tracks a large bear, and it agrees to give him its life (178–184). He is also a favorite of the old Spanish priest, Fray Nicolas, who is rumored to have been his father (184). The old priest rejects the boy after Francisco becomes a man, for he sees that Francisco is a longhair, "one of them & goes often in the kiva & puts on their horns & hides & does worship that Serpent which even is the One our most ancient enemy" (50).

From the old priest's point of view, there is no good in paganism; it is all of the devil. But from a tribal point of view, all paganism is sorcery; if one accepts tribalism as a way of life, then one must accept "devil" worship or "witchcraft" with the same reverence and respect as one accepts other rites. This is something that Francisco is able to do throughout his life, but it is beyond Abel's ability without his first suffering greatly for his psychological inflexibility.

Colonization does not, after all, affect people only economically. More fundamentally, it affects a people's understanding of their universe, their place within that universe, the kinds of values they must embrace and actions they must make to remain safe and whole within that universe. In short, colonization alters both the individual's and the group's sense of identity. Loss of identity is a major dimension of alienation, and when severe enough it can lead to individual and group death. When an individual's sense of self is, like Abel's, distorted by the impact of contradictory points of view, colonization and its terrible effects will not be assuaged by mere retention of land rights or economic self-sufficiency. The whites either fear paganism greatly (Fray Nicolas) or simply dismiss it as superstition (Fr. Olguin and even Tosamah). Faced with an assessment of his tribal identity that either damns or discounts it, Abel reacts to socially induced loss of identity with growing violence. First he murders the pagan albino. Then he antagonizes the Los Angeles cop into nearly killing him.

Abel must come to terms with the reality of paganism and its requirements so that the terror that has haunted him and the rage that is his response to it can be harmonized into their proper form and he can take his proper place in the universe. In the end, Abel understands and accepts the ancient tribal order, its beauty, its fearfulness, its significance, and its pattern. And in the end, as he runs to join the Runners-After-Evil, whom Momaday also calls the Dawn Runners, he backs up his understanding with action, demonstrating that he is truly restored to wholeness, to health.

James Welch's *Winter in the Blood* (1974) is no happier a book than *House Made of Dawn*, though it is appreciably more comic.[10] Welch skillfully disguises the ritual basis of his novel within a style that is witty and satiric and a form that can be seen as surreal. It is important to keep in mind that surrealism is a European mode that derives from psychoanalytic notions about the nature of the mind; the style and form of the American Indian writers, however, are based on the tribal notion about the nature of existence. It happens that both see dream as a primary vehicle of creative power, but they approach the dream differently and understand the nature and source of creative power differently. In the arcane tradition from which Welch writes, dream and vision are synonymous. For men, obtaining a vision is related to the warrior tradition, and a man who has had a vision is a fully functioning adult, possessing an identity that is of both ritual and practical significance to himself and his peers.

Both of Welch's novels (*Winter in the Blood* and *The Death of Jim Loney*) are developed along the general lines of vision-questing or "crying for pity" as it is practiced on the Northern Plains. As the plot of *Winter in the Blood* unfolds, the nameless protagonist, who is also the narrator, locates the balance and sense of identity that the ritual is designed to bring about.[11] Seeking a vision, or "crying for pity," is a ritual practiced widely among traditional Native Americans. In different forms it is done by both women and men, though its male form is the one that Welch uses in his work. In the ritual a youth goes out to find himself through prayer, fasting, wandering, and, in some traditions, mutilation. The seeker hopes to gain a vision because through doing so he will also gain a secure adult identity and some "medicine," that is, some personally owned item that will empower him in certain ways. He might get a song or a ritual. He might get a powerful crystal, a particularly charged stone, or a spirit guide who is some creature like an eagle, a wolf, a coyote, an ant, but who in any case counsels the seeker in certain crucial situations that have bearing on the seeker's "path." Until he has a vision the youth is not an adult, that is, a ritually acknowledged member of his community. He has no adult name, a circumstance that marks him as a "child" who cannot take on his adult responsibilities in the community.

In *Winter in the Blood*, the Blackfeet protagonist, in accordance with the dictates of the vision quest, is seeking his adult identity. Until he finds it he will be required to live in his mother's house, work for her, and in general take the part of a child. In his mid-thirties, he is not a youth but neither is he yet an adult.

He brings a Cree woman home to his mother's house, saying she is his wife, but she leaves when he is out on a drinking spree, taking his gun and razor with her. His grandmother is distressed by the Cree woman's presence because the Cree are the traditional enemy of the Blackfeet. The nameless protagonist spends the rest of the story driving between his mother's home and nearby Havre, Montana, trying to locate the woman and get his gun and razor back. During his wanderings he meets a mysterious white man who talks about good fishing in the river, which has been bereft of fish for some time. He joins forces with the white man, a trickster figure who offers him a new car and who exhibits uncanny skill at gambling. He also engages in a number of sexual escapades. He does find his "wife," but her brother beats him, preventing him from finding out where his gun and razor are as well as from connecting with the Cree woman again.

In the course of the novel the protagonist follows the vision quest ritual: he is mutilated and he seeks an older man who can serve as his guide. He wanders the "surrealistic" streets of Havre, encountering a number of strange beings; he is connected to animal guides throughout the story—a spinster cow, a horse named Bird, a duck called Amos, and the perplexing fish who magically appear and disappear from the filthy river. Most significantly, he is required to consider the place of tradition in his life. Tradition, for him, comes through his grandparents, as it does in most tribal traditions, and his grandmother's death at the end of the novel signifies that he has incorporated the traditions she represents into his own psyche, making her transition from the material to the nonmaterial world possible and proper.

The novel follows the ritual tradition in structure as well as in theme, for it incorporates dream/vision, the clown (or trickster), reflection or meditations, seeking, adventure, humiliation, suffering, desire, ritual accoutrements (such as the stolen gun, the razor, and the tobacco pouch his grandmother was never without), humor, insight, ancient lore, and tribal history. Like stories from the oral tradition, it meanders through time with little regard for chronology, beginning in the center, the here and now, and moving around it in widening circles. By the end of the story, the interrelationships of the events chronicled in the narrative have become clear. The reason for their occurrence is largely a matter of their interrelationships and the significance of the events taken as a whole rests on their relationship to the nonrational or "mysterious" aspects of being as tribal people see it, so readers can understand the significance of the events and can see how the narrator has located himself, has found a center of balance from which he can move into adulthood.

Like *Winter in the Blood,* Welch's second novel, *The Death of Jim Loney* (1979), is based on vision ritual. Like a questor who seeks his vision alone and far from his community, Loney is isolated, abandoned, neglected. He is mutilated, thirsty, and starving, is entirely poverty-stricken in mind, body, and heart. In this condition he obtains a vision that becomes the guiding force in his life and his death, and he dies like a warrior in a place and at a time of his own choosing.

In his early thirties, Loney, who was one of the abandoned children of a full-blood mother and an Irish father, has lived alone since high school. He has a girlfriend, a Texas schoolteacher, and though he knows most of the people in the small town in Montana where he grew up, he has no close friends. He is isolated from all the communities he might be connected to: the small town community he lives in, the Indian community his mother came from, the Catholic community he was raised by, even the men's community of ex–basketball stars and their onetime fans. The novel makes it clear that ritual does not necessarily lead to a sense of community; indeed, Loney's quest for understanding of himself, his history, and his life leads him away from community. And his quest is largely ritually embraced and prescribed. He makes his search because he is having visions and waking dreams that he cannot control or change and that he does not understand. His desire to understand the significance of his visions leads him to the wilderness pass where he dies, killed by a high school classmate, a full-blood who has become a tribal cop.

Welch finds his resolutions in self-knowledge gained in traditional ways that are adapted to modern contexts. His characters go through a period of intense self-examination and reflection about their lives and the universe they live in. In the end, after a series of magical and extraworldly encounters, they come to terms with their existence and with their personal histories. Welch's novels are best understood in the context of the dream/vision ritual structure of Plains tribal life, for they are structured along the lines of the vision rather than on the chronological lines of mundane or organizational life, and the structure of the works holds the major clue to the nature of the novels as primarily tribal documents.

Like Momaday, Welch follows the accretive narrative structure of the oral tradition. Their novels weave in and out of past, present, and future, incorporating vision and dream into the action as the story moves toward its inevitable conclusion. Because the novels are designed to reflect ritual or tribal world-views, the distinctions usually made between "realism" and "surrealism" are inverted, reversed, or ignored entirely. In accordance with ritual literature of the oral tradition, in these novels the time line is achronological; that is, the ritual nature of time is the measure used, so action sequences include memories, legends, histories, dreams, and visions, the combination of which suggests the integrative nature of ritual consciousness. So crucial is the difference between mundane timekeeping and ritual time that the sense of time used in tribal novels determines what kind of consciousness is reflected in the novel—western, industrial, secular or tribal, wilderness, ritual consciousness.

In *House Made of Dawn* Momaday makes direct reference to the centrality of ritual time for an understanding of tribal literature and tribal life. He describes a time when Francisco took his grandsons, Abel and Abel's brother Vidal, out to Campo Santo, "south and west of the Middle." There Francisco instructed the boys in the importance of ceremonial time telling:

> There, at the rounder knoll, it was time to plant corn and there, where the highest plane fell away, that was the day of the rooster race, six days ahead of the black bull running and the little horse dancing, seven ahead of the Pecos immigration; and there, and there, and there, the secret dances, every four days of fasting in the kiva, the moon good for hoeing and the time for harvest, the rabbit and witch hunts, all the proper days of the clans and societies; and just there at the saddle, where the sky was lower and brighter than elsewhere on the high black land, the clearing of the ditches in advance of the spring rains and the long race of the black men at dawn. (p. 177)

Francisco thus shows that the significance of the lives of individuals in a tribal setting is inextricably linked to ritual. Pointing to different spots on black mesa, which is the geological calendar of the Walotowa, he shows his grandsons how to determine what time it is, "for only then could they reckon where they were, where all things were, in time." (pp. 177–178)

Leslie Marmon Silko and Gerald Vizenor: Healing and Ritual

And in the belly of this story
  the rituals and the ceremony
    are still growing.
    —Leslie Marmon Silko, *Ceremony*

Whose dream is this, anyway?
    —Gerald Vizenor, *The Darkness*
      in Saint Louis Bearheart

The novels of Leslie Marmon Silko and Gerald Vizenor[12] move deeply into the traditional world. Their concern with tribal perspectives is even more overt in plot, style, and structure than is Welch's and Momaday's. Both *Ceremony* (1977) and *The Darkness in Saint Louis Bearheart* (1978) are noticeably closer to wilderness and farther from civilization in setting and in content. But they are situated along a continuum from tribal narrative and ritual to western narrative and have structural features in common with their predecessors' books. Like Momaday and Welch, Silko uses short blocks of narrative and pays little attention to chronological timing. Locating events within the ritual context that supports them, she relies on accretive structuring to build toward comprehensive significance in her novel, as do traditional storytellers. Some sections in her narrative do not have any overt connection to the story being told. One is about a small boy, Tayo, who lives in the Gallup arroyo with his mother and a number of homeless Indians. Another is about a young woman who went to boarding school and tried to become white. These stories are analogues within the narrative; the former gives the reader a clear picture of the protagonist Tayo's early life before he was taken to live permanently at the pueblo with his mother's sister, and the latter describes a process analogous to the one that caught Tayo's mother in a world she could neither enter nor leave.

Silko also inserts a clan story from Laguna set in short poetic lines into the conventionally set prose of the novel, adding a definite traditional flavor and providing a text by which to determine the significance of ritual tradition in the novel. The clan story is about Reed Woman and Fly, the rainbearers in both the narrative and ritual versions of the rain-bringing event. Silko uses this clan ritual narrative in a ceremonial way as an analogue to her own story about Tayo and the long drought he helps the region recover from, thus illuminating the connection between the ritual tradition, the storytelling tradition, and a contemporary working out in a novel of both tribal forms. By using a nonsequential structure that is accretive, achronological, and interspersed with the traditional clan ritual narrative about how the rain is made to return to the village, Silko shows that clear understanding of a given narrative depends on proper understanding of the stories attached to each significant word. In this way stories are themselves ritual events (though their ritual power comes from their relation to the actual rituals they refer to). Silko explains the process in the following sequence, in which Ku'oosh, a Laguna priest ("medicine man") tells the seriously ill Tayo how the world works and how the words that connect a person with the world work:

> But you know, grandson, this world is fragile. The word he chose to express "fragile" was filled with the intricacies of a continuing process, and with a strength inherent in spider webs woven across paths through sand hills where early in the morning the sun becomes entangled in each filament of web. It took a long time to explain the fragility and intricacy because no word exists alone, and the reason for choosing each word had to be explained with a story about why it must be said this certain way. (p. 35)

Two of *Ceremony*'s major themes are the centrality of environmental integrity and the pacifism that is its necessary partner, common motifs in American literature in the last quarter of the twentieth century. Silko develops them entirely out of a Laguna/Keres perspective, for both themes are fundamental to the fabric of Keres pueblo life and thought. She also takes up witchcraft as a central theme, and in turn weaves these strands into the design laid down in the clan story, which itself is the prose account or prescription for a ceremony.

Momaday was the first American Indian novelist to take up the subject of ritual as witchcraft in considering its effect on Abel and his people in *House Made of Dawn*. There he explored the tribal mode of perceiving the conflict between good and evil as a complementary dialogue and compared it both to the Christian belief that all pagan ritual is evil and is by nature opposed to the good and to the contemporary feeling of some Christians and urban Indians that beliefs in ritual or witchcraft are primitive and have been culturally inculcated into members of a cultural system. In *Ceremony* Silko continues this exploration, positing a ceremony that will counter the "witchery." Like Momaday, she sees ritual as having dual faces, one evil, one good. Unlike Momaday's protagonist, Silko's protagonist is required to choose between good and bad, and the survival of his people rests on his decision. Abel is required to understand that all ritual is sacred and leads to the continuance of the tribe.

Gerald Vizenor reconciles the opposing forces of good and evil in the manner of his Anishinabe (Chippewa) people. He evokes the power of Wenebejo, Trickster, who is the personification of the chaotic creative power that accompanies his main characters on their pilgrimage to find "nothing more than a place to dream again" (206). With this tribal and ritual device, Vizenor cuts through Christian-based dichotomies about good and evil, creative and destructive forces, and their analogues. Thus far the funniest and most brutal American Indian novel written, *Bearheart* reflects the facts of Indian life more faithfully than its predecessors and removes Indian fiction entirely from its colonizer-influenced frameworks.

Like all trickster narratives, *Bearheart* is obscene and occasionally scatological because it is founded on the tribal perception of the essential humor of earthly life. As is usual in trickster rituals such as those enacted by clown societies in the Southwest and Northwest or by false-faces in the Northeast, every aspect of contemporary American and American Indian life, even the sacred, is targeted for ridicule. But it is also a serious and profoundly reverent book, and in joining these usually divergent impulses, Vizenor establishes the kind of chaotic equilibrium that the wilderness itself establishes.

Its thirteen pilgrims, each of whom reflects some aspect of Wenebejo's nature, are led by an old Anishinabe shaman, Proude Cedarfair. Along with seven "clown crows" and one shaman-dog, Pure Gumption, they journey across the Plains from the Mississippi to northwestern New Mexico where they find their new place to dream. Along the way all but two of the pilgrims die, including the clearest Wenebejo figure, Double Saint Plumero Bigfoot. A total innocent whose lust knows no bounds, Bigfoot responds to death and danger with whatever sexual activity occurs to him. Like the Winnebago Trickster Wenebejo, Bigfoot is graced with an oversized penis (which matches his oversized feet) named "president jackson." As with Trickster, Bigfoot suffers most of his grief because of his penis, and again like Trickster, Bigfoot and his penis are immortal. The night after his murder he is still alive, though not in the flesh, and spends the night tumbling joyously with Rosina, the bear-shaman Cedarfair's wife, in her dreams.

Because *Bearheart* is written in the trickster-clown mode, much of the novel is offensive, however one looks at it. Vizenor leaves no icon unbroken in his mad pursuit of primordial balance. Like the sacred clowns of the Pueblos, he suggests that nothing is sacred, and with them he walks us backward through a futuristic scenario into the ancient past of the earth. Cedarfair and the stranger become bears, and with a "haa ha haa" they enter the fourth world, leaving us to contemplate ourselves in their absence.

Paula Gunn Allen:
Generation, Regeneration, and Continuance

> And they will take you by the hands and lead you forward
> into the dark that will seem as bright as day. They will take
> you to the heart of midnight, the heart of the sun. They will
> charm your heart away.
> —Paula Gunn Allen,
> *The Woman Who Owned the Shadows*

My own novel, *The Woman Who Owned the Shadows* (1983), looks specifically to women's traditions for its ritual foundations.[13] Long ignored by white and Indian writers alike, these traditions are the basis for much of tribal society in the Americas. My choice is not surprising: as a daughter of Laguna, a Keres pueblo, I was raised with a gynocratic perspective, one not unmixed with patriarchal views, however.

As already mentioned, women's rituals are traditionally centered on continuance. While women experience transformations accompanied by danger, blood, and death, they also create life from their own flesh. The transformative phases of a woman's life alter the degree of power (in the medicine or sacred sense) that she possesses, bringing to her increased power with each of the four female life phases.[14]

The Keres conceptualize the supreme being as a puzzling figure commonly referred to as Old Spider, Grandmother Spider, or Spider Woman. Spider Woman's Keres name is translated as Thought Woman (it can be better understood if translated as Creating-through-Thinking Woman). She is the Dreamer, the ritual center, who sang her sister goddesses Uretsete and Naotsete into life and taught them the rituals they used to sing everything in their baskets, their medicine bundles, into being. Among the things in their baskets were the heavens, the waters, the mountains, the earth, the katsina (spirit messengers and protectors), the creatures, and the plants. In ensuing times they change: Uretsete becomes Iyatiku and as such is the Mother of the people, the gods, and the animals. She, like her agricultural analogue the corn, is the power of self-generation and regeneration. It is this power or force that binds the people together, that empowers their rituals and customs and provides them with social systems, village plans, sustenance, and all else they might need to live in harmony and reasonable plenty on earth. Eventually Uretsete leaves the people and goes to Shipap, the ceremonial or dream/vision center of the tribe's ritual life, from whence she guides the people, aided by the cacique and counseled by the Spirit of Thought, Spider Woman, who sits near her or on her shoulder.

My novel centers on woman lore and the relationships it bears to the events in the life of an individual. It is concerned with the journey of the half-breed protagonist Ephanie Atencio toward psychic balance and describes how the parallels between her life and the lives of the god-women (as they are preserved in the oral tradition) aid her finding that balance.

Ephanie traces her experience in four directions: New Mexican colonial history, her intercultural family life, tribal tradition, and personal emotion and perception. Living in Albuquerque with her two children, Ephanie suffers a mental breakdown after her husband abandons her. Stephen, her cousin and lifetime friend, comes to stay with her to help her recover her balance. At first unable to distinguish dream from reality or memory from fantasy, she gradually begins to recover, until Stephen devastates her by having sex with her. Enraged, she leaves Albuquerque for San Francisco, where she gets a job, brings her children Agnes and Ben to live, joins a therapy group, spends time at the Indian Center, attends powwows, and becomes involved in urban life. She also makes friends with a white woman, Teresa, and eventually marries Nisei Japanese-American, Thomas Yoshuri. When that marriage begins to founder, she leaves Thomas and takes her children to live in Oregon where her twin sons are born, one of whom dies. Shortly afterward, she divorces Thomas.

When, years later, she returns to San Francisco, her older children are with her parents much of the time and the surviving twin, Tsali, lives with his father. Ephanie spends much of her time alone, communicating mostly with Teresa, reading and studying, trying to discover the history, the ritual traditions, and the family and personal events that led her to this lonely life and that will, perhaps, enable her to take charge of her fate. On one occasion she attempts suicide but finds within herself a fierce determination to live. She finally uncovers the source of her despair and isolation and is drawn into the spiritual life of the women of her people.

Ephanie's search for psychic unity is founded in ritual awareness which, in turn, is embedded within the adaptive and inclusive properties of the oral tradition as well as the ritual of her Guadalupe people. Ephanie learns to understand how her life and the lives of her mother and grandmother parallel the tribal narratives. As she understands this and as she lives out the implications of that understanding, she is able to accept her place within the ritual tradition of her people and her responsibility to continue it. As a breed Ephanie is raised outside of the formal tradition of her people, but inwardly she is ritual-oriented. Her difficulty, which she shares with Loney, Tayo, Abel, Cedarfair, and Welch's nameless protagonist, is finding a point of entry into the ritual patterns of her people.

One function of the storytelling part of the oral tradition is to give people a basis of entry into the more obscure ritual tradition. Entry into the narrative tradition enables individuals to realize that the significance of their own lives stems in large part from their interlocking connections with the lives of all the others who share a particular psychospiritual tradition. It lets people realize that individual experience is not isolate but is part of a coherent and timeless whole, providing them with a means of personal empowerment and giving shape and direction to their lives. The seamless web of human and nonhuman life, which is simultaneously the oral tradition and the thought of Old Spider Woman, is neither causal nor sequential. It is achronological and ahistorical, and it is simultaneously general and highly specific.

These universal characteristics of life are embodied in the oral tradition, which is composed of the rituals and their narrative counterparts, stories, and which is based in the dream/vision tradition that informs the life of tribal people in the Americas. The conflict between western ways and those of the tribes has been a major theme in all the novels by and about American Indians, but that theme has been treated increasingly as a part of an ancient cyclical pattern of cultural dissolution and revival by contemporary American Indian novelists. The novels and other contemporary literature function, in a sense, as a mapping of the possibilities, an exploration of our options as native peoples as we enter the twenty-first century surrounded by non-Indians. The novels respond to the question of whether we can remain Indians and still participate in and influence western culture or whether we will be junked or enshrined in museums of culture, victims of what Gerald Vizenor has named the "word wars" and "terminal creeds."

Indians, as Acoma poet Simon J. Ortiz says, are everywhere, and nowhere more articulate than in their novels. They are just a few years short of five hundred years since first contact with Europeans. In those five centuries, massive change has come upon the native peoples of the western hemisphere, change that they did not seek and did not control. But they have survived as cultural entities, as McNickle strongly argues in his histories of native peoples of Canada and the United States. As a consequence of this persistence, which is a primary fact of Native American life, the most important theme in Native American novels is not conflict and devastation but transformation and continuance. We change, of course, which is one very important meaning of men's ritual traditions, and of course we remain the same, which is one meaning of women's ritual traditions. When seen together, the significance of the ritual, ceremonial traditions of the tribes becomes clear. The nature of the cosmos, of the human, the creaturely, and the supernatural universe is like water. It takes numerous forms; it evaporates and it gathers. Survival and continuance are contingent on its presence. Whether it is in a cup, a jar, or an underground river, it nourishes life. And whether the ritual traditions are in ceremony, myth, or novel, they nourish the people. They give meaning. They give life.

Something Sacred Going on Out There: Myth and Vision in American Indian Literature

It is difficult if not impossible at the present time to speak coherently about myth because the term has become so polluted by popular misuse. Yet no discussion of American Indian literature is complete without an examination of what mythic narrative and the concept of myth itself mean in a tribal context.

Popularly among Americans, *myth* is synonymous with *lie*; moreover, it implies ignorance or a malicious intent to defraud. Thus, any attitude or idea that does not conform to contemporary western descriptions of reality is termed myth, signifying falsehood. Labeling something a myth merely discredits the perceptual system and world-view of those who are not in accord with the dominating paradigm. Thus, current dictionary definitions of *myth* reinforce a bias that enables the current paradigm of our technocratic social science–biased society to prevail over tribal or poetic views just as it enables an earlier Christian biblical paradigm to prevail over the pagan one. Indeed, terms such as *pagan, tribal,* and *poetic*—often used interchangeably— imply ignorance, backwardness, and foolishness. They allow dismissal by western readers, just as their allied term, *myth*, does. A definition such as the following makes it clear that any story called a myth is not to be taken seriously.

1. a traditional or legendary story, usually concerning some super-human being or some alleged person or event, with or without a determinable basis of fact or a natural explanation, esp., a traditional or legendary story that is concerned with deities or demigods and the creation of the world and its inhabitants. 2. stories or matter of this kind . . . 3. any invented story, idea or concept . . . 4. an imaginary or fictitious thing or person. 5. an unproved collective belief that is accepted uncritically and is used to justify a social institution.[1]

Essentially, all parts of the definition indicate a prevailing belief in the fictitiousness of myth; such terms as "alleged," "determinable," "factual," and "natural explanation" imply falsity or, at least, questionable accuracy. This meta-myth is deceptive, for it imputes factualness to certain assumptions that form the basis of western perceptions without acknowledging that it does so. Part of this meta-myth is the belief that there is such a thing as determinable fact, natural—that is, right—explanations, and reality that can be determined outside the human agency of discovery and fact finding.

This attitude falls more along the lines of uncritical acceptance used to justify the social institutions of contemporary societies than of proven belief attested to by many physicists, psychoanalysts, visionary mystics, poets, artists, and Indians as well as human experience of thousands of years and thousands of cultures.

Be that as it may, *myth* has not been considered synonymous with *belief* until recently. Earlier it was synonymous with *fable*, from the Greek, where it had the connotation of moral story. The Greek terms μύ-σ-τησ and μυ-σ-τήρου meant "one who is initiated" and "a mystery, secret (thing muttered)," respectively, and are based on the Indo-Germanic root, *MU*. Another Greek term, μύ, μû, "a sound of muttering," and its Latin forms, *muttum* or *mutum*, meaning "a slight sound," both signify muttering and muteness.[2]

So while μûûοσ is translated as "fable," it is more accurately translated as "ritual," that is, as a language construct that contains the power to transform something (or someone) from one state or condition to another. Of course it reflects belief, at least in the sorcerer's or magician's sense, but it is at base a vehicle, a means of transmitting paranormal power.

The mythic narrative as an articulation of thought or wisdom is not expressible in other forms; it must be seen as a necessary dimension of human expression, a dimension that is categorically unique. It is in this sense that facts or explanations of various phenomena such as "how the Loon got its white neck" or "why coyote has a ragged coat" can be incorporated into mythic structures. These pourquoi elements are signals of the kind of reality myth inhabits, rather than statements about social and material reality; their referent is to the sacred world of ritual magic rather than to the external world of machine-verifiable facts.

In this regard, the American psychoanalyst Rollo May defines myth "in its historically accurate sense of a psycho-biological pattern which give meaning and direction to experience."[3] In other words, the mythic dimension of experience—the psychospiritual ordering of nonordinary knowledge—is an experience that all peoples, past, present, and to come, have in common. As Thomas Mann observes, myth and life are identities:

> Life, then—at any rate—significant life—was in ancient times the reconstitution of the myth in flesh and blood; it referred to and appealed to the myth; only through it . . . could it approve itself as genuine and significant. The myth is the legitimization of life; only through and in it does life find self-awareness, sanction, consecration.[4]

Myth may be seen as a teleological statement, a shaped system of reference that allows us to order and thus comprehend perception and knowledge, as Mann suggests. The existence of mythic structures supposes a rational ordering of the universe. The presence of myth in a culture signifies a belief in the teleological nature of existence and indicates that powers other than those of material existence, or what Carlos Castaneda calls "ordinary reality," guide and direct the universe and human participation in it. As such myth stands as an expression of human need for coherence and integration and as the mode whereby human beings might actively fill that need.

Yet myth is more than a statement about how the world ought to work; its poetic and mystic dimensions indicate that it embodies a sense of reality that includes all human capacities, ideal or actual. These, broadly speaking, are the tendency to feel or emotively relate to experience and the tendency to intellectually organize it—the religious, aesthetic, and philosophical aspects of human cultures. Human beings need to belong to a tradition and equally need to know about the world in which they find themselves. Myth is a kind of story that allows a holistic image to pervade and shape consciousness, thus providing a coherent and empowering matrix for action and relationship. It is in this sense that myth is most significant, for it is this creative, ordering capacity of myth that frightens and attracts the rationalistic, other-centered mind, forcing it into thinly veiled pejoration of the mythic faculty, alienistic analysis of it, and counter myth-making of its own.

Myth, then, is an expression of the tendency to make stories of power out of the life we live in imagination; from this faculty when it is engaged in ordinary states of consciousness come tales and stories. When it is engaged in nonordinary states, myth proper—that is, mystery mumblings—occur. It is of course the former relationship between myth and imagination that has caused myth to be regarded as "a wholly fictitious story" as the *Oxford English Dictionary* puts it or, as in the standard *French Dictionary of Littre*, "that which has no real existence."

In the culture and literature of Indian America, the meaning of myth may be discovered, not as speculation about primitive long-dead ancestral societies but in terms of what is real, actual, and viable in living cultures in America. Myth abounds in all of its forms; from the most sacred stories to the most trivial, mythic vision informs the prose and poetry of American Indians in the United States as well as the rest of the Americas.

An American Indian myth is a story that relies preeminently on symbol for its articulation. It generally relates a series of events and uses supernatural, heroic figures as the agents of both the events and the symbols. As a story, it demands the immediate, direct participation of the listener.

American Indian myths depend for their magic on relationship and participation. Detached, analytical, distanced observation of myth will not allow the listener mythopoeic vision. Consequently, these myths cannot be understood more than peripherally by the adding-machine mind; for when a myth is removed from its special and necessary context, it is no longer myth; it is a dead or dying curiosity. It is akin, in that state, to the postcard depictions of American Indian people that abound in the southwestern United States.

Only a participant in mythic magic can relate to the myth, can enter into its meaning on its own terms. This is not to say that only a devout Oglala can comprehend the Myth of White Buffalo Woman or that only a practicing Cheyenne can comprehend the presence of Sweet Medicine. It does mean that only those who experientially accept the nonmaterial or nonordinary reality of existence can hope to comprehend either figure in their own terms; all others are, of necessity, excluded.

I have said that an American Indian myth is a particular kind of story, requiring supernatural or nonordinary figures as characters. Further, a myth relies on mystical or metaphysically charged symbols to convey its significance, and the fact of the mystical and the teleological nature of myth is embodied in its characteristic devices; the supernatural characters, the nonordinary events, the transcendent powers, and the pourquoi elements all indicate that something sacred is going on.

On literal levels of analysis, the myth tells us what kind of story it is. It focuses our attention on the level of consciousness it relates to us and relates us to. Having engaged our immediate participation on its own level, the myth proceeds to re-create and renew our ancient relationship to the universe that is beyond the poverty-stricken limits of the everyday.

Mythologists have long noticed a connection between ritual and myth. Some believe that ritual is an enactment of a myth, while others feel that myth tells about the ritual in story form. Neither explanation seems satisfactory to all parties, and for a very good reason: these speculations are based on Greek and Roman mythologies, the only kind that the Church did not suppress totally, and on extant histories of rituals in Greek and Roman cultures. The materials thus left available for students of the mysteries, coupled with analytical methods developed over two millennia of churchly control of academic research, led to fundamental misperception and misrepresentation of ritual and mythic modes.

> It was precisely because the classics were based upon fictive themes that they survived the mythoclastic rigors of early Christianity. Myths were pagan, and therefore false in the light of true belief—albeit that true belief might today be considered merely another variety of mythopoeic faith. Here is where the game of debunking starts, in the denunciation of myth as falsehood from the vantage-point of a rival myth.
>
> Classical myths could be rescued by allegory, prefiguration, or other methods of reinterpretation; but they could not be accepted literally.[5]

Other material that has come to light more recently in this regard has been forced to conform to the preconceived theories of Christian enculturated mythologists prior to Sir James Frazer, the Scottish classicist and anthropologist who compiled *The Golden Bough*, his study of magic and religion. But an alternative explanation to those popularly held is possible, based on an examination of actual contemporary Native American practices. This explanation coincides, in some significant ways, with contemporary psychoanalytical observation. Its ultimate proof, of course, lies in the actual practice among mythopoeic peoples around the world.

Briefly stated, myth and ritual are based on visionary experience. This simple observation has apparently escaped notice because generally neither mythologists nor social scientists credit visionary experience with the same validity given them by visionary peoples, including some artists and poets. Yet a careful look at Native American cultures reveals evidence of direct vision as central to religious practice, ritual, and literature. In most Indian societies, the vision is actively pursued and brought back to the people as a gift of power and guidance.

A significant example of the relationship of vision to myth and ritual is in the story of Sweet Medicine, a central figure in the Cheyenne religion. Called a "culture hero" by anthropologists and a prophet and savior by the Cheyenne, Sweet Medicine brought religion, religious rituals, and social laws to the Cheyenne people.[6] He received them from the Sacred Ones who live on the mountain that the Cheyenne call Noahvose (Sacred or Holy Mountain)[7] and is known to whites as Bear Butte, in the Black Hills country. Revealed to him at this place were the religion of the Sacred Arrows, the religious and political organization the Cheyenne would adopt, the proper marriage ritual, the correct way to trap eagles to obtain the emblem feathers the chiefs wore, and many other things. "There was no end to all the things the people learned from him."[8] Sweet Medicine lived to be very old, outlasting four generations of Cheyenne. At his death he told the people how they must live if they wanted to be sure of plenty of game and other food; he prophesied their future, telling them of the coming of the whites and of the horse, the disappearance of the buffalo, and the ultimate loss of the true Cheyenne way. After he died, his body was said to have disappeared. All that remained was the tipi he had died in. The spot was marked with a stone cairn, the historical marker of the Cheyenne.[9]

Sweet Medicine came to the Cheyenne "many centuries ago"; a more recent example of the visionary source of a myth is found in the life and experience of Black Elk. Ultimately, I suppose, Black Elk will be seen as a prophet and a savior of his people, just as Sweet Medicine is seen by his. Presently Black Elk is considered a sage, a prophet, and healer, a wicasa waka̱n, sacred or holy man. The fact that he has heirs to his visionary power attests to the enormity of his gift.

Black Elk was a very young boy when his vision came to him. The Oglala, along with many eastern, midwestern, northwestern, southwestern, and southern Indians actively seek visions. The ability to achieve a vision is a mark of maturity, a kind of rite of passage. Usually a man or woman goes after a vision by performing a particular ritual called hanblecheya or Lamenting for a Vision. (Actually, there are two separate rituals involved in this rite as purification—inipi—precede the vision quest.)[10] But Black Elk was much younger than the age when hanblecheya is practiced. He was called by the powers that are usually sought, and his vision was bestowed on him without his asking. In this respect also his experience parallels Sweet Medicine, who was also given to vision and miracles before he reached maturity.

In *Black Elk Speaks*,[11] Black Elk tells of his initial vision and the subsequent visions during the years of his growing up. This singularly complete account of a holy man's vision, the ceremonies performed in reenacting the vision, and the powers held by the person who had the vision all indicate the centrality of vision to ritual, song, and myth. In fact, if Black Elk as narrator were removed from his own account and Black Elk as mythic character left in and if the point of view of the narrative were shifted from first-person personal to third-person omniscient, the vision would become identical in form and symbolic content to those great myths that have come down to us not only from the Oglala but from peoples as diverse as the Tlingit of Alaska, the Hopi of Arizona, the Cherokee of the Carolinas and Georgia, and the Iroquois of New York and Canada. Certainly, with the exception of the narrator's presence, the story is in the most proper sense a myth. Consisting of a logical progression of symbol, it is in truth a metaphysical statement that is significant in its cosmological implications, its prophetic content, its narrative sequence, its sense of timelessness, its characters, and, ultimately, its meaning for people all over this country. Seen that way, it is an example of myth at its most sacred and abstract.

Every element in such a story is meaningful on the deepest levels of human understanding. Thus it is that the true significance of Black Elk's vision is yet to be discovered; the meaning of the vision has not yet been explicated in terms of ordinary human consciousness, and the great sweep of history it encompasses has not yet been lived. Yet much of it has been lived, and those parts are undeniably true. This gives us another clue to the true nature of the prophetic aspect of the myth. White researchers have supposed that a myth was a story intended to explain and record events after they had happened so that they would be remembered. Working from this assumption and allied misunderstandings, anthropologists and mythologists have supposed an astounding chain of "facts" about the lives, movements, and ultimate origins of Indian people and about their cultures, world-view, and even their bodies. Yet this primary assumption is false. No Indian who is even peripherally aware of the Indian idea of things can muster much more than contempt for the ideas advanced by the literary curio hunters of the white world. Yet few white investigators who profess to be aware of and concerned with Indian attitudes are willing to listen, even provisionally, to the Indian account of these matters. It is assumed that Indians are "making believe" for religious, political, or existential reasons or that they are simply ignorant of the real truth about how the world works. It is seldom assumed that a given tribal version of its own history is true or that it might be seen as true from some perspective other than the social science paradigm common to western ideas of fact finding.[12]

Black Elk's vision offers an opportunity to demonstrate that the American Indian position is neither romantically primitive nor realistically absurd; and because it is written, the factualness of this account can be examined and verified in time. An examination of its elements and their arrangement can be made to discover the workings of a metaphysical statement and how myth relates to sacred songs, rituals, objects, and ornaments.

The vision begins when Black Elk is guided to the other world by two men who move down through the sky like "arrows slanting down."[13] The long spears they carry emit flashes of "jagged lightning."[14] From the beginning of this vision we are told the kind of vision it will be; visions that include the powers associated with Thunder and the West indicate a highly sacred or powerful vision and signify revelation, introspection, and deep change.[15] Because of these qualities, the Thunder and the West are said to be terrifying because they have the power to "make live" and the power to destroy. These powers are conferred on Black Elk, and are such as to terrify any man.

This vision is of or from the West. Its major symbolic theme is Thunder and what is associated with it: horses, lightning, rainbow, water. The other symbols occur in the context of these. And each action or speech occurs from the West, which is not the usual sequence in Oglala practice.

The directions themselves are the major motif, as they generally are in Oglala rituals. Orienting oneself to the directions is basic to all Native North American peoples and appears to be as important in South America.

The presence of different troops of horses, one troop from each direction, indicates that the vision will be comprehensive. The powers that will derive from it will include war and healing, knowledge and life. The poems and text will, like the actions and sacramental objects, be related to this whole and to these powers. All the powers that a man can possess will be represented here, and Black Elk will carry them back to his people, to use on their behalf. The primary thrust of the vision, in keeping with its western point of view, will be that of revelation, self-awareness and deep personal experience, and supernatural truth.

The Grandfathers of Powers of the Six Directions are the agents of this vision and its power. The First Grandfather, the Power of the West, tells Black Elk what will be given him:

> "Behold them yonder where the sun goes down, the thunder beings! You shall see, and have from them my power; and they shall take you to the high and lonely center of the earth that you may see; even to the place where the sun continually shines, they shall take you there to understand."
>
> And as he spoke of understanding, I looked up and saw the rainbow leap with flames of many colors over me.
>
> Now there was a wooden cup in his hand and it was full of water and in the water was the sky.
>
> "Take this," he said. "It is the power to make live, and it is yours."
>
> Now he had a bow in his hands. "Take this," he said. "It is the power to destroy, and it is yours."[16]

Each of the Grandfathers plays a role in this vision. The Sixth Grandfather represents Black Elk himself. He shows Black Elk the reality of humanity and its true power by transforming himself into a youth:

> and when he had become a boy, I knew that he was myself with all the years that would be mine at last.[17]

He shows himself as Black Elk's body because Black Elk represents all his people; he will be required to take this vision and its powers to his people and use both on their behalf. In no other way can such a vision become actual or positive. Without this sharing of what is conferred on one for the benefit of many, the vision itself will turn on the visionary, making him ill or even killing him, as later events show.

But while the body or person of Black Elk is like that of the Sixth Grandfather, the spirit of Black Elk (the spirit form in which he will experience the rest of the vision) is that of the Power of the West; for after giving Black Elk the power to make live and the power to destroy, the First Grandfather shows him a remarkable thing:

> Then he pointed to himself and said: "Look close at him who is your spirit now, for you are his body and his name is Eagle Wing Stretches."[18]

And in this mystic body, or mythic character, Black Elk goes through the rest of the vision.

The Grandfathers give Black Elk the power to make live, the power to understand and to know, the power to destroy, the power to purify, the power to feed and nurture, and the power to heal. Each of these powers is signified with an emblem or sacramental object, and some are accompanied by a song to be sung when calling on that power.[19] Most of all, he was given the gift of prophecy, the power of the universe itself.

> Now the fifth Grandfather spoke, the oldest of them all, the Spirit of the Sky. "My boy," he said, "I have sent for you and you have come. My power you shall see!" He stretched his arms and turned into a spotted eagle hovering. "Behold," he said, "all the wings of the air shall come to you, and they and the winds and the stars shall be like relatives. You shall go across the earth with my power." Then the eagle soared above my head and fluttered there; and suddenly the sky was full of friendly wings all coming toward me.[20]

In the next sequence, Black Elk learns the immediate future of the Oglala Lakotas. In the person of Eagle Wing Stretches, the Grandfather of the West, he journeys over a "distant landscape," rescuing the people from threatened annihilation by war, disease, and massacre. He restores for them the ancient way, the Path of the Sacred Pipe, the holy tree, the nation's hoop.[21] Then he discovers the farther future of the people, revealed once again symbolically. He is shown the means of saving the people of the earth from the great destructive forces that would overcome them, which is the sacred flower, the "herb of understanding."[22] He learns songs of power and sees the people calling the powers of the cosmos.[23] That power comes to their aid at the end of the fourth ascent in the guise of "the chief of all the horses, and when he snorted, it was a flash of lightning and his eyes were like the sunset star."[24]

> My horses, prancing they are coming;
> My horses, neighing they are coming;
> Prancing, they are coming.
> All over the universe they come.
> They will dance; may you behold them.
> They will dance; may you behold them.
> They will dance; may you behold them.
> They will dance; may you behold them.
> A horse nation, they will dance. May you behold them.
> A horse nation, they will dance. May you behold them.
> A horse nation, they will dance. May you behold them.
> A horse nation, they will dance. May you behold them.[25]

The last major sequence of the vision consists of a summarization of the vision and a return to more or less normal consciousness. In it Black Elk, as Eagle Wing Stretches, returns to the sacred tipi of the Six Grandfathers, where his triumph is acknowledged, the nature of his mythic identity, journey, and powers are explained once more, and he is returned to earth. His journey has lasted twelve days, during which the small boy's body had been lying, comatose, in the tipi of his parents.

The vision, which lasted twelve days, is divided into six parts, another indication of the depth of its significance and its inclusiveness: the first part has two aspects, the vision of the Horse Nation and the meeting with the Six Powers of the Universe. The second, broadly speaking the Prophecy, is divided into prophetic vision of the immediate, the near, and the distant future. The first part has since been lived on earth, as has much of the rest. The last major division, divided into two parts, consists of summary and return.

This sequence reveals to Black Elk that his body is painted in a special manner, signifying the kind of vision or kind of power he has had:

I had not noticed how I was dressed until now, and I saw that I was painted red all over, and my joints were painted black, with white stripes between the joints. My bay had lightning stripes all over him, and his mane was cloud. And when I breathed, my breath was lightning.[26]

He is assured of his triumph after painful experience; his powers are affirmed and their emblems shown again. He learns the songs, the way to dress when acting as an agent of the supernatural, the movements and sequences that will ensure his success in these matters, and, most of all, the meaning of his experience in terms of the people, living and yet unborn.

Had Black Elk had this vision under more normal circumstances, he would have returned from his vision and recounted it to an older holy man, the one who had directed his quest. Then, with the holy man's help, he would have enacted significant portions of that vision in a ceremony for the people. In this way, the power bestowed on him during the vision would have been diffused, confirmed, intensified or amplified, and rendered real and functional on material and human levels. But he was very young. It frightened him, made him feel separated from his family and friends, burdened him with a knowledge that he was not old enough to use or understand. Some Indians feel that the disasters that befell Black Elk's people subsequently were a result of his failure to follow the usual pattern; yet it seems that, had this been necessary or wise, the Grandfathers either would have waited several years before calling Black Elk or would have chosen someone who was of the right age to give that vision to. Eventually Black Elk did what he should have done, and the account of the ceremonies held in enacting the vision (actually parts of it) clarify for us the relation between ritual, myth, and vision.

When Black Elk was sixteen, the time when young Oglalas prepare for their first hanblecheya, he began to be haunted by a fear.[27] The thunder, lightning, and clouds called him continuously; the coyotes and birds reminded him that it was his time. He didn't know what to do, and because of his growing fear and distraction, he became more and more fearful, behaving strangely and worrying those around him. When he was seventeen his parents asked an old medicine man, Black Road, to help Black Elk. Black Elk told the old man about his vision, and the old man arranged a ceremony because Black Elk had to do what the bay horse wanted him to do. The old man said he "must do [his] duty and perform the vision for [his] people upon earth."[28]

The Horse Dance that Black Road and another wise man, Bear Sings, designed with Black Elk incorporated all the symbols and personages in the parts of the vision pertaining to the horses, which are scattered throughout the account.[29] The songs that Black Elk had heard in the vision were sung, and all the people participated in the ceremony. Black Elk was painted red, the color of the earth and of the East, and the color of what is sacred, and black, the color of the West, of truth, revelation, and destruction. The horses were painted to show their relationship to the lightning, and the riders were dressed to indicate the various symbols that the vision horses had carried or worn or that were associated with them. Young women, virgins, enacted the part played by their supernatural counterparts, their faces painted scarlet. Six old men were the Six Grandfathers, and a sacred tipi was erected and painted to conform to the one in Black Elk's vision, a rainbow over the door.

Thus, in particular details of design and ornamentation, in movements and action and in characters, the vision was reconstructed as closely as may be done of the nonordinary in this material plane. The people and Black Elk were reenacting the vision so that its power would be revealed and renewed on earth. Black Elk comments on the strength or truth of this enactment: as they were praying and dancing he once again saw the sacred tipi as in his vision—the rainbow door, the horses, and the Six Grandfathers sitting inside. He even saw himself on the bay in front of the tipi. As the vision faded, it began to storm; wind and hail struck.

> The people of the village ran to fasten down their tipis, while the black horse riders sang to the drums that rolled like thunder . . . And as they sang, the hail and rain were falling yonder just a little way from us, and we could see it, but the cloud stood there and flashed and thundered, and only a little sprinkle fell on us.[30]

That Black Elk's ceremony was true and effective can hardly be doubted: after it was over, the people came up to him and told him how they or their relatives were well again after being sick, and they gave him presents.[31] More significant, perhaps, was what they saw in the tipi they had erected:

> Then the horses were all rubbed down with sacred sage and led away, and we began going into the tepee to see what might have happened there while we were dancing. The Grandfathers had

sprinkled fresh soil on the nation's hoop that they had made in there with the red and black roads across it, and all around this little circle of the nation's hoop we saw the prints of tiny pony hoofs as though the spirit horses had been dancing while we danced.[32]

And Black Elk himself felt renewed; the fear that had dogged him for two years was gone. He was accepted as a wicasa wakan by the other holy men.

This reenactment is normal procedure for a vision of this type. Such a ceremony, or at least use of revealed songs, power objects and animals, costume and emblematic designs, is incorporated into the visionary's daily life after a successful hanblecheya. Sometimes these things are kept privately by the seer, sometimes they are made public, in part at least, as in Black Elk's case, but always the mental or spiritual phenomena are made physical.

For example, the vision of Wovoka, the Paiute holy man and prophet, became the Ghost Dance. It was danced all over the Plains during the most destructive years of the wars. Other visions, received during the dancing by participants, were incorporated into the ceremony as it was practiced in any locale, but it was through the agency of direct vision that the clothing worn, the songs sung, the dance itself, the rules for the behavior of the dancers, the articles they carried and the ornamentation they used were determined.[33]

As in the case of Sweet Medicine Man and the religion of the Sacred Arrows, all areas of behavior that were touched on in the vision were incorporated into the religious and social behavior of the people the vision was meant to serve. Because of his vision and his enactment of it, Black Elk became a powerful healer. He also gained invulnerability in battle when he imitated the geese, the symbols or emblems of purification and wisdom.[34]

Presumably he would have achieved the status of a great leader, as did Crazy Horse and Sitting Bull, had not white wars and government systems, rules, and prohibitions intervened. As it is, through the agency of the books he dictated, the personal aid he gave his people, and the heirs he left, his influence extends across the world; his vision was enacted in the Lakota way and recorded in the white man's way, thus reaching far beyond the small hoop of the Lakota across the hoops of many nations, just as the Grandfathers had showed him it would.[35]

Sweet Medicine Man was an ancient, traditional figure, and the dances, societies, laws, and truths he brought have become the traditional ways of the Cheyenne. Black Elk's vision has had neither time nor appropriate circumstances to become embedded in a people's way, but the processes of the transformation of vision into thought and action are the same. Those processes themselves are traditional in Indian America, as attested to in the ethnographies and collections of such people as Ruth Underhill, Alice Marriott, James Mooney, Franz Boas, Natalie Curtis, Jack and Anna Kilpatrick, John Stands-in-Timber, Lame Deer, Paul Radin, and so many more. Their testimony is clear: the Indian way includes ample room for vision translated into meaningful action and custom and thought, and it is because of the centrality of the vision to the life of the peoples of America that the religious life of the tribe endures, even under the most adverse circumstances. Vision is a way of becoming whole, of affirming one's special place in the universe, and myth, song, and ceremony are ways of affirming vision's place in the life of all the people. Thus it renews all: the visionary and his relatives and friends, even the generations long dead and those yet unborn.

The vision, however, as vision, can be experienced only by one person directly. Yet it, like all aspects of Indian life, must be shared; thus myth. Myth is a story of a vision; it is a presentation of that vision told in terms of the vision's symbols, characters, chronology, and import. It is a vehicle of transmission, of sharing, of renewal, and as such plays an integral part in the ongoing psychic life of a people.

In *Love and Will*, Rollo May recounts an experience he had with a Cézanne painting, contending that the painting was "mythic" because it encompassed "near and far, past, present and future, conscious and unconscious in one immediate totality of our relationship to the world."[36] In this way, myth acts as a lens through which we can discover the reality that exists beyond the limits of simple linear perception; it is an image, a verbal construct, that allows truth to emerge into direct consciousness. In this way, myth allows us to rediscover ourselves in our most human and ennobling dimensions. Through it we are allowed to see our own transcendent powers triumphant; we know, experientially, our true identity and our human capacity that is beyond behaviorism, history, and the machine.

Myth functions as an affirmation of self that transcends the temporal. It guides our attention toward a view of ourselves, a possibility, that we might not otherwise encounter. It shows us our own ability to accept and allow the eternal to be part of our selves. It allows us to image a marriage between our conscious and unconscious, fusing the twin dimensions of mind and society into a coherent, meaningful whole. It allows us to adventure in distant, unfamiliar landscapes while remaining close to home. Thus myth shows us that it is possible to relate ourselves to the grand and mysterious universe that surrounds and informs our being; it makes us aware of other orders of reality and experience and in that awareness makes the universe our home. It is a magic: it is the area of relationship between all those parts of experience that commonly divide us from ourselves, our universe, and our fellows. In the myth, and especially the mythopoeic vision that gives it birth, past, present, and future are one, and the human counterparts of these—ancestors, contemporaries, and descendents—are also one. Conscious and unconscious are united through the magic of symbolic progression so that the symbols can convey direct, rational meanings and stir indirect memories and insights that have not been raised to conscious articulation. In mythopoeic vision and its literary counterparts, the near and the far must come together, for in its grasp we stand in a transcendent landscape that incorporates both. Lastly, the mythic heals, it makes us whole. For in relating our separate experiences to one another, in weaving them into coherence and therefore significance, a sense of wholeness arises, a totality which, by virtue of our active participation, constitutes direct and immediate comprehension of ourselves and the universe of which we are integral parts.

The Feminine Landscape
of Leslie Marmon Silko's
Ceremony

There are two kinds of women and two kinds of men in Leslie Marmon Silko's *Ceremony* (New York: Viking, 1977). The figures of Laura, Night Swan, Grandmother, Betonie's Grandmother, and Ts'eh represent one kind of woman, while to some extent Auntie, Betonie's grandfather's wives, and grandfather's mother represent the other. Josiah, the Mountain Spirit, Betonie's grandfather, Ku'oosh, Betonie, Robert, and Tayo represent a kind of man associated with the first category of women, while Rocky, Emo, Pink, Harley, and the witches represent men associated with the second. Those in the first category belong to the earth spirit and live in harmony with her, even though this attunement may lead to tragedy. Those in the second are not of the earth but of human mechanism; they live to destroy that spirit, to enclose and enwrap it in their machinations, condemning all to a living death. Ts'eh is the matrix, the creative and life-restoring power, and those who cooperate with her designs serve her and, through her, serve life. They make manifest that which she thinks. The others serve the witchery; they are essentially inimical to all that lives, creates, and nurtures.

While *Ceremony* is ostensibly a tale about a man, Tayo, it is as much and more a tale of two forces: the feminine life force of the universe and the mechanistic death force of the witchery. And Ts'eh is the central character of the drama of this ancient battle as it is played out in contemporary times.

We are the land, and the land is mother to us all. There is not a symbol in the tale that is not in some way connected with womanness, that does not in some way relate back to Ts'eh and through her to the universal feminine principle of creation: Ts'its'tsi'nako, Thought Woman, Grandmother Spider, Old Spider Woman. All tales are born in the mind of Spider Woman, and all creation exists as a result of her naming.

We are the land. To the best of my understanding, that is the fundamental idea that permeates American Indian life; the land (Mother) and the people (mothers) are the same. As Luther Standing Bear has said of his Lakota people, "We are of the soil and the soil is of us." The earth is the source and the being of the people, and we are equally the being of the earth. The land is not really a place, separate from ourselves, where we act out the drama of our isolate destinies; the witchery makes us believe that false idea. The earth is not a mere source of survival, distant from the creatures it nurtures and from the spirit that breathes in us, nor is it to be considered an inert resource on which we draw in order to keep our ideological self functioning, whether we perceive that self in sociological or personal terms. We must not conceive of the earth as an ever-dead other that supplies us with a sense of ego identity by virtue of our contrast to its perceived nonbeing. Rather, for American Indians like Betonie, the earth *is* being, as all creatures are also being: aware, palpable, intelligent, alive. Had Tayo known clearly what Standing Bear articulated—that "in the Indian the spirit of the land is still vested," that human beings "must be born and reborn to belong," so that their bodies are "formed of the dust of their forefather's bones"—he would not be ill. But if he had known consciously what he knew unconsciously, he would not have been a major agent of the counterceremony, and this tale would not have been told.

Tayo's illness is a result of separation from the ancient unity of person, ceremony, and land, and his healing is a result of his recognition of this unity. The land is dry because earth is suffering from the alienation of part of herself; her children have been torn from her in their minds; their possession of unified awareness of and with her has been destroyed, partially or totally; that destruction characterizes the lives of Tayo and his mother, Auntie and Rocky, Pinky and Harley, and all those who are tricked into believing that the land is beyond and separate from themselves.

The healing of Tayo and the land results from the reunification of land and person. Tayo is healed when he understands, in magical (mystical) and loving ways, that his being is within and outside him, that it includes his mother, Night Swan, Ts'eh, Josiah, the spotted cattle, winter, hope, love, and the starry universe of Betonie's ceremony.

This understanding occurs slowly as Tayo lives the stories—those ancient and those new. He understands through the process of making the stories manifest in his actions and in his understanding, for the stories and the land are about the same thing; perhaps we can best characterize this relation by saying that the stories are the communication device of the land and the people. Through the stories, the ceremony, the gap between isolate human being and lonely landscape is closed. And through them Tayo understands in mind and in bone the truth of his and our situation.

Tayo is an empty space as the tale begins, a vapor, an outline. He has no voice. "He can't talk to you. He is invisible. His words are formed with an invisible tongue, they have no sound," he tells the army psychiatrist (p. 15).

Invisible and stilled, like an embryo, he floats, helpless and voiceless, on the current of duality, his being torn by grief and anger. Love could heal him—love, the mountain spirit Ts'eh, the "wonder" being, who was the manifestation of the creator of the waters of life that flow from a woman and bless the earth and the beloved with healing, with rain. It is loving her that heals Tayo, that and his willingness to take up her tasks of nurturing the plant and beast people she loves. And he had loved her from "time immemorial," unconsciously. Before he knew her name, he had given her his pledge of love, and she had answered him with rain:

> So that last summer, before the war, he got up before dawn and rode the bay mare south to the spring in the narrow canyon. The water oozed out from the dark orange sandstone at the base of the long mesa. He waited for the sun to come over the hills . . . The canyon was full of shadows when he reached the pool. He had picked flowers along the path, flowers with long yellow petals the color of the sunlight. He shook the pollen from them gently and

sprinkled it over the water; he laid blossoms beside the pool and waited. He heard the water, flowing into the pool, drop by drop from the big crack in the side of the cliff. The things he did seemed right, as he imagined with his heart the rituals the cloud priests performed during the drought. Here the dust and heat began to recede; the short grass and stunted corn seemed distant. (p. 93)

As Tayo completes his prayer and begins to descend the mountain, he sees a bright green hummingbird and watches it as it disappears: "But it left something with him; as long as the hummingbird had not abandoned the land, somewhere there were still flowers, and they could all go on" (p. 96). Forty-eight hours after Tayo makes his prayer, the sky fills with clouds thick with rain. The rain comes from the west, and the thunder preceding it comes from the direction of Mount Taylor, called Tse-pi'na in Laguna (Woman Veiled in Clouds), a mountain that is blue against the sky, topped in white when it rains or snows. Having prayed the rain in, Tayo must experience its power personally as the next step in the ceremony. The rain makes it necessary for Josiah to miss his date with Night Swan, so he sends Tayo to the nearby village of Cubero with a message for her. He writes the message on "blue-lined paper" (p. 96).

Night Swan is a mysterious and powerful woman. We know that she is associated with Ts'eh by her circumstances and the colors with which she surrounds herself. Many signs indicate that she is associated with the ceremony of which Tayo was an integral (through unknowing) part: the color of her eyes, her implication in the matter of the spotted (half-breed) cattle, Auntie's dislike of her, and her mysterious words to Tayo when he leaves her. Additionally, her room is filled with blue: a blue armchair, curtains "feeling colored by the blue flowers painted in a border around the walls," blue sheets, a cup made of blue pottery painted with yellow flowers. She is dressed in a blue kimono when Tayo enters her room, and she wears blue slippers (p. 98). Most important, she is associated with a mysterious power that Tayo associates with whatever is behind the white curtain:

He could feel something back there, something of her life which he could not explain. The room pulsed with feeling, the feeling flowing with the music and the breeze from the curtains, feeling colored by the blue flowers painted in a border around the walls. He could feel it everywhere, even in the blue sheets that were stretched tightly across the bed. (p. 98)

This woman, who appeared out of the southeast one day and took up residence in Cubero, on the southern slope of the mountain, and who disappears as mysteriously after Josiah is buried, is surrounding with emblems of the mountain rain. She takes Tayo to bed. This is not an ordinary coupling, for nothing about Tayo's life is ordinary while the counterceremony moves toward resolution:

> She moved under him, her rhythm merging into the sound of the rain in the tree. And he was lost somewhere, deep beneath the surface of his own body and consciousness, swimming away from all his life before that hour. (p. 99)

The encounter with Night Swan sets the seal of Tayo's destiny in those moments. Through her body the love that Ts'eh bears for him is transmitted. Night Swan is aware of the significance of her act and tells Tayo, "You don't have to understand what is happening. But remember this day. You will recognize it later. You are part of it now" (p. 100).

These passages tell of the ceremonial nature of man and woman; they embody the meaning of the action of the relation between the characters and Thought Woman that is the basis of Laguna life:

> In the beginning Tse che nako, Thought Woman, finished every-thing, thoughts, and the names of all things . . . And then our mothers, Uretsete and Naotsete, said they would make names and they would make thoughts. Thus they said. Thus they did.
> —Laguna Thought Woman Story

From the foregoing it is clear that the Lagunas regard the land as feminine. What is not so clear is how this might be so. For it is not in the mind of the Laguna simply to equate, in primitive modes, earth-bearing-grain with woman-bearing-child. To paraphrase grandma, it isn't that easy. If the simplistic interpretation were accurate to their concept, the Lagunas would not associate the essential nature of femininity with the creative power of thought. The equation is more like earth-bearing-grain, goddess-bearing-thought, woman-bearing-child. Nor is ordinary thinking referred to here, that sort of "brain noise" that passes for thinking among moderns. The thought for which Grandmother Spider is known is the kind that results in physical manifestation of phenomena: mountains, lakes, creatures, or philo-sophical-sociological systems. Our mothers, Uretsete and Naotsete, are aspects of Grandmother Spider. They are certain kinds of thought forces if you will. The same can be said of Ts'eh; indeed, it must be said of her if the tale that Silko tells, that Spider Woman thinks all into being, is to have its proper significance. Psychoanalytically, we might say that Tayo's illness is a result of the repression of his anima and that through his love of Ts'eh he becomes conscious of the female side of his own nature and accepts and integrates feminine behavior into his life. This Jungian interpretation of the process of Tayo's healing is accurate enough, though it misses an essential point of the story: Tayo's illness is connected to the larger world. The drought-stricken land is also ill, perhaps because the land has also repressed its anima.

Silko illustrates this nexus with the metaphor of the witchery and the ceremony used to contravene its effects. Through the vehicle of the story, Ts'its'tsi'nako's thought, Silko explains how the witchery could be responsible for sickness in individuals, societies, and landscapes simultaneously:

> Thought-Woman, the spider
> named things and
> as she named them
> they appeared.
>
> She is sitting in her room
> Thinking of a story now.
> I'm telling you the story
> she is thinking. (p. 1)

After Tayo completes the first steps of the ceremony, he is ready to enter into the central rituals connected with a ceremony of cosmic significance, for only a cosmic ceremony can simultaneously heal a wounded man, a stricken landscape, and a disorganized, discouraged society.

He becomes a warrior, thus dissociating himself from the people. A warrior in a peace-centered culture must experience total separation from the tribe. He has been prepared for his role by the circumstances of his birth and upbringing: Auntie was especially forceful in propelling him away from the heart of what he was. By virtue of his status as an outcast who, at the same time, is one of the Laguna people in his heart, he is able to suffer the ritual of war and dissolution. Only total annihilation of the mundane self could produce a magic man of sufficient power to carry off the ceremony that Tayo is embroiled in.

At the opening of the story, Tayo is still experiencing this stage of the ceremony. He is formless, for his being is as yet unshaped, undistinguished from the mass it sprang from. Like rainless clouds, he seeks fulfillment—a ceremony, a story about his life that will make him whole. He has the idea that if he had died instead of Rocky or Josiah, the land would be full of rain. This "story" of his is inappropriate. Perhaps because of his status as an outcast, he does not understand the nature of death, nor does he know that it is not in the deaths of two individuals that the prosperity or the suffering of the people rests. Perhaps no one has told him that the departed souls are always within and part of the people on earth, that they are still obligated to those living on earth and come back in the form of rain regularly (when all is well), so that death is a blessing on the people, not their destruction. What Tayo and the people need is a story that will take the entire situation into account, that will bless life with a certain kind of integrity where spirit, creatures, and land can occupy a unified whole. That kind of story is, of course, a ceremony such as Betonie performs with Tayo as the active participant, the manifester of the thought.

After Tayo walks through Betonie's ceremony, finds the cattle, and puts them in a safe pasture, after he has confronted the witchery and abandoned all thought of retaliating against it, after he has been transformed by these efforts and his meeting with Ts'eh from isolated warrior to spiritually integrated person, after he has taken on the aspect of unity termed naiya (mother) in Laguna, he is free to understand the whole thing:

> He would go back there now, where she had shown him the plant. He would gather the seeds for her and plant them with great care in places near sandy hills . . . The plants would grow there like the story, strong and translucent as stars. (p. 254)

"But you know, grandson, this world is fragile," old Ku'oosh had told Tayo, and having entered the ways of unification of a fragmented persona, Tayo is free to experience that fragility directly:

> He dreamed with his eyes open that he was wrapped in a blanket in the back of Josiah's wagon, crossing the sandy flat below Paguate Hill . . . the rumps of the two gray mules were twin moons in front of him. Josiah was driving the wagon, old Grandma was holding him, and Rocky whispered "my brother." They were taking him home. (p. 254)

The fragility of the world is a result of its nature as thought. Both land and human being participate in the same kind of being, for both are thoughts in the mind of Grandmother Spider. Tayo's illness is a function of disordered thinking—his own, that of those around him, and that of the forces that propelled them all into the tragic circumstances of World War II. The witchery put this disordered thinking into motion long ago and distorted human beings' perceptions so that they believed that other creatures—insects and beasts and half-breeds and whites and Indians and Japanese—were enemies, rather than part of the one being we all share, and thus should be destroyed. The cure for that misunderstanding, for Tayo, was a reorientation of perception so that he could know directly that the true nature of being is magical and that the proper duty of the creatures, the land, and human beings is to live in harmony with what is. For Tayo, wholeness consists of sowing plants and nurturing them, caring for the spotted cattle, and especially knowing that he belongs exactly where he is, that he is and always has been home. The story that is capable of healing his mind is the story that the land has always signified:

> The transition was completed. In the west and in the south too, the clouds with round heavy bellies had gathered for the dawn. It was not necessary, but it was right, even if the sky had been cloudless the end was the same. The ear for the story and the eye for the pattern were theirs; the feeling was theirs; we came out of this land and we are hers . . . They had always been loved. He thought of her then; she had always loved him, she had never left him; she had always been there. He crossed the river at sunrise. (p. 255)

So Tayo's initiation into motherhood is complete, and the witchery is countered for a time, at least for one human being and his beloved land. Tayo has bridged the distance between his isolated consciousness and the universe of being, because he has loved the spirit woman who brings all things into being and because he is at last conscious that she has always loved them, his people, and himself. He is able at last to take his normal place in the life of the Laguna, a place that is to be characterized by nurturing, caring for life, behaving like a good mother. Auntie can now treat him as she treats the other men, not as a stranger but as a friend whom it is safe to complain about, to nag, and to care for. Even Grandmother knows that he is no longer special after he returns from the Paguate hills, where he became simply a part of the pattern of Laguna life and the enduring story within the land, and she comments that "these goings-on around Laguna don't get me excited any more" (p. 260). Perhaps she is also implying that ordinariness can replace the extraordinary nature of life while the ceremony is being played out. Tayo has come home, ordinary in his being, and they can get on with serious business, the day-to-day life of a village, which is what the land, the ceremony, the story, and time immemorial are all about.

A Stranger in My Own Life: Alienation in American Indian Poetry and Prose

Although one of the major themes in contemporary American Indian literature is alienation, traditional American Indian literatures display an attractive absence of a sense of otherness. Indeed, the overwhelming message of belonging, of enwholement, that characterizes traditional American Indian literature makes it and the tribes to which it belongs appealing to the American and European mind.

Belonging is a basic assumption for traditional Indians, and estrangement is seen as so abnormal that narratives and rituals that restore the estranged to his or her place within the cultural matrix abound. The primary thrust of traditional narratives and chants is wholeness because relationship is taken as fundamental to creaturely existence. Aliens are so designated because they belong to another group of people, not because they are excluded from group membership altogether. Their alien condition is thus normal. It occasions no intrapsychic conflict because the basic assumption of belonging is not in question. The rules for dealing with strangers are clear in tribal traditions, and the normative bias remains unchallenged. Even when a group member is ostracized for severe violations of tribal laws, the narratives point to his or her eventual return to the people, often bringing new laws or rituals, like Handsome Lake of the Seneca or

Kochinnenako of the Keres, or coming as a leader of great stature, like Sweet Medicine of the Cheyenne.

A tribal member's estrangement from the web of tribal being and the conflict that arises are the central preoccupations of much of contemporary American Indian literature. The ancient thrust toward integration of the individual within the common whole is not lost in modern American Indian literature, but it is a movement fraught with pain, rage, and angst, beset by powerlessness, denial, loss of self, normlessness, and anomie, and often characterized by political and personal violence.

Within longer works, violence usually leads to some sense of integration for the protagonist. In shorter works the conflicting forces of absorption and the fear of it are expressed in terms of the bloody history of colonization, of rage at the white man, of despair; often these are accompanied in the same work or in the same writer's body of work by poems or stories replete with sentimental idealizations of the old ways. In brief, what is too often portrayed in shorter works is a world that might have been or that might yet be, but not one that was or is.

The process of creating an American Indian world-that-is-not began with earliest Anglo and European travelers and raconteurs, who took all manner of tales about American aboriginal life back to England and Europe (or, later, back to the white colonial settlements). These stories were all untrue to a greater or lesser extent because they were partial, they reflected the values and perceptions of the travelers and their world-view, and they were bereft of context. However, the conventions developed through these accounts continue to inform present political, social, creative, religious, and educational writing about American Indian life, past and present. And these conventions are followed in one way or another by Indian and non-Indian writers alike.

For instance, consider Peter Martyr, the first historian of the "New World":

> I wolde think their life moste happye of all men, if they might therwith enjoye their auncient libertie . . . Emonge these simple sowles, a fewe clothes serue the naked; weightes and measures are not needefull to sure as can not skyll of crafte and deceyte and haue not the vse of pestiferous monye . . . they seeme to lyue in that goulden worlde of the whiche owlde wryters speake so much; wherein men lyued simply and innocentlye without inforcement of lawes, without quarrelingue Iudges and libelles, contente onely to satisfie nature.[1]

In the main, the writing of these and other non-Indians raises the noble savage convention to a mystical and spiritual height from which the Indian falls at his or her great peril. But whites are not the only writers trapped in the Romantic Fallacy, as I term it: a week spent sampling entries in the proliferation of anthologies, journals, and literary magazines devoted to American Indian writing and in perusing a few of the many American Indian novels will assure a reader that Indians are without fail innocent and magical beings who have run afoul of fate and that the ways of tribal life were simple, stark, and pure, guided by a few simple philosophical principles and a transcendent comprehension of the laws of the universe which the Indians, in their simple but pure way, adhered to unfailingly.

While this portrayal provides little factual evidence for the spiritual, social, or material life of aboriginal Native Americans, Martyr raised this convention to the exalted status of fact. As a consequence, little material that placed tribal life and persons into a context that was their own found its way to popular outlets or critical circles. Indeed, white writers and poets garnered attention by virtue of their ability to manipulate Martyr's view for white pleasure.

Idealization of a group is a natural consequence of separation from the group; in other words, it is a by-product of alienation. Based on denial, it arises from a split-off of element from context. In literary terms, decontextualization of tribal elements that are recombined to suit a nontribal perceptual mode gives rise to alienation as the dominant theme of literature of and about American Indians.

Aside from the historical reasons for this—which are undeniable, numerous, and at base genocidal—the contemporary Indian writer's preoccupation with alienation in its classic dimensions of isolation, powerlessness, meaninglessness, normlessness, lowered self-esteem, and self-estrangement, accompanied by anxiety, hopelessness, and victimization, may be so pervasive because the writers are one way or another predominantly breeds themselves. Exactly what this means in terms of writers' rendering of personal experience is necessarily a central concern of American Indian literary criticism.

What is the experience that creates this sense of alienation? The breed (whether by parentage or acculturation to non-Indian society) is an Indian who is not an Indian. That is, breeds are a bit of both worlds, and the consciousness of this makes them seem alien to traditional Indians while making them feel alien among whites. Breeds commonly feel alien to themselves above all. The Indian world informally classifies individuals according to their "Indianness." No one is exactly sure what the qualifying characteristics are (though various definitions have been advanced, most recently during congressional hearings that sought to establish a definition of Indian, and there is common agreement that blood quantum and community membership or recognition are the most significant qualifiers), nor is the content of the definitions to the point.

But this classification imposes on people the need to conform to the qualifying standards, often without knowing more than vaguely what these might be or how conformance may be signaled. Then, too, one can meet the formal standards and still find oneself excluded from the community on social levels. Or one might change communities and find oneself forced to reestablish one's Indian identity, often with respect to unfamiliar standards and norms. This is particularly true for those who come into a strange urban environment, though it is not as fraught for rural people, who conform to physical standards of appearance, speak an Indian language or use English in the way that bilingual Indians of whatever tribal antecedents do.

Nor is it clear whether norms on reservations are more or less stringent than those applied in urban areas or whether traditional full-blood Indians make the same demands for "purity" that partial-bloods or acculturated full-bloods make (though a number of my aquaintance do).

It is very clear that belonging to the tribe in modern times is precariously dependent on vague norms of others or on clear (but unmeetable) standards officially declared by tribes, individuals, or the U.S. government. The pervasive sense of uneasiness, of having been shut out or disenfranchised, of anger at circumstances that have resulted in overt or covert alienation from the basic source of one's consciousness, informs the greater body of Native American writing, though its expression is often disguised by historically justified anger and culturally supported romanticizing of the old ways. The subject of Indianness generates intense response because when belonging is a central value, the excluded, who are likely to feel keenly the importance of the value in question, are necessarily maimed by separation. Thus we have the dimensions of alienation and the poetry and fiction that ensue from the position of outsider—a position that is all the more painful when the perceived right to belong is greatest.

One poem that directly addresses the issue while acknowledging its complexity is nila northSun's "the way and the way things are," addressed to her grandmother. Gramma has complained that her grandchildren don't speak "indian" and that no one is near to buy her tobacco. The poet replies,

> but gramma
> you told your daughters
> marry white men
> told them they would have
> nicer houses
> fancy cars
> pretty clothes
> could live in the city
>
> gramma your daughters did
> they couldn't speak indian anymore
> how could we grandchildren learn
> there are no rabbits to skin
> in the city
> we have no gramma there to
> teach us the ways[2]

The poem articulates the frustration of normlessness, for while the speaker is aware of the norms, they are meaningless in her personal context. For what use is it to know, vaguely, that there are songs one might sing or dances one might dance, that there is a language to speak and customs to follow, when one knows little more about them than a common tourist. Jeff Saunders observes:

> I came far today
> from where winds are white . . .
> We came circus
> trying to crawl down streets.
> I left . . .
> I felt like a tourist.[3]

Simon J. Ortiz writes in "Toward Spider Springs":

> Our baby, his mother,
> and I were trying to find
> the right road . . .
> We were trying to find
> a place to start all over
> but couldn't.[4]

The impact of normlessness and estrangement from oneself and people is referred to many times by Ortiz in *Going for the Rain* as well as by other poets. Ortiz is better able than many to resolve the conflict by retreating into Indianness, but his retreat inevitably lacks the conviction possessed by Pueblo Indians of earlier generations who did not face the question in its recent, profoundly disorganizing form.

Other poets who are not fully at home in either world have less ease than Ortiz in pretending to discover balance through identifying as purely Indian in their work. (Nor is Ortiz faced with an easy task; writing poetry and stories and being actively involved in radical politics are not traditional Acoma pursuits.) Other poets express their anguish, anger, and dislocation more polemically than he, and with less poetic finesse.

Politically conscious, romanticizing stances characterize much of the work of contemporary American Indian writers. In that work, alienation is everywhere in evidence, for political activism is one way younger Indian writers (and older Indians just beginning to get politically involved) can get a hearing, and their own sense of alienation is often the motivating force that propels them into writing to begin with. But it also tends to produce a poetry that slides into easy oppositions: the red man as noble and persecuted, an innocent victim of a fate he was and is powerless to meet. Opposed to him (seldom *her*) is the greedy and ignorant white man (seldom white woman) whose dominant characteristic is his unmitigated evil. While the historical facts, when viewed in a large scope that blurs individual details, are largely about the theft of an entire hemisphere by alien invaders (who might just as well have come from outer space for all they and the native people had or have in common), the pain and anxiety engendered by not having a secure sense of place and identity cannot be assuaged by reducing a multifaceted history and many human interactions to one-dimensional or cartoonish stereotypes.

Nor does portraying the Indian as a helpless, innocent, highly exotic victim do much for the image of Indian people as complex and intelligent human beings. If we're so smart, why did we lose two whole continents? The question must enter the minds of readers at least vaguely when they are confronted with the noble innocent red man in place of a human being.

There are ways to write about colonization, the disasters and the misery and disorganization that have flowed in its wake, that do justice to the enormity of the tragedy while maintaining a sense of the humanity of those involved. That means treating the subject of colonization and of alienation with respect for the complexity of it. And there are plenty of poets and writers who do so with great competence, in some cases with brilliance.

The themes of loss, anger, and brutalization form the body of the work of poets such as nila northSun and Marnie Walsh. NorthSun writes of her cousin, shadow:

> shadow is
> my cousin
> shadow was
> my cousin
> hated herself
> because
> others hated her
> whites hated her
> indians hated her
> called shadow
> apple indian
> whites saw only INDIAN
> fat drunk greasy squaw
>
> shadow didn't know
> what she was
> my cousin killed herself
> nothing new
> we have lots of cousins
> both dead & alive
> sometimes
> both
> with the same shadow[5]

With the same tone of understatement, the almost brutal flippancy of northSun, Walsh writes of Aunt Nettie, who went to Catholic school and then to college for a while, but when she came home "she got a baby / but give it away." Aunt Nettie liked to talk about what she'd done in college. "She don't tell though why she come home / nathan say she stole money / and got throwed out." Aunt Nettie liked to tell poetry that she learned in college, "about love and some lady in a tower / by a lake," and this love was to be her undoing on the reservation:

5
when aunt nettie got too drunk
she told poetry
and oh she knowed it good
but all the people laughed
and she took to crying a lot
wouldn't eat
just drank whisky all the time . . .
no mama to care and no papa to beat her
they dead and her alone

6
yesterday they find her
all crazy
screaming and naked
she say she lost
and cant find her tower
by the lake
some people take her away
but not her poetry
i stole it
and she wont miss it   where she went[6]

Aunt and cousin, caught in the same ambiguity; unable to be Indian, unable *not* to be Indian, they go the same route: drunk, crazy, isolated, having no point of reference that is meaningful to all their experience. Neither Indian nor white can accept all parts of these unfortunates' experiences, so they fall into tragedy along with their people.

The crucial factor in the alienation so often treated in American Indian writing is the unconscious assumption that Indians must ally with one particular segment of their experience and not with another. The world is seen in terms of antagonistic principles: good is set against bad, Indian against white, and tradition against cultural borrowing; personal significance becomes lost in a confusion of dualities. For many, this process has meant rejection of Indianness. The "apples," who categorically reject the Indian culture they were born to, choose one side, the white. The personal war waged by those who choose to perceive themselves as thoroughly westernized is often worked out in bouts of suicidal depression, alcoholism, abandonment of Indian ways, "disappearance" into urban complexes, and verbalized distrust of and contempt for longhairs, John "Big Bluff" Tosamah in N. Scott Momaday's *House Made of Dawn* represents this response to the forces of alienation.

Others, aware that one cannot reject one's race and culture, either because the winds of fashion and politics have so convinced them or because they are aware that such an action is in reality impossible, choose the other course of self-rejection. These persons often work out their struggle through rage directed against whites and "apples." Their violence tends to be other-directed, and they are the most likely to engage in abuse of wives and children.

A third category of victims of alienation are people caught between two cultures. These are the most likely to be suicidal, inarticulate, almost paralyzed in their inability to direct their energies toward resolving what seems to them an insoluble conflict. Their lives are, as they see it, completely beyond their control and any hope of reconciling the oppositions within and outside themselves seems beyond their reach.

James Welch writes about those who choose to cling to their Indian heritage in his moving "Winter Indian":

> Happy to think of good times
> buffalo fat to fall in jumps.
> When war was still a game and berries
> stained a face fierce,
> white women slaved to laughing squaws.[7]

Unlike many who write about the past with longing, Welch sees the terms of the conflict and in his anger and grief finds wit for honesty, though the dire need of his people does not escape his notice:

> If we raced a century over hills
> that ended years before, people couldn't
> say our run was simply poverty of promise
> for a better end. We ended sometime
> back in recollections of glory, myths
> that meant the hunters meant a lot
> to starving wives and bad painters . . .
>
> Comfortable we drink and string together stories
> of white buffalo, medicine men who promised
> and delivered horrible cures for hunger,
> the lovely tales of war and white men massacres.

> Meaning gone, we dance for pennies now,
> our feet jangling dust that hides the bones
> of sainted Indians.[8]

Welch directs his anger equally against white and Indian. He does not sentimentalize his forebears as noble savages, nor does he bow in shame at a history that is his birthright. But for many, writers and activists among them, unity with Indian roots is sought in the humorless repudiation of the experiences that form a large part of their cultures. In the attempt to integrate a fragmented personality, many choose violent rejection of what they know and intensely cling to dreams of lost glory, lost traditions, and a fantasized past of plenty, justice, and rectitude that may or may not have existed.

The better part of integration of oneself lies in a careful reclamation of whatever facts are relevant to one's present circumstances, though such a reclamation can hardly be pleasant when the facts themselves are so brutal. Many Indians do recognize the realities of their existence; the realization often produces a tragic vision because there is no way to be acceptably Indian (with all the pain that implies) and acceptable to whites at the same time.

The other-directedness of Indian life dictates against the inherently self-serving kind of autonomy that self-acceptance implies. The attempt to reconcile the irreconcilable often results in events such as those described in Marnie Walsh's "Vickie Loans-Arrow, 1972":

> I
> this morning
> me and my cousin
> charlene lost-nation
> are in to bobby simons bar
> and charlene say
> i tired of living
> there aint nothing in it
> and bobby simon
> behind the bar
> goes ha ha ha
> when she fall off
> the stool
> im laughing too
> she so drunk
> she funny
> . . .

IV
we drink and she pulls
her face up tight
tells me it dont pay to think
theres something to it
cause there aint
and says wont nobody
never believe her
what she says
i just laugh
she so drunk
she funny

V
well me and bobby simons
drink some more
i seen charlene
when she gone to the can
she dont come back
pretty soon bobby simon
say i better check her out
so i go to see
i find her all right
sitting in a corner
theres blood on her mouth
and her chin
and down her dress

VI
she looks at me
and i see the knife
sticking out between her teeth
and remember what that means
and i know shed like to die
but can't
so she killed her tongue
instead
i leave her there
i go out the door
and down the street
and the yellow wind
make me shiver and sweat

because now i believe her
but wont never say so[9]

Tonguelessness. A dimension of alienation that is not mentioned in the literature concerning it but that occurs frequently in the work of American Indian poets and novelists. The inability to speak is the prime symbol of powerlessness in the novels of Momaday, Welch, and Leslie Marmon Silko. Abel, in *House Made of Dawn*, is essentially an outsider to his people even before he is drafted, but by the time he returns he has lost the power of speech. Estranged from his own people as well as from himself, he lives his days remembering events that marked his strangeness and his isolation from all that should have been familiar to him.

As a youngster, he is unable to perceive the geese as his brother, Vidal, perceives them. He seems to be haunted, and the deaths of his mother and soon after of his brother intensify his preoccupation with the terrors of the unseen evil that seems to stalk him. His grandfather, Francisco, no stranger to evil, has made an uneasy peace with it, but perhaps he has been cursed: his crippled leg, the deaths of all those he loved with the exception of Abel, whose crippling is less visible but more complete, indicate that he is a victim of some supernatural ill will.

Francisco's involvement with evil is echoed by his grandson's inability to participate in the ceremonial life of the village. He is isolated from the traditions that organize the seasons and human relationships into significant patterns. Even his participation with the Bakyush in their eagle hunt is flawed by his inability to accept necessary pain: when the eagle has been captured, he cannot bear her captivity and the change that comes over her as a result. He strangles her, thus violating the ceremony and separating himself further from the religious/ceremonial life of the tribe.

Abel has no norms, no means of understanding and naming his experience. He cannot structure what happens to him or around him. His only response to events is violence, as he attempts to destroy what is destroying him.

In the inarticulateness of his powerlessness and isolation, he first talks to and then murders the albino, believing him a witch, responsible for all the pain and grief that Abel has suffered. Abel struggles with the stark facts of the destruction that colonization brings, and he displaces his terror onto the strange being who has humiliated him as the white soldiers humiliated him during his tour of duty.

One of the arms lay out from the body; it was there, in the pale angle of the white man's death, that Abel knelt . . . The white, hairless arm shone like the underside of a fish, and the dark nails of the hand seemed a string of great black beads.[10]

So Abel tries to murder the alien other that he cannot accept and integrate within his own psyche and that he perceives to be the source of his pain and terror. Certainly, the albino in his death resembles the white man, the Church, and the unseen, nameless evil that Abel seeks to destroy or evade, and Abel is destroyed in his struggle to make sense of modern imperatives and history. He has no tradition to which he can relate and no words in which to articulate his perception. He lacks the security of self-knowledge and belonging that Francisco possesses; his memories are not those of a priest or of an Indian raised securely within a village untouched by tragedy. In his attempt to reconcile opposites that he cannot control, he murders the albino and ensures his own exile.

The violence in which Abel finds himself involved is a result of the collision of tradition and history. The novel, in its careful recounting of conquest and the religious transformation that ensues and with it the witchcraft that withers the village and blasts Abel's youth, makes this collision and its consequences clear.

Some within the novel do not accept violent solutions to grief; like Francisco, they find their acknowledgment of the unknown to be "nothing more than a dull, intrinsic sadness, a vague desire to weep,"[11] and they find it possible to live out their lives in relative tranquility.

There are several kinds of breeds in *House Made of Dawn*. Benally, the relocation Navajo who finds a middle ground between his economic need and his tradition, Tosamah, who attempts to connect his Indian self and his white self by becoming a Christian minister and a Peyote priest, and the lost men who listen to Tosamah preach and who attend his Peyote services all represent varying characterizations of the central theme. They all suffer from some degree of alienation and attempt, through drink and powwows on the Los Angeles hills, to accommodate it and its attendant anguish.

Only Abel finds no way to bridge the enormous gap between self and white. He, neither Christian nor pagan, neither soldier nor warrior, neither brother nor son, can find nothing within himself to form such a bridge but murderous rage. For him alcohol is no tranquilizer, but a fire that feeds his sullen, speechless rage until he explodes in a violence that results in his near-fatal beating by the *culebra* policeman

Martinez. When he returns home, broken and diseased, to preside over his grandfather's death, he returns speechless—all power of any kind, even that of his body, gone from him.

Tayo, the half-breed protagonist of Silko's *Ceremony*, also suffers from speechlessness. He will not speak because he believes that he is invisible. He was in the war, saw his cousin Rocky die, watched Japanese soldiers who looked like his own people dying. He cursed the rain, believing that if it would stop, Rocky would live.

He thinks he is responsible for the drought at home, on the Laguna reservation, because he went to war and might have killed somebody. His uncle Josiah died while Tayo was in the Philippines, and Tayo thinks he is responsible for Josiah's death as well.

Feeling completely powerless over the tragic events surrounding him and convinced that he has somehow caused them, he retreats into a dream life in which he believes himself to be invisible, unable to speak because he has no tongue, unable to make a sound because he has no voice.

Tayo's suffering is caused by his status as a half-breed in a tribe that does not approve of mixed blood. His mother, a lost Laguna woman who had tried to fit into the white world as a result of her experiences at white schools, turned to alcohol and a bitter form of prostitution when her attempts to be accepted in the white man's world failed. She died of exposure or alcohol, and her breed son Tayo was raised by her sister and brother in Laguna. Because he was a breed, Tayo was not taught Laguna traditions and did not share the arcane knowledge of his Laguna people. He was treated as an outsider, mocked for his green eyes. Auntie watched him carefully, always remembering the circumstances of his birth and his low status because of his white father, reminding him through her actions how alien he was. She did not treat her son Rocky the same way but encouraged him to emulate whites—seeing in him some hope of salvation, some restoration of the respect she believed lost by Laura's transgressions. Tayo saw his place in the family as the shadow of his successful and handsome cousin-brother Rocky.[12] He believed that he would take Josiah's place in tending the cattle and fields because Rocky seemed destined for college and a job in the white man's world.

With Josiah and Rocky dead, Tayo's sense of where he fits in is gone. The guilt and loss of self that their deaths arouse are more than he can bear. He retreats into psychosis that manifests itself as "invisibility" and the belief that he can neither speak nor be heard.

Many of the characters in *Ceremony* suffer from the effects of alienation, which they experience in their perceived powerlessness to control their own destinies, their isolation from the old ways and its attendant homogeneity, the growing meaninglessness of the traditions and traditional understandings, and the lowered self-esteem that being an Indian in a white man's world too often creates.

Rocky shows the effects of the process by determining to study scientific methods of ranching, spurning the older ways of dealing with weather, disease of livestock, and breeding. He feels that his people are superstitious and ignorant, and he does not intend to be like them. His mother turns from a tribal connection and acceptance of herself to Christian modes of thought. She models her life on simple concepts of good—sacrifice, struggle, and quiet martyrdom, "wishing to show those who might gossip that . . . above all else, she was a Christian woman."[13]

But if Tayo and his counterparts at Laguna are examples of the destructive aspects of alienation caused by half-breed status, Betonie, the breed Navajo shaman, is an example of the creative possibilities of mixed blood. Betonie accepts his heritage for the strength it gives him and looks to basic causes for the situation the whole world is in. Betonie is aware that alienation is a common sickness, not confined to the reservation or its urban extensions, and he identifies "the witchery" as its source. Because he is comfortable with his integrated cultures and because ceremonialism has been his mainstay throughout his life, he is able to heal Tayo and to help him find the mission he was meant to complete. Betonie's magic propels Tayo along his ceremonial journey which takes him to Ts'eh, the mountain spirit woman. Through her aid Tayo finds and rescues Josiah's breed cattle, and through loving he finds his own completeness.

The solution Silko offers, the acceptance of self through ceremonial rite, is not one that is likely to occur for the average half-breed. Welch poses the same situation in both his novels, *Winter in the Blood* (1974) and *The Death of Jim Loney* (1979), and resolves it in very different ways, though the final resolution is, in both cases, a matter of personal integration through insight and action.

In *Winter in the Blood*, the symptom of speechlessness is somewhat a quality of the protagonist, but it is most characteristic of his grandmother who sits in her chair day after day and seldom says anything. The powerlessness of the narrator is symbolized in the theft of his razor and his gun by his Cree sweetheart and by his bum knee, which prevents him from walking with strength. His namelessness is also significant—showing both the degree of his lack of power (an Indian without a name is powerless indeed) and the extent of his self-estrangement.

He is isolated from his family and his tradition as the novel opens; even his history has been cut off by the exigencies of history and his grandmother's past. His father, First Raise, and his brother, Mose, are both dead. As the novel progresses, he discovers his grandfather, a solitary man who converses with the animals and the weather and only very occasionally with other human beings. Through Yellow Calf, the narrator recovers his family history, though this discovery does not at first appear to lessen his isolation.

His mother, Teresa, decides to marry a man she has been seeing for some time, and by this marriage effectively conveys to the narrator his ineffectiveness as rancher and man. The narrator does not like his new stepfather but works alongside him when necessary. Between times, he goes to town to try to find the Cree girl and persuade her to return to him. He gets involved in a series of sexual encounters that are distinguished mainly by their lack of caring and by his observation of pain in the lives of the women he meets.

The Cree woman's brother beats him up, and he joins with a white man who seems even more surreal than himself. None of the encounters in the novel are notable for their meaningfullness except those with Yellow Calf and Teresa. The nameless narrator is so out of touch with himself that his long past relationships with his dead brother and father have more meaning for him than any of his contemporary ones, and he is adrift in a life that lacks shape, goal, understanding, or significance.

In the end, it is his recognition of his estrangement that leads him through his impasse and allows him to reintegrate his personality around realistic perceptions of himself and the reality he inhabits. "I wondered if Mose and First Raise were comfortable. They were the only ones I really loved, I thought, the only ones who were good to be with."[14]

Lying in the rain, stiff and unwilling to move, the narrator finally confronts himself. It is a gentle encounter that enables him to understand that acceptance is the better part of grief. "Some people, I thought, will never know how pleasant it is to be distant in a clean rain . . . It's not like you'd expect, nothing like you'd expect."[15]

In *The Death of Jim Loney*, Jim does not come to self-realization and the healing that accompanies it so gently. Haunted by the absence of a past or of any lasting relationships, Jim's search for significance, for meaning, flows in a downward spiral into alcoholism, delusion, vision, and death. This most brutal and honest of the novels written about alienated mixed-blood Indians portrays the exact process of an alienation that offers no possibility of relief.

Jim Loney's father was an Irish-American ne'er-do-well, his mother a reservation Indian woman who studied to be a nurse. When Jim's sister was five or six and Jim a toddler, his mother abandoned them. After a few years the father left as well, and Jim's sister Kate took care of herself and her brother until social welfare intervened and placed the children in a foster home. At this point, Kate left to attend mission school, and a woman Jim remembers with love and grief took the boy in. Jim saw his time with her as the only happiness he'd ever felt.

The woman, Sandra, had been the elder Loney's mistress, and whether through pity or love, she offered his children a home. She was eventually forced to give Jim up, although he didn't know why until many years later. He was sent to live with the Catholic brothers at a nearby mission school until he ran away in high school. The years went by, and his father returned to town, but he never spoke to Jim. He lived in a trailer at the edge of town, got drunk regularly at his crony's bar, and listened to the radio. Rumors said Jim's mother was dead, that she had gone insane, that she had moved south. His sister graduated and then moved east. She had an important job for the Indian bureaucracy in Washington and visited Jim once or twice.

This novel is the most difficult of the four to understand. Written to match the seamless web of loss Loney is entrapped in, it does not easily give up its secrets. The emotive content is of pain, grief, despair, loss of hope, of self, of past, and of future. Its victim-protagonist knows what is happening but is powerless to change anything. The fragmented structure of the text underlines the shattering impact of alienation on Jim's psyche, and the painfully clear diction intensifies the almost perfect stasis of Loney as he approaches the moment when he must encounter his isolated reality and come to terms with a life entirely devoid of human contact and personal significance.

Like the nameless narrator in Welch's *Winter in the Blood*, Loney is driven beyond despair into decision by lack of love. Indeed, while lovelessness is not usually named by sociologists as an aspect of alienation, it may be the primary factor. For without relationships with significant others, meaning, self-esteem, a sense of belonging expressed in the establishment of norms and experienced as a sense of power cannot exist. And for one like Loney, who has been severely deprived of close, nurturing relationships with others he could depend on, the crippling effects of alienation must necessarily cast a shadow on an entire life.

The absence of love is not a mere matter of sexual intimacy. Loney has a lover, Reah, who cares deeply for him. But Loney, wounded beyond repair in childhood, cannot experience the bonding, the dependence, the knowing of self through another that a meaningful human relationship requires.

He had two chances to learn about loving, about being loved and cared for, but both came to an end before he developed a sense of what belonging, what meaning something to another human being might signify. He ran out of time. The first time, while Jim was still very young, his sister had decided to teach him what she learned at school. It became an obsession with her, and she continued it for several years. Then, when their father left, she thought, "for a few exhilarating days . . . that she would raise her brother herself."[16] But that proved impossible—the authorities wouldn't allow it, though by then she was fifteen and Jim was ten. So his father's lover offered to take them in. Kate refused, because "she had felt she would lose her brother and she couldn't take that."[17]

The two years Jim spent with Sandra were his only experience of warmth and caring. He thought of those years as being "like a dream."[18] He didn't remember how she died, did not even know what happened to her. He did not remember her name until Kate reminded him of it years later. But he remembered certain moments—drinking hot chocolate, brushing her hair. She was, he decided, "the woman he had tried hardest to love, throughout the years, and now."[19]

Thus, fatherless, motherless, abandoned by sister and friend, he grew into an adult who was lonely to the core, unable to be nurtured by anyone. Anomie was his chief characteristic.

In many respects, Jim Loney, Tayo, Abel, and the nameless narrator of *Winter in the Blood* are alike. All have been severely damaged by death, all are parentless except the narrator in *Winter in the Blood*, whose mother, though still alive, cannot communicate love or closeness to her son. Most important, none of these protagonists has a clear sense of belonging to a people, a tradition, or a culture.

The conflict is resolved variously: the southwestern authors, Momaday and Silko, choose traditional Indian modes of resolution, while the northern author Welch chooses realism. The difference in choice can at least be partly ascribed to the differences in perception of options among Pueblo, Navajo, or other southwestern tribes and those of the Plains or more eastern tribes. As the acculturation processes have been different in the two regions, the degree of alienation, as reflected in these novels, has also been different. In addition, romanticism of American Indians is endemic to the Southwest, while brutalization and degradation of them is common on the Plains.

Thus, it seems that alienation is a political issue. Among others, Silko and Momaday make this point as part of their plots. In *House Made of Dawn*, police brutality is a significant factor in Abel's destruction, as is the lack of comprehension by liberal sympathizers like Fr. Olguin and Milly. Beyond these elements, Momaday's portrayal of Abel as lost because he has been cut away from his sources by colonization and genocide clearly focuses on alienation as a political theme. Silko also uses political arguments throughout *Ceremony*. The ideas and values of the ecology, antiracist, and antinuclear movements inform much of her narrative, giving it a topical quality while advancing the plot and major themes of the novel.

The tragic vision of Welch may best portray the ultimate condition of the Indian people in the United States, although his novels reach resolution in singularly white ways. The protagonist in *Winter in the Blood* achieves a sort of sanity, a balance between his anguish and his need, that allows him to make plans for a future that will not be as blighted as his past. But Jim Loney chooses a warrior's death—one that is simple and clean, that comes of his own choice, and that singularly fits the circumstances of his life. Loney chooses to die on the reservation he never lived on. He is killed by an Indian, a tribal policeman who believes that Loney murdered his high school friend, Pretty Weasel.

Jim Loney has his own reasons for allowing the police to believe him a murderer. He would like to live, to survive, but he can't survive in a world that is not meant for him, a white world that rejects him, an Indian world that abandons him. He can belong to neither, and his memories, like the black birds he sees, are too painful for him to continue recalling. He hopes to be remembered as an Indian, not as a man who was seen "with a bottle and a gun"[20] like a white man, but "carrying a dog that I was taking to higher ground."[21]

Loney dies like a warrior, out of choice, not out of defeat. Though he could not plan or control his life, he could, finally, determine his death. Perhaps the most destructive aspect of alienation is that: the loss of power, of control over one's destiny, over one's memories, thoughts, relationships, past, and future. For in a world where no normative understandings apply, where one is perceived as futile and unwanted, where one's perceptions are denied by acquaintance and stranger alike, where pain is the single most familiar sensation, the loss of self is experienced continually and, finally, desperately.

To be sure, American Indians are not the only people who suffer alienation in the modern world, but they are among the most beleaguered, the most wounded by it. For, like the protagonists in their novels, and like the speakers in their poems, they live in a land that is no longer their home, among strangers who determine, senselessly, the patterns of their lives. And they are, for the most part, powerless to do much more than determine the cause of their deaths.

The Ceremonial Motion
of Indian Time:
Long Ago, So Far

The traditional tribal concept of time is of timelessness, as the concept of space is of multidimensionality. In the ceremonial world the tribes inhabit, time and space are mythic.

Years ago Fred Young, the Navajo mathematician and physicist, explained to me the essential movement of time and space. He said that if you held time constant, space went to infinity, and when space was held constant, time moved to infinity. That was why it was not possible to determine the exact location of a particle on a grid. The tribal sense of self as a moving event within a moving universe is very similar to the physicists' understanding of the particle within time and space. There is plenty of time in the Indian universe because everything moves in a dynamic equilibrium and the fact of universal movement is taken into account in the ritual life that is tribal existence.

Achronology is the favored structuring device of American Indian novelists since N. Scott Momaday selected it for organizing *House Made of Dawn*. Particularly in that novel, Leslie Marmon Silko's *Ceremony*, and my own *The Woman Who Owned the Shadows*,

---

Lagunas start their stories by saying "humma haa," which means "long ago, so far," among other things.

events are structured in a way that emphasizes the motion inherent in the interplay of person and event. In them the protagonist wanders through a series of events that might have happened years before or that might not have happened to him or her personally, but that nevertheless have immediate bearing on the situation and the protagonist's understanding of it.

The death of Francisco in *House Made of Dawn*[1] underscores the difference in perception of time between tribal people and nontribal ones. Fr. Olguin wants to know what time it is when Abel wakes him to tell him that Francisco has died. He is unhappy with being awakened at that ungodly hour—whatever it is exactly. "Good lord, what time is it, anyway?" he complains. "Do you know what time it is?" Then, aware that his response is improper, out of place, he says, "I can understand how you feel, but—" As Abel leaves him standing in the predawn doorway, Fr. Olguin shouts after him, "I understand! *Oh God! I understand—I understand!*" (p. 190). But he doesn't, of course. He does not know that the time is Francisco's death time.

House Made of Dawn revolves around the axis of time as motion. It opens with Abel running, and it closes the same way. The novel's epiphany occurs when Abel, maimed and near death on the Los Angeles beach, comprehends the point of the Runners-after-Evil (p. 96). Scene after scene revolves around the thematic preoccupation with the nature of time—Indian time, industrial time, pastoral time, ceremonial time, institutional time. Momaday pursues his story, placing moving particle against eternal field and counterposing still particle against moving field. When moving particle and moving field are in harmony, joy is the result: Benally riding to the squaw dance, singing a riding song; Ben and Milly on the beach, running; Francisco leading the runners in the ritual race, drumming perfect time of the dance. In the end, the understanding Abel reaches is the understanding that all who live in harmony and balance with their universe must reach. And it is the same understanding that contemporary physicists had to reach as they learned to describe the universe of particles that move within moving time and space. Fr. Olguin does not understand, for he confuses emotion with motion, just as he confuses motivation with season and death with life.

Francisco understands, and in the end he moves from this world into another. He runs into death as he ran into life as a young man (pp. 186–188). He moves with what moves. And in the end Abel understands, finally, after a lifetime of not understanding, that the difference between a witch-inspired death and a harmonious, healing death is the difference between stopped movement and balanced motion with what moves. "He was alone and running on. All of his being was concentrated in the sheer motion of running on, and he was past caring about the pain" (p. 191).

The achronological time sense of tribal people results from tribal beliefs about the nature of reality, beliefs based on ceremonial understandings rather than on industrial, theological, or agricultural orderings.

Chronological time structuring is useful in promoting and supporting an industrial time sense. The idea that everything has a starting point and an ending point reflects accurately the process by which industry produces goods. Western industrialists engage in time-motion studies hoping to enhance profits. Chronological organization also supports allied western beliefs that the individual is separate from the environment, that man is separate from God, that life is an isolated business, and that the person who controls the events around him is a hero. (*Woman* seldom—indeed virtually never—is addressed or referred to in western theological or philosophical speculations.) That understanding, which includes a strong belief in individualism as well as the belief that time operates external to the internal workings of human and other beings, contrasts sharply with a ceremonial time sense that assumes the individual as a moving event shaped by and shaping human and nonhuman surroundings. The difference in the two concepts of time gave rise to my poem, "Hoop Dancer":

> It's hard to enter
> circling clockwise and counter
> clockwise moving no
> regard for time, metrics
> irrelevant to this place
> where pain is the prime number
> and soft stepping feet
> praise water from the skies:
>
> I have seen the face of triumph
> the winding line stare down all moves
> to desecration: guts not cut from arms,
> fingers joined to minds,

together Sky and Water
one dancing   one
circle of a thousand turning lines
beyond the march of gears—
out of time   out of
time,   out
of time.[2]

"Hoop Dancer" came at least in part out of the conversations I had with Fred Young, the Navajo theoretical physicist and mathematician I spoke of earlier, several years before I wrote it. It concerns itself with the psychic fragmentation of factory time compared with the psychic integration of ceremonial time. It seemed to me then, as it does now, that the basis of Indian time is ceremonial, while the basis of time in the industrialized west is mechanical. I also implied that motion that is in balance is integrating and empowering, while the other kind is fragmenting and disempowering.

The difference between these concepts of time is embodied in the function of the dances: the green corn dances, the deer dances, and the Feast Day dances are all symbolized, held, in the hoop dance I was watching in my imagination when I wrote the poem. The sky and water joining into rain clouds are characteristic of the time at home when the green corn dances are danced. "Hoop Dancer" is a rendering of my understanding of the process by which one enters into timelessness— that place where one is whole.

Achronicity is the kind of time in which the individual and the universe are "tight." The sense of time that the term refers to is not ignorant of the future any more than it is unconscious of the past. It is a sense of time that connects pain and praise through timely movement, knitting person and surroundings into one. Dancing in the midst of turning, whirling hoops is a means of transcending the limits of chronological time and its traumatizing, disease-causing effects. Chronological time denies that an individual is one with the surroundings. The hoop dancer dances within what encircles him, demonstrating how the people live in motion within the circling spirals of time and space. They are no more limited than water and sky. At green corn dance time, water and sky come together, in Indian time, to make rain.

While the time structuring used in novels by American Indian writers is a technical problem, it is also a factor in the ultimate significance of the book. It determines which kind of consciousness will be reflected in the novel—western industrial consciousness or Indian consciousness. Momaday and Silko opt for Indian consciousness, but earlier novelists like D'Arcy McNickle and Mourning Dove chose western consciousness. One result of the earlier novelists' choice is that they wrote easily readable books. But the other consequence is that they furthered the stereotyping tendencies of American readers and made their version of Indians conform to the version of those who see Indians as dying victims of the white man's world.

I am suggesting that there is some sort of connection between colonization and chronological time. There is a connection between factories and clocks, and there is a connection between colonial imperialism and factories. There is also a connection between telling Indian tales in chronological sequences and the American tendency to fit Indians into the slots they have prepared for us. The Indians used to be the only inhabitants of the Americas, but times change. Having perceived us as belonging to history, they are free to emote over us, to re-create us in their history-based understanding, and dismiss our present lives as archaic and irrelevant to the times.

Not surprisingly, both of McNickle's novels, *Wind from an Enemy Sky* and *The Surrounded*, are about the loss of hope for the Indians. Both protagonists are caught in a web of actions and reactions that can be understood by comparing the cultural understandings of the Indians and those of the whites. Both books imply that while the Indians are sincere and much more humanely intelligent than the whites around them, their tribal sense of propriety and timing leads them into deadly conflict with the whites. Mourning Dove's protagonist in *Cogewea, the Half-Blood* suffers a happier fate: her experience with the wily white man is devastating, but it could have been avoided had she understood the situation as the grandmother does, ceremonially. But neither Cogewea nor any other Indian in Mourning Dove's novel is murderer or murdered, and Cogewea herself finally understands the true point of the Stemteema's teachings. Nor is Mourning Dove as comfortable with chronological ordering as McNickle. While *Cogewea, the Half-Blood* is told in chronological sequence, Mourning Dove makes massive interruptions for sociopolitical ruminations. These stop the flow of the story, to be sure, but they also point to Mourning Dove's uneasiness with the simple ordering and interpreting of events that chronological organization imposes.

The contemporary novels of Leslie Marmon Silko and James Welch are composed of a series of short vignettes. Welch sticks to a nearly chronological narrative line, but both his narratives are full of flashbacks and rely heavily on surrealistic methods of solving the problem posed by differing Indian and white understandings of the relationship and nature of time and event. Welch uses dream or quasi-dream sequences as well as flashbacks to further the plot in ways that make an Indian's experience comprehensible to white readers. But because he relies heavily on chronological, cause-and-effect ordering, his protagonists do not experience a reintegration of self within their surroundings. The ways by which the nameless hero of *Winter in the Blood* and Jim Loney locate themselves in their lives are alienating. At the end of *Winter in the Blood*, the protagonist still has no name, and Jim Loney dies hoping Amos After Buffalo will remember him in ways he never was.

Silko's *Ceremony*[3] is organized mainly around motion and ritual. She makes several references to industrial notions of time, notably in the collection of calendars amassed by the maverick healer Betonie. One time referent she takes is galactic: the placement of stars is the basis of what time it is. The other is ceremonial: it is time for the witchery to be undone. The role of the protagonist Tayo is to behave in a proper ritual manner, and to this end he loses his mechanical time sense in the void, his mechanical space sense in the Philippines, and his sense of his identity as isolated in his movement within the mountain and within the ceremony he must enact. That his proper ritual role is primarily one of motion is suggested by the amount of walking, riding, searching, and learning to be a Pueblo man that he engages in. The traditional medicine man Ku'oosh explains to him, "But you know, grandson, this world is fragile" (p. 36).

With my own novel, I had difficulty with at least two publishers because I chose Indian time over industrial time as a structuring device. Their comments on *The Woman Who Owned the Shadows*[4] sounded very much like those of my students attempting to read and understand *House Made of Dawn* and *Ceremony*. Their distress stemmed from their inability to locate the particle (protagonist) on a background grid (setting). They wanted the hero to be foregrounded and the events, understandings, and other characters to be clearly delineated back-drops. While they wanted the protagonist to have a heritage, replete with lore, she or he must have a "personal story" that places these other elements in their proper background relationship to the main action.

Indian tales, however, don't really work that way. The structure of the stories out of the oral tradition, when left to themselves and not recast by Indian or white collector, tend to meander gracefully from event to event; the major unifying device, besides the presence of certain characters in a series of tales, is the relationship of the tale to the ritual life of the tribe.

In my novel, I told a number of stories, some from the Keres oral tradition, some from Keres and Navajo history, some from contemporary happenings around Indian country, some from the life of the protagonist, Ephanie Atencio, and some from her grandmother's life. I selected the "heritage and lore" sections for their direct bearing on the events Ephanie herself experiences, so that each kind of story relates to and illuminates the rest. The plotting is as near to a conversation with Indians as I could make it, and the style is "legendary" (as one reader phrased it) to further the reader's sense of the underlying structure. Time is a central theme of the book, and understanding temporality and chronology is an obsession that moves Ephanie through every experience she has. The problem of understanding clock time comes up early in the story:

> Four o'clock. The brass handle was cold in her hand. They'll be here pretty soon. The others. She thought. She crossed the room, smoothing her disorderly black hair as she again walked toward the door. No, they just left. I thought I heard them talking, coming up the walk. She turned again, pulling the door shut behind, vagueness hunching her round shoulders, her brown arms raising to circle her for warmth. Slowly she sat in the nearest bright orange chair. What time is it? (p. 3)

In the book, dream, "actual" event, myth, tale, history, and internal dialogue are run together, making it evident that divisions do not lead to comprehension. The structure reflects the point that particles move in moving time and space and that individuals move in a moving field. One passage in particular relates this idea:

> All is very still. There is sky leading everywhere. Or nowhere. And the woman in a beige dress is telling Ephanie she is too meek. That she lets them run over her. That she must take charge . . .
> Ephanie sat the afternoon pondering the window, its light. The reflection of the yellowed tree. Branches standing as if on the threshold of awareness. Throwing light at the sky. Fall now, winter soon. Time a floating crap game. (p. 15)

The section title that follows this passage, "If She Remembers, She'll Know The Time," captures the essence of Indian time.

Ultimately, Indian time is a concept based on a sense of propriety, on a ritual understanding of order and harmony. For an Indian, if being on time means being out of harmony with self and ritual, the Indian will be "late." The right timing for a tribal Indian is the time when he or she is in balance with the flow of the four rivers of life. That is, Indian time rests on a perception of individuals as part of an entire gestalt in which fittingness is not a matter of how gear teeth mesh with each other but rather how the person meshes with the revolving of the seasons, the land, and the mythic reality that shapes all life into significance.

What Fred Young showed me, drawing careful though incomprehensible formulas on the chalkboard in some dusty classroom of the Physics Building at the University of New Mexico sometime long ago so far, was how an Indian tells time. He said it was the right theoretical way to do it, and he was right.

**Answering the Deer:
Genocide and Continuance
in the Poetry of
American Indian Women**

In the ancient bardic tradition the bards sang only of love and death. Certainly these twin themes encompass the whole of human experience. Loving, celebrating, and joining are the source of life, but they necessarily occur against a background of potential extinction. Thus, these themes become the spindle and loom of the poets' weavings, for from the interplay of connection and disconnection come our most significant understandings of ourselves, our fellow creatures, and our tradition, our past. The American Indian women who write poetry do so in that ancient tradition, for like the bards we are tribal singers. And because our tribal present is inextricably bound to our continuing awareness of imminent genocide, our approach to the themes of love and death takes on a pervasive sense of sorrow and anger that is not easily reconciled with the equally powerful tradition of celebrating with the past and affirming the future that is the essence of oral tradition.

We are the dead and the witnesses to death of hundreds of thousands of our people, of the water, the air, the animals and forests and grassy lands that sustained them and us not so very long ago.

"Blessed are they who listen when no one is left to speak," Chickasaw poet Linda Hogan writes in her poem "Blessing."[1] The impact of genocide in the minds of American Indian poets and writers cannot be exaggerated. It is a pervasive feature of the consciousness of every American Indian in the United States, and the poets are never unaware of it. Even poems that are meant to be humorous derive much of their humor directly from this awareness. American Indians take the fact of probable extinction for granted in every thought, in every conversation. We have become so accustomed to the immediate likelihood of racial extinction in the centuries since Anglo-European invasion, that we can allude to it in many indirect ways; its pervasive presence creates a sense of sorrow in even the funniest tales.

Mary Randle TallMountain, Athabascan poet born in the Koyukon village of Nulato, Alaska, writes of a wolf companion in her poem "The Last Wolf." The speaker is lying in a hospital in a devastated San Francisco, waiting for the last wolf to make his way to her through the "ruined city." She hears

> his baying echoes
> down the steep smashed warrens
> of Montgomery Street
> . . . and at last his low whine as he came
> . . . to the room where I sat
> I watched
> he trotted across the floor
> he laid his long gray muzzle
> on the spare white spread
> and his eyes burned yellow
> his dotted eyebrows quivered.
>
> Yes, I said.
> I know what they have done.[2]

The question that the writers face again and again, pose in a multitude of ways, answer in a multitude of ways, is this: How does one survive in the face of collective death? Bearing witness is one solution, but it is singularly tearing, for witnessing genocide—as with conversion—requires that someone listen and comprehend.

The American Indian poet is particularly bereft of listeners. The Indian people, who form a tiny subpopulation in the United States and who don't buy modern poetry or literary novels in large numbers, are very busy trying to preserve the elements of culture and tribal identity that are left them, while accommodating these elements to the larger American society around them. Audiences for the American Indian writer from among other Americans are sparse because of the many large and trivial differences in assumptions, expectations, experiences, and symbol structures between Indian and non-Indian. The American Indian writer has difficulty locating readers/listeners who can comprehend the significance of her work, even when she is being as clear and direct as she can be, because these differences in experience and meaning assigned to events create an almost impossible barrier.

What we bear witness to is not easily admissible into the consciousness of other Americans, and that inadmissibility causes us difficulty in articulation and utterance signified by Hogan's plaint and by these lines from "I expected my skin and my blood to ripen" by Hopi-Miwok poet Wendy Rose:

> I expected my skin and my blood
> to ripen
> not to be ripped from my bones;
> like green fruit I am peeled
> tasted, discarded; my seeds are stepped on
> and crushed
> as if there were no future. Now
> there has been
> no past.
> My own body gave up the beads,
> my own hands gave the babies away
> to be strung on bayonets . . .
> as if the pain of their birthing
> had never been.[3]

Perhaps the knowledge of the real possibility of total extinction spurs one to perceptions that transcend the usual political, sociological, psychological, or aesthetic responses to pain or rage. Certainly the knowledge of continuance is difficult to cling to. We cling to it nevertheless; for as Rose writes at the end of her poem, the speaker would have protected the baby:

> if I could, would've turned her
> into a bush or rock if there'd been magic enough
> to work such changes. Not enough magic
> to stop the bullets, not enough
> magic to stop the scientists, not enough magic
> to stop the money. Now our ghosts dance
> a new dance, pushing from their hearts
> a new song.[4]

The new song our ghosts push from their hearts is a song of bitterness and grief, to be sure; but it is also a song of sanity, balance, and humor.

Humor is widely used by Indians to deal with life. Indian gatherings are marked by laughter and jokes, many directed at the horrors of history, at the continuing impact of colonization, and at the biting knowledge that living as an exile in one's own land necessitates. Thus, Leslie Marmon Silko updates Coyote tales to reflect modern life at the pueblo of Laguna, an eastern pueblo that is a crossroads of southwestern Anglo, Chicano, and Indian cultures:

> Some white men came to Acoma and Laguna a hundred years
>   ago
> and they fought over Acoma land and Laguna women and
> even now
> some of their descendents are howling in
> the hills southeast of Laguna.[5]

This short story tells the tale that what is important at Acoma is land, and at Laguna it is women (said to be some of the most attractive women around) and that mixed-bloods are likely to be howling around in the hills because they are the offspring of the wily and salacious Coyote. Indeed, "coyote" to many Hispanic Americans refers to a half-breed, and that idea is also present in this poetic joke.

Coyote is a tricky personage—half creator, half fool; he (or she in some versions) is renowned for greediness and salaciousness. Coyote tales abound all over native America, and he has been taken up by contemporary American Indian poets as a metaphor for all the foolishness and the anger that have characterized American Indian life in the centuries since invasion. He is also a metaphor for continuance, for Coyote survives and a large part of his bag of survival tricks is his irreverence. Because of this irreverence for everything—sex, family bonding, sacred things, even life itself—Coyote survives. He survives partly out of luck, partly out of cunning, and partly because he has, beneath a scabby coat, such great creative prowess that many tribes have characterized him as the creator of this particular phase of existence, this "fifth world." Certainly the time frame we presently inhabit has much that is shabby and tricky to offer; and much that needs to be treated with laughter and ironic humor; it is this spirit of the trickster-creator that keeps Indians alive and vital in the face of horror.

The stance of bitter irony characterizes the poetry of Crow Creek

Sioux poet Elizabeth Cook-Lynn, as this excerpt from her poem "Contradiction" indicates:

> She hears the wolves at night
> prophetically. Put them behind,
> the legends we have found,
> care not a bit,
> go make a night of it! . . .
> She wonders why you dress your eyes
> in pulsing shades of Muscatel,
> while wailing songs of what-the-hell
> make essences to eulogize.[6]

When the traditions that inform the people with life and inform that life with significance are put behind, not much but Muscatel and "songs of what-the-hell" are left. Aside from the obvious emotional, social, and psychological considerations implied in this observation, the interesting thing about the use of humor in American Indian poetry is its integrating effect: it makes tolerable what is otherwise unthinkable; it allows a sort of breathing space in which an entire race can take stock of itself and its future. Humor is a primary means of reconciling the tradition of continuance, bonding, and celebration with the stark facts of racial destruction. It is used in that way by many Indian poets, as in nila northSun's poem "moving camp too far":

> i can't speak of
>   many moons
>   moving camp on travois
> i can't tell of
>   the last great battle
>   counting coup or
>   taking scalps
> i don't know what it
>   was to hunt buffalo
>   or do the ghost dance
> but
> i can see an eagle
>   almost extinct
>   on slurpee plastic cups
> i can travel to powwows
>   in campers & winnebagos

> i can eat buffalo meat
>   at the tourist burger stand
> i can dance to indian music
>   rock-n-roll hey-a-hey-o
> i can
>   & unfortunately
>   i do[7]

Surely this poem is a mourning song, as it is one of a stunted and trivialized vision made to fit a pop-culture conception of Indian, earth, and extinction; certainly it highlights some of the more enraging aspects of American culture as they can appear only to an American Indian: among Indians, a Winnebago is a member of a tribe that lives in Iowa; among non-Indians it is a recreation vehicle—aptly enough. An eagle is a symbol of the spirit, of vision, of transcendence to many American Indian traditionals, but it is also an emblem that bedecks a plastic cup. And the buffalo signified an entire culture, a way of life for numerous tribes once upon a time; now it is a consumer curiosity one can purchase at a tourist foodstand.

Many of the poems written by American Indian women address the stark fact of extinction directly, with a vigor and resilience that does not merely bewail a brutal fate but directs our attention to a kind of hope born of facing the brutal and bitter facts of our recent history and present condition. This sense of hope is characteristic of the peoples whose history on this continent stretches beyond the dimmest reaches of time, winding back through history to time immemorial; it is a hope that comes about when one has faced ultimate disaster time and time again over the ages and has emerged stronger and more certain of the endurance of the people, the spirits, and the land from which they both arise and which informs both with life.

The metaphors that most appeal to American Indian poets are usually those that combine elements of tribal tradition with contemporary experience: thus the poetry of Creek poet Joy Harjo finds itself entwining ancient understandings of the moon, of relationship, of womanhood, and of journeying with city streets, rodeo grounds, highways, airports, Indian bars, and powwows. From the meeting of the archaic and the contemporary the facts of her life become articulate, and the fact that modern American Indians are both Indian and American becomes very clear, as in the wry, laconic lines from "3 AM":

3 AM
in the albuquerque airport
trying to find a flight
to old oraibi, third mesa
TWA
    is the only desk open
bright lights outline new york,

                                    chicago

and the attendant doesn't know
that third mesa
is a part of the center
of the world
and who are we
just two indians
at three in the morning
trying to find a way back.[8]

A contemporary American Indian is always faced with a dual perception of the world: that which is particular to American Indian life, and that which exists ignorant of that life. Each is largely irrelevant to the other except where they meet—in the experience and consciousness of the Indian. Because the divergent realities must meet and form comprehensible patterns within Indian life, an Indian poet must develop metaphors that not only will reflect the dual perceptions of Indian/non-Indian but also will reconcile them. The ideal metaphor will harmonize the contradictions and balance them so that internal equilibrium can be achieved, so that each perspective is meaningful and that in their joining, psychic unity rather than fragmentation occurs.

Fortunately, modern life, like modern poetry, provides various means of making the dichotomy clear and of reconciling the contradictions within it. Airports, traveling, powwows, burger stands, recreation vehicles, and advertising layouts all provide ways to enter the contradictions and resolve them. The increasingly common images from the more arcane aspects of western traditions—alchemy, postindustrial science, electronic technology and the little-changing chores of housework and wifery—provide images that are common denominators in the experiences of Indian and non-Indian alike, making unitary perception and interpretation possible. The poetry of Oneida (Wisconsin) poet Roberta Whiteman Hill exemplifies this reconciliation, as in this fragment from "Leap in the Dark":

—Then she sealed her nimble dreams
with water from a murky bay. "For him I map
this galaxy of dust that turns without an answer.
When it rains, I remember his face in the corridor
of a past apartment and trace the anguish around his mouth,
    . . . With the grace that remains
I catch a glint around a door I cannot enter.
The clock echoes in dishtowels; I search love's center
and bang pans against the rubble of my day, the lucid
grandeur of wet ground, the strangeness of a fatal sun
that makes us mark on the margin of our loss,
trust in the gossamer of touch, trust in the late-plowed field.
I hug my death, my chorus of years, and search
and stretch and leap, for I will be apprentice to the blood
in spite of the mood of the world
that keeps rusting, rusting, the wild throats of birds.[9]

Transformation, or, more directly, metamorphosis, is the oldest tribal ceremonial theme, one common to ancient Europe, Britain, and America. And it comes once again into use within the American Indian poetry of extinction and regeneration that is ultimately the only poetry a contemporary Indian woman can write. Poets who have located a means of negotiating the perilous path between love and death, between bonding and dissolution, between tribal consciousness and modern alienation must light on the transformational metaphor to articulate their experience. Or as Whiteman writes:

. . . Oh crazy itch that grabs us beyond loss
and let us forgive, so that we can answer birds and deer,
lightning and rain, shadow and hurricane
Truth waits in the creek, cutting the winter brown hills:
it sings of its needles of ice, sings because of the scars.[10]

And, in a recent poem, "Morning: The World in the Lake," Linda Hogan uses the metaphor of transformation to celebrate the duration and persistence that are the basic characteristics of continuance and of love:

Beneath each black duck
another swims
shadow
joined to blood and flesh.
There's a world beneath this one.
The red-winged blackbird calls
its silent comrade down below . . .

And then it rises, the blackbird
above the world's geography of light and dark
and we are there, living
in that revealed sliver of red
living in the black
something of feathers,
daughters all of us,
who would sleep as if reflected
alongside our mothers,
the mothers of angels and shadows,
the helix and spiral of centuries
twisting inside.
Oh the radiant ones are burning
beneath this world.
They rise up,
the quenching water.[11]

Reconciling the opposites of life and death, of celebration and grief, of laughter and rage is no simple task, yet it is one worthy of our best understanding and our best effort. If, in all these centuries of death, we have continued to endure, we must celebrate that fact and the fact of our vitality in the face of what seemed, to many, inevitable extinction. For however painful and futile our struggle becomes, we have but to look outside at the birds, the deer, and the seasons to understand that change does not mean destruction, that life, however painful and even elusive it is at times, contains much joy and hilarity, pleasure and beauty for those who live within its requirements with grace. I have written a series of poems about assimilation and colonization, laying these against arcane and land-centered understandings, trying to articulate the balance between despairing reality and the hope that continued existence requires, as in these lines from "Transformations":

> Out in the light or sitting alone,
> sorting, straightening tangled skeins
> (they're always tying lives in knots)
> I would like to be sleeping. Not
> dreaming, just blacked out:
> no one bumping around in my brain—
> no tangles, no deaths, just quiet
> empty nests, just threads
> lying straight and ordered and still.
> Outside the window I can see
> sweet winter birds
> rise up from tall weeds
> chattering. They fly
> into sunrisen sky that holds them
> in light.[12]

The information and the patterns for continuance are all around us, if we will accept them for what they can signify and use them to lend vitality and form to our life. Certainly in the long ago that's what they did, and that's what they can do now as well.

This Wilderness in My Blood: Spiritual Foundations of the Poetry of Five American Indian Women

In contradistinction to other American poets and writers, American Indian women writers have as our first and most significant perceptual characteristic a solid, impregnable, and ineradicable orientation toward a spirit-informed view of the universe, which provides an internal structure to both our consciousness and our art. This view is not merely private, for it is shared by all the members of tribal psychic reality. It is not exactly personal, for it reaches far beyond the simple confines of mortal flesh and individual nervous system. It is, however, subjective, for it seems apparent that all matters concerning the non-material realms of being must be experienced within the subjective mind of each individual at least as much as within the particular part of the tribal gestalt that is activated by ceremony, ritual, and vision. It should be noted, however, that the subjectivity of this process derives from internalization of tribal oral traditions rather than from a purely private, emotionally subjective bias. This distinction is important, for it distinguishes the poetry of American Indian women from that of our non-Indian colleagues and is, I think, the difference that makes our work less accessible to non-Indian readers, editors, and audiences. Certainly, this mode of objective/internal perception of spiritual forces and entities leads American Indian women to write a poetry and fiction that is internally more coherent and unified than that of other American writers because it is always based on a group-shared understanding of private and public events.

The American Indian women who wait, watch, and write are keenly aware of the inner truth of the spiritness of the tribal universe. Their conviction in the spiritness of all-that-is prevents the development of self-cannibalizing neurotic musings, emotionally biased, raging polemic, or purely aesthetic self-indulgence. The best Indian writers can and do engage in any and all of these stances in their work, but they seldom maintain these purely self-aggrandizing postures for more than a few lines or paragraphs.

The Arms of Another Sky: Joy Harjo (Creek)

Joy Harjo, a poet whose work is concerned with metaphysical as well as with social connections, comments that the spirit people are all around her, crowded around, when she writes. "Sometimes," she says, "I can almost see them. And my work is powerful when I'm able to see them. Sometimes I get kind of scared. And sometimes I think, 'Well, all of these things are going on, how come I can't see them?' Sometimes I get all obsessed with not seeing. Maybe that's why I write. I keep wanting to see. And I keep wanting to see more, but I know that I can only see what I'm able to see. And I won't see anything else until I'm ready. So I get really frustrated. There's so much I want to see, but I have to take that responsibility too. I feel like my poetry is a way to see, because I have a sense of how I keep going deeper and deeper. It's not like into a hole, maybe like the center of the earth like a star, which is really the outside but it's the inside. It has that duality, the polarity, which drives me crazy. But I also know, in another sense, there are worlds in which polarity isn't the law. You don't have good/evil, sun/moon, light/dark. And I have a sense of that other place, sometimes. When I really feel that other place, this place seems insane. That's why I wrote 'She Had Some Horses.' I wrote to name those horses. And then I said, 'she had some horses she loved, she had some horses she hated,' which is a polarity. And these are the same horses."[1]

Interestingly, Harjo believes that the view she describes of the inside being the outside has come to her from American feminists. However accurate that belief may be, it is an understanding inherent to certain of the tribes, her people the Creek among them. In traditional times they even institutionalized that understanding, designating certain officials as inside chiefs and others as outside chiefs. Harjo is obviously angered at the apparent polarity of life in the modern world, and her thrust, in her work as well as in her discussion of it, is toward reconciliation of the polarities into an order that is harmonious, balanced, and whole. One way she articulates her understanding of this wholeness is in terms of the physiology of the female body. "Look at it in terms of physiology," she says. "I always see it as very spiritual. A woman contains herself inside herself, and others, too. But the men— it's like their sex roles are all external. But a woman has to push outward from herself, so she has to go constantly outside of herself to find herself."[2]

Another way she articulates her certain understanding of the spherical unity of the universe, its essential "spiritness," is in her poetry. Of particular interest are her poems that use the moon as their central conceit (if such a term is appropriate within the context of uses she selects). She says, "I have this image. It's not a generator, it's not a power plant. But it's like they have these different points in between. So it's a place, it's a poem, like a globular, like a circle with center points all over. And poems are like that. They have circuits."[3]

And the circuits are evident in their connections in her poem "Moonlight":

> I know when the sun is in China
> because the night shining other-light
> crawls into my bed. She is moon.
> Her eyes slit and yellow she is the last
> one out of a dingy bar in Albuquerque—
> Fourth Street, or from similar avenues
> in Hong Kong. Where someone else has also
> awakened, the night thrown back and asked,
> Where is the moon, my lover?
> And from here I always answer in my dreaming,
> The last time I saw her was in the arms
> of another sky.[4]

The sense of the connectedness of all things, of the spiritness of all things, of the intelligent consciousness of all things, is the identifying characteristic of American Indian tribal poetry. These features link American Indian literary work to that of tribally inspired poetry around the world.

Let Us Hold Fierce:
Linda Hogan

Like Joy Harjo, Linda Hogan (Chickasaw) directly integrates a spirit-based vision in her work. She is conscious of its vibrant spherical power to unify divergent events and conflicting views. Like all the American Indian women writing poetry and fiction, Hogan is conscious of the real nature of spirit presence in the world and so includes it as a basic assumption about reality in all of her work.

Hogan speaks of a phase she went through when she was first conscious, in an adult's way, of having visions. Because she had not been raised by traditional Indian people within a traditional tribal framework, she did not know that her experience was quite normal.

"It took years before I realized that there wasn't anything wrong with me," she says. "It was just that I was set up my whole life to be that way. An Indian friend of mine made this clear to me. She was telling me about how she finally realised the same thing was true of her. She had been having visions of spirit people, or events that had taken place in the past, and one night she talked to her mother about it. Her mother was a full-blood, and understood these things. Later, when she was just lying in bed, she said she realized that she wasn't crazy, just an Indian. Anyway, she told me about it and said I should have known it years ago; that I was different from others around me because I am an Indian, and that was why I didn't fit into the white-dominated world I was living in. I try to turn that into strength now."[5]

Hogan has used her spirit-centered consciousness to develop a growing feminist consciousness and activist orientation. Her recent work is consciously directed toward the politics of Indian survival, which she, like many Indian activists, believes includes the survival of the natural world. She is involved in these movements, she says, "because of the destruction I have feared all my life—the animals and all life, not because I love politics. I don't want that devastation. I've been this way all my life. People used to think I was a very strange person, because when I was a child, I was speaking out for the animals, and I always will. I was in a workshop once, and they said, oh, is this another animal poem that you're bringing in today?

"But I also grew up with these visions of destruction. I feel that what people are doing from the very beginning of the mining process all the way to the final explosion is that they're taking a power out of the earth that belongs to the earth. They're taking the heart and the soul of the earth."[6]

Hogan's current poetry and fiction clearly reflect her concern with the presence of spirits in the land and among the people and her continuing concern with the political issues of our time. In her work she carefully fuses her vision to her tribal-based understanding, so that her work does not exhibit the awkwardnesses common to writers who are not so strongly aware of the spirit-based consciousness that necessarily must underlie the political involvements of an Indian. The fundamental tribal understanding that Hogan possesses also protects her from falling into the simplistic rhetoric of activist propaganda; her politics are deeply knitted to her vision, and her vision, as her friend observed, is a result of her being an Indian. Being an Indian enables her to resolve the conflict that presently divides the non-Indian feminist community; she does not have to choose between spirituality and political commitment, for each is the complement of the other. They are the two wings of one bird, and that bird is the knowledge of the interconnectedness of everything. That awareness gives rise to a deep confidence that we will survive because the consciousness possessed by tribal people is now spreading throughout the nontribal, post-Christian, postindustrial general populace.

"White people are waking up," she says. "I have been traveling, and everywhere I go I see that people are really developing an older consciousness and they are paying attention to what's going on in the world, understanding what needs to be spoken and heard. And the people are starting to see the animals, the insects, the trees, as equal to themselves."[7]

In her journals, Hogan has written powerfully and lyrically, articulating the connection that she so clearly perceives between the alienated vision of the technocracy she lives in and the living world of creatures, human and nonhuman, within which she also dwells.

In an entry dated January 4, 1979, she writes:

Sunday morning. More snow. This has been the coldest hardest winter I remember and the snow scares me when I think of the radiation plumes coming out of the plant in Pennsylvania. We will never be told the results of this accident but maybe now people will begin to think about the consequences of their actions and inactions.

There are so many things going on in the world, I feel guilty when I write about myself or my family. We are all small. A million people are nothing on this earth, not even as important as the plants, the water, the animals. Maybe it is this knowledge that gives us our need to destroy them all. There must be something like fear behind the minds of so many men, something that directs them toward a detached destruction.[8]

And two years later, while in Chicago on a Tribal Historian Fellowship, she wrote in an entry dated April 17, 1981:

I don't know why I grieve and mourn so much when other people don't. The story of Oppenheimer and the bomb was just on television here in Chicago and I wept through the entire show. I do not know how those men could smile, could say they did what was best. That they got used to the suffering after a few days in Hiroshima when they went to see what they had done.

A man in Alamogordo [New Mexico] smiled when he said the sides of cattle turned white and that a black cat turned white and its owner sold it to a tourist for five dollars. The men also told of machine-gunning the antelope to pass the time.[9]

She talks about her feelings of alienation while in the city, of how difficult it is for her to understand the thinking that city people engage in, and writes, "Yesterday a woman looked at the violets in the grass and said, 'How lovely,' and then she walked on them." After making this observation, she continues her remarks on the Oppenheimer television show, which she concludes with a quote from one of the men who was interviewed for the program: "'I never thought we would flatten all those people.'" Then, Hogan observes, "And he smiled. That is why I howled and cried."[10]

The unity of Hogan's vision is vitalized by her determination to articulate that vision accurately. In a series of recent poems she gives voice to her deep, intensely personal sense of the exact measure of global destruction we all face. In one of the poems, "The Women Speaking," she articulates her fear, rage, and celebration of love within the spectre of annihilating light. The women are speaking, for in her work women signify what is connected:

And the Russian women in blue towns
are speaking.
The flower-dressed women of Indian
women in orange tents,

dark women
of the Americas
who sit beside fires,
have studied the palms of their hands
and walk toward one another.

It's time to bless this ground.
Their hair is on fire
from the sun
and they walk narrow roads
toward one another.
Their pulses beat
against the neck's thick skin.
They grow closer.

Let us be gentle
with the fiery furnaces
smelling of hay and rum,
gentle with the veils of skin
that bind us
to the world.
Let us hold fierce
the soft lives of our children,
the light is inside them
and they are burning
in small beds of straw,
beds of scorched white sheets,
newspaper beds with words
wrapped against skin
the light burns through.

The women cross their hands
on their chests
and lie down to sleep a moment
along dust roads.

In the dark, Japanese women
light lanterns
the shape of children.
They blow gently
on the sides of hills,
the roads
illuminated by the bodies of children
that enter our eyes.

At night there are reflections of skin
filled with muscle, lung,
nerve, that flash of dark and light skin,
shadows we love
that belong to us all.

Daughters, the women are speaking.
They arrive
over the wise distances
on perfect feet.
Daughters, I love you.[11]

Out of a Dark and Different Time:
Mary TallMountain

The work of Mary TallMountain (Athabascan) reveals a deeply
spiritualized sensibility. Her tribal consciousness is tempered with a
mystical Roman Catholic perspective, and this makes for a difficult
and uneasy alliance between the pagan awareness that characterizes
tribal thought and the less earthy, more judgmental view of medieval
Christianity. Yet at times her purely Indian awareness and the unity of
thought that distinguishes it from that of more secularized political
consciousness overwhelms her Christianized sensibility. The poem
titled "The Last Wolf" is based on the appearance of a spirit wolf who
saw her through a time of deep personal difficulty and serious illness.
Along with that poem, she has also recorded incidents of tribal consciousness, as in the following synopsis I've made of a personal memoir
she wrote in 1980, titled "There Is No Word for Good-Bye." Tall-
Mountain had returned to the Alaskan Koyukon village of her birth
after an absence of fifty years. She was talking to a nun with whom she
was staying during her visit, and they began to talk about spirits that
have been spotted recently around the village. The nun mentioned a
beaver who had come up out of Mukluk Slough that spring and had
clearly said "Do in tsa" ("hello" in Koyukon) to some children. Then
she told TallMountain about the appearance of a Christmas tree in the
ice seen by one of the men that winter when he was getting water. A
pilot who flies a bushplane to Nulato also spotted the tree, "shining out
there in the middle of the river," the nun said. In response to these tales,
TallMountain recounted a dream she had had around that time, about
a Raven flying upside down. "It's a message," she observes.

And certainly her awareness of spirit runs through her work like a bright thread, or sometimes like a note fraught with dread and fear. Her journals are full of notes about nonphysicals around her, and they are often directed toward her mother, who died years ago but whose presence is often very close to TallMountain. But side by side with these pagan awarenesses, she reveals a great deal of conflict within her own mind. She has a personal spirit who has often spoken to her. His name is Naagudzaah, or Owl. She speaks of him often in her conversation and in her journal, but she quietly writes that he is "really the Lord Jesus" and that she is aware of that fact. And most of her journal entries, which date from 1973 to the present, are filled with impassioned meditations on the meaning of Catholicism, on the teachings of the Church, and on what the Lord Jesus Christ wants of her. For first and foremost, TallMountain is a devout Roman Catholic, like her Koyukon mother before her; but unlike her mother, TallMountain is a Catholic deeply steeped in the mystical literature and liturgy of her faith.

Her poetry is an odd assortment of poems that dart quixotically among her disunified, fragmented perceptions of the world and her place within it. It is disconcerting in many ways, for she is not easily placed in one camp or another—politically, socially, or poetically. It must be said, though, that her finest poetry springs out of her Catholic mysticism, through which, it seems, she realizes the true reach of her considerable powers of contemplation, comprehension, and poignant longing for a clear, solid ground on which to stand.

The Figure in Clay

Climbing the hill
When it was time,
Among sunken gravehouses
I filled my fists with earth
And coming down took river water,
Blended it,
Shaped you, a girl of clay
Crouched in my palms
Mute asking
To be made complete.

Long afterward
I buried you deep among
Painted masks.

Yet you ride my plasma
Like a platelet,
Eldest kinswoman.
You cry to me through smoke
Of tribal fires.
I echo the primal voice,
The drumming blood.

Through decades waiting
Your small shape remained
In morning ritual
You danced through my brain,
Clear and familiar.
Telling of dim glacial time,
Long perilous water-crossings,
Wolf beasts
Howling the polar night,
Snow flowers changing.

Now watching you in lamplight,
I see scarlet berries
Ripened,
Your sunburned fingers plucking them.
With hesitant words,
With silence,
From inmost space
I call you
Out of the clay.

It is time at last,
This dawn.
Stir. Wake. Rise.
Glide gentle between my bones,
Grasp my heart. Now
Walk beside me. Feel
How these winds move, the way
These mornings breathe.
Let me see you new
In this light.

You—
Wrapped in brown,
Myself repeated
Out of dark and different time.[12]

There Has to Be Someone to Name You: Wendy Rose

Conflict such as that articulated by Harjo, Hogan, and TallMountain is a feature of the work of virtually every Indian woman writer. Each experiences it differently, and each has her particular way of addressing it and, within her work, of resolving it. Wendy Rose, a Hopi-Miwok woman, speaks poignantly of the conflict as it works itself out in her life. Born and raised in Richmond, California, completely estranged from any tribal traditions from birth, Rose exhibits the greatest polemical tendencies of contemporary Indian women writers. Yet she is also one of the clearest about the exact nature and degree of the conflict she must live with. She is aware of the spiritual and mystical nature of her Hopi people and of her enforced distance from them. Because she has been educated as an anthropologist, much of the material in her poetry comes from her ethnographic knowledge. Because she was raised a Roman Catholic, much of the spiritual content of her work is phrased within Catholic structures. And because she was a dropout into the mad, hippy world of Berkeley in the 1960s, much of her work is informed with a militant, radical polemic.

Nevertheless, Rose's work exhibits the peculiar unitariness of consciousness, despite surface contradictions, that marks American Indian poetry in the late 1970s and 1980s. The oral tradition, based on a mystical understanding of unity that is not as material as it is psychic, provides an axis for the work of contemporary American Indian writers, and this axis is as present in the work of "marginal" Indians like Rose, Hogan, Harjo, and TallMountain as it is in the work of the more traditional women writing today. And while her enforced distance from her people grieves and angers Rose, she writes poetry that does not fall into suicidal bitterness on the one hand or radical excess on the other. Rather, it hews a clear line toward her understanding of her position, illuminating in that clarity the position of all who are dispossessed.

Affirmative Action
Berkeley, 1977

Us riffraff,
you and me,
they let us in.

You're okay
but I'm wedged
tight like
I belonged here
sort of blind
pretending
I was cut to plan
the worst part being
the direction, that
wide white path
on which I step
across broken
beer bottles, cracked
pow wow drumsticks,
tiny spots of blood
leading into books.
They imagine
in their tower
that if I come
to the top
of their mountain
I will not turn around
tumble back down
with a PhD stuck
uselessly in
my fossilized ribs.
But I know
a sheepskin-degree
will not turn me white
as turquoise never
turned me red.
We slip into the current
crashing along parallel
to striped red
and white path.
We have no names
but are swept along
because inside the dictionaries
we have turned to thieves.
Without compass
or daystar or dipper
I sail on past the port.

Like Magellan I miss
entire continents
landmasses sliding
by in the fog
like planets
galaxies apart,
molecules apart.
Shall I stop
and count my losses
here? Shall I go
mumbling into my knees?
Shall I sleep
through the handgame
gambling my dreams?
Shall I back up bare-assed
against the mesquite?
Shall I cast myself
a spell
to be born again
not as a Christian girl
but as a Bear Clan boy
destined to be loved,
fullblooded and fluent,
truly Hopi
and useful, holder
of a sacred trust?
Shall I lean toward earth
from space like this
or miss myself
floating by,
surround myself
with deceptively
white moons?[13]

    In poems that speak to her dispossession, as in most of her work, Rose maintains a clear, steady, spiritual basis. She often furthers her point with spirit-based imagery, so that the thrust of her work moves steadily toward a nonmaterial, nonsocial, and nonpolitical significance. The social, political, interpersonal, and personal images and statements she forms become metaphors for spirit-infused consciousness—a thrust toward uniting fragmented elements of her life that she shares with the other Indian women writers.

This Wilderness in My Blood:
Carol Lee Sanchez

One of the most problematic of Indian women writing today, Carol Lee Sanchez (Laguna/Sioux) writes intellectually abstract, direct, and often jarring poetry. She combines images, ideas, and insights from a variety of sources without regard to western categories. Her tone, posture, and point of view combine a wry sense of humor with a directness of statement that is often very disconcerting, and her work exhibits a marked disdain for conventional lyric rhythm. Students of mine have remarked that Sanchez is the most alien of Indian women writers and the most Indian. On the surface, this observation might seem extreme, but a closer examination of Sanchez's work reveals its deep connections to Laguna thought-styles and world-view.

Certainly Sanchez's poetry has received the least notice of those writers who have steadily produced work over a number of years. While she has published three books, *Conversations from the Night-mare, Message Bringer Woman,* and just recently *Excerpts from a Mountain Climber's Handbook,* she has published very seldom in journals and magazines. Of the Indian anthologies, her work has appeared only in *The Remembered Earth.* My students believed that this lack of public recognition is directly related to the fact that she does not use western forms in her work. Indian poets are expected to write certain kinds of poetry. Those who don't are not widely published or read.

Sanchez, who is also an artist of considerable ability, was raised first on the Laguna Reservation in the village of Paguate where she ran freely through the village, a welcome guest in whatever home she decided to visit. Later her family moved from Paguate to a small land-grant Chicano village nearby, where she lived until her marriage at eighteen. But Sanchez was not raised in a traditional Indian home; her mother, a Laguna, married a non-Indian, and so Sanchez was raised in a distinctly multicultural, multilinguistic, Roman Catholic environment. Her Laguna grandmother, who lived next door, had married a Jewish immigrant from Germany (her second marriage), and Sanchez's father is an Arabic- and Spanish-speaking Lebanese-American. The languages she heard from infancy were English, Spanish, Arabic, Laguna and Acoma, German, and occasionally Navajo and Zuni. Her home mixed the foods and knowledge, viewpoints and customs of most of these groups and did so often with little regard for

178

their derivation. If her poetry reflects a multiplicity of consciousness, it simply reflects her early life. But beneath that multiplicity rests a single-minded bias toward Laguna understandings and values, a bias that shows most clearly in her continuing insistence on proper order and in the very complexity of her thought.

Sanchez's work is difficult for many because it is so blatantly Indian; it does not bow to common misconceptions about Indian people, ever. She seldom panders to popular stereotypes about Indians; her poetry never wears feathers, and she never says "ugh," except to laugh ironically at notions of Indianness that have been formulated by non-Indian apologists and borrowed from them by Indian writers. While many Indians writing contemporary poetry and fiction use white-generated stereotypes in their work with ho apparent sense of the source of those images, Sanchez does not. As a result, her work can be dismissed as "not Indian." Many believe that to be Indian is to be romantic, naive, inarticulate, and intellectually primitive (or noble, depending on the mode of dismissing our intelligence).

In Indian cultures in general, abstract thinking was practiced by women while representational thought was practiced by men. The pottery designed by women, as well as the belts, baskets, blankets, and beadwork, all exhibit a marked sense of abstraction. Sanchez, a daughter of one of the most adamantly matriarchal of the tribes, adheres to this sensibility. Her work is abstract in the extreme, demanding careful thought and a well-trained ear. And while her cadences are not lyric in the western Romantic sense, they are closely attuned to the rhythms of Pueblo dance. To understand her rhythms one must carefully study Pueblo music, especially the green-corn dances.

Sanchez never questions her own identity; she knows that she is one of the people and that as such her obligation is to maintain a sense of traditional propriety. In an interview I had with her, she specified this clearly, describing the organization of one of her manuscripts: "I want to unify [the book], to give it the sense of proper ritual. That's what I am really concerned about doing with these poems, that there is that proper order. That proper event taking place. That's what Indians have held on to. Even though they've gotten urbanized and acculturated, and even assimilated, they have held to those particular titles, or names of things that become ceremony, that become ritual; that those directions, or whatever little fragment they've got to hang on to, it orders. It gives proper order. It also gives a connecting point to the spirit world. It is our bridge, our little rope bridge back into tradition. And that I think will be handed on. And the idea, I think, is for us in a transition period to place that tradition in the literary format so that it is comprehensible enough for Indians to grab it. Because genetically we respond to it."[14] She continues this thought in reference to her artwork, which she says is also about "redefining, reinterpreting. As we become westernized, as we go into that form of acculturation where we have been for a long time to probably total assimilation, then again there are those visual reference points that 'click.' That kick you up. That startle your soul. That make you remember. Not the artifacts of a dead society, but the reworking of the symbol of that civilization, and those cultures. So there is a place to connect to."[15]

Sanchez writes as a way of connecting to her people. She does not write so that white editors and other poets will feel sympathetic toward Indians; she does not attempt to create "clicks" in white readers. What she does is what Indian matrons have always done: knit the old ways to the new circumstances in such a way that the fundamental world-view of the tribe will not be distorted or destroyed. In her task she uses every resource of her present existence: technology and myth, politics and motherhood, ritual balance and clearsighted utterance, ironic comment and historical perspective.

the Song   the Dance   the Poem

1) i toil   in the field
    syllable into line
    through the breath
    the breathing is
    difficult
    the birthing.

    i dreamed of you   mamma
    far away,   talking hours
    into the night.
    the breathing was difficult
    and you changed again
    trying to tell me something
    i couldn't remember   —except
    the field was there and
    stretched on and on.

    the stubble would not
    be replaced with new corn
    and spring is soon.

the breathing is
difficult at times
from syllable into line.

2)   i am sent to the fields
to labor one more time.
the breathing will not
discover the line.
my land races visions
before my eyes
—tunes these senses i possess
to smell and taste and touch
yet   the solidity of
a sandstone boulder
will not be painted without a brush.

my pen is frozen
in some ancient mold,
the image lost wants only to hide
in my palette's colors
—will not be found
to mould a line.

what syllable then can best convey
the ochre/umbers of that ground?
and choking dust that's interspaced
with sunburst prism
on window glass?

i swell with visions
erupting rocks and clouds
within my mind.
i know   this wilderness in my blood
and cannot sing it
into line.

3)   as climate reaches roots
together with polar infinities
moss springs from the cracks
in the line
grasps energy seeded in context
replaced as a function
for internal rhyme.

these roots go back somewhere.
related through syllable
through time
connect with a script not known.
some form that communicated
alternative meanings
still held in this construct
in this time.

that master who began to define this form
remarked on the search:
the detective part of the work any
creation comes from.

the *doing* will suffice,
the momentum of the forward push
—cause of the breath:

life is the breathing/breathing life
embues each syllable chosen
energized
embodied within the construct
jam/packed into content.

that moss will recede—that remark
made to remember the roots.

trace the roots from the branches
from the leaves
each word floats   caught
suspended in time
will reveal energy connected ancestors
moved through each syllable selected
more living breath through the line.[16]

As the work of these five women shows, the lives of Indian women in America are multidimensional. The breakup of ancient orders of life, the change in custom and language occasioned by the vast change in lifestyle, white education and occupation, social structures and ritual life have left tribal life in shambles. But the fragmentation of consciousness that might be expected to result from this massive cultural breakdown is a surface breakdown.

Indians are remarkably resilient, and their ways are remarkably durable. And while the white government and churches have made it their business for centuries to assimilate Indians into American life, Indian values, perceptions, and understandings have clung tenaciously to life, informing the work of writers and artists as they inform the lives of all Indian people in the United States today. Certainly, our ancient bond to the land and to the spirit world is in large part responsible for this tenacity, and the strength of spirit presence speaks powerfully in all the works of contemporary American Indian writers.

There is a permanent wilderness in the blood of an Indian, a wilderness that will endure as long as the grass grows, the wind blows, the rivers flow, and one Indian woman remains alive.

Pushing Up
the Sky

In the years since I first wrote "The Sacred Hoop" and "Grandmother of the Sun," my attention has turned more and more to the literature and lives of American Indian women. In part this has been a result of my involvement in the feminist movement, particularly lesbian feminism, in part a result of the increase in published poetry, fiction, and novels by American Indian writers. That increase in sheer volume has required that I narrow my focus to manageable proportions, largely because the literature and lore of American Indian women strikes me as some of the most engaging, far-reaching, and significant literature being written in America today. It is in the work and lives of American Indian women that I find myself most fully realized as scholar, writer, and woman, and it is in their work and the lives that their work grows out of that the strands of my personal inclinations, accidental lessons, and formal training come together in the kind of dynamic whole that is the sacred hoop. It is not coincidental that the symbol of the wholeness and vitality of the nations is a female symbol or that the woman who taught me the meaning of that symbol was a Laguna Indian woman—daughter of one of the last great gynocracies.

The essays in this section are devoted to our lives as we live them in a contemporary setting. The section touches on our traditions through a study of a Keres woman's story; articles about politics and Indian women's issues; a history of women, gays, and lesbians, and the impact of colonization on them; an essay on the relationship between American Indian women's social status and the development of feminism in the United States; an analysis of lesbianism in tribal cultures, and some recommendations and speculations on our futures as we retake the ground we have lost as women in the centuries of white male-centered domination.

The years between time immemorial and the present are long and bloody and filled with despair. But we cannot despair, we children of the mother, Earth Woman, and the grandmother, Thought Woman.

American Indian women not only have endured, but we have

grown stronger and more hopeful in the past decade. Our numbers grow, our determination to define ourselves grows, and our consciousness of our situation, of the forces affecting it, and of the steps we can take to turn our situation around grows. The women and the men of Native America are busily rebuilding their traditions, and the one most in need of rebuilding at this time is the way of the mothers and the grandmothers, the sacred way of the women. When Grandmother returns (and she's coming soon) we want to be ready; we intend to be ready. We are recovering our heritage and uncovering the history of colonization—the history of gynocide that weakened the tribes almost to death. And we are busily stealing the thunder back, so it can empower the fires of life we tend, have always tended, as it was ever meant to.

Angry Women Are Building: Issues and Struggles Facing American Indian Women Today

The central issue that confronts American Indian women throughout the hemisphere is survival, *literal survival*, both on a cultural and biological level. According to the 1980 census, population of American Indians is just over one million. This figure, which is disputed by some American Indians, is probably a fair estimate, and it carries certain implications.

Some researchers put our pre-contact population at more than 45 million, while others put it at around 20 million. The U.S. government long put it at 450,000—a comforting if imaginary figure, though at one point it was put at around 270,000. If our current population is around one million; if, as some researchers estimate, around 25 percent of Indian women and 10 percent of Indian men in the United States have been sterilized without informed consent; if our average life expectancy is, as the best-informed research presently says, 55 years; if our infant mortality rate continues at well above national standards; if our average unemployment for all segments of our population—male, female, young, adult, and middle-aged is between 60 and 90 percent; if the U.S. government continues its policy of termination, relocation, removal, and assimilation along with the destruction of wilderness, reservation land, and its resources, and severe curtailment of hunting, fishing, timber harvesting and water-use rights—then existing tribes are facing the threat of extinction which for several hundred tribal groups has already become fact in the past five hundred years.

In this nation of more than 200 million, the Indian people constitute less than one-half of one percent of the population. In a nation that offers refuge, sympathy, and billions of dollars in aid from federal and private sources in the form of food to the hungry, medicine to the sick, and comfort to the dying, the indigenous subject population goes hungry, homeless, impoverished, cut out of the American deal, new, old, and in between. Americans are daily made aware of the worldwide slaughter of native peoples such as the Cambodians, the Palestinians, the Armenians, the Jews—who constitute only a few groups faced with genocide in this century. We are horrified by South African apartheid and the removal of millions of indigenous African black natives to what is there called "homelands"—but this is simply a replay of nineteenth-century U.S. government removal of American Indians to reservations. Nor do many even notice the parallel or fight South African apartheid by demanding an end to its counterpart within the borders of the United States. The American Indian people are in a situation comparable to the imminent genocide in many parts of the world today. The plight of our people north and south of us is no better; to the south it is considerably worse. Consciously or unconsciously, deliberately, as a matter of national policy, or accidentally as a matter of "fate," *every single government*, right, left, or centrist in the western hemisphere is consciously or subsconsciously dedicated to the extinction of those tribal people who live within its borders.

Within this geopolitical charnel house, American Indian women struggle on every front for the survival of our children, our people, our self-respect, our value systems, and our way of life. The past five hundred years testify to our skill at waging this struggle: for all the varied weapons of extinction pointed at our heads, we endure.

We survive war and conquest; we survive colonization, acculturation, assimilation; we survive beating, rape, starvation, mutilation, sterilization, abandonment, neglect, death of our children, our loved ones, destruction of our land, our homes, our past, and our future. We survive, and we do more than just survive. We bond, we care, we fight, we teach, we nurse, we bear, we feed, we earn, we laugh, we love, we hang in there, no matter what.

Of course, some, many of us, just give up. Many are alcoholics, many are addicts. Many abandon the children, the old ones. Many commit suicide. Many become violent, go insane. Many go "white" and are never seen or heard from again. But enough hold on to their traditions and their ways so that even after almost five hundred brutal years, we endure. And we even write songs and poems, make paintings and drawings that say "We walk in beauty. Let us continue."

Currently our struggles are on two fronts: physical survival and cultural survival. For women this means fighting alcoholism and drug abuse (our own and that of our husbands, lovers, parents, children);[1] poverty; affluence—a destroyer of people who are not traditionally socialized to deal with large sums of money; rape, incest, battering by Indian men; assaults on fertility and other health matters by the Indian Health Service and the Public Health Service; high infant mortality due to substandard medical care, nutrition, and health information; poor educational opportunities or education that takes us away from our traditions, language, and communities; suicide, homicide, or similar expressions of self-hatred; lack of economic opportunities; substandard housing; sometimes violent and always virulent racist attitudes and behaviors directed against us by an entertainment and educational system that wants only one thing from Indians: our silence, our invisibility, and our collective death.

A headline in the *Navajo Times* in the fall of 1979 reported that rape was the number one crime on the Navajo reservation. In a professional mental health journal of the Indian Health Services, Phyllis Old Dog Cross reported that incest and rape are common among Indian women seeking services and that their incidence is increasing. "It is believed that at least 80 percent of the Native Women seen at the regional psychiatric service center (5 state area) have experienced some sort of sexual assault."[2] Among the forms of abuse being suffered by Native American women, Old Dog Cross cites a recent phenomenon, something called "training." This form of gang rape is "a punitive act of a group of males who band together and get even or take revenge on a selected woman."[3]

These and other cases of violence against women are powerful evidence that the status of women within the tribes has suffered grievous decline since contact, and the decline has increased in intensity in recent years. The amount of violence against women, alcoholism, and violence, abuse, and neglect by women against their children and their aged relatives have all increased. These social ills were virtually unheard of among most tribes fifty years ago, popular American opinion to the contrary. As Old Dog Cross remarks:

Rapid, unstable and irrational change was required of the Indian people if they were to survive. Incredible loss of all that had meaning was the norm. Inhuman treatment, murder, death, and punishment was a typical experience for all the tribal groups and some didn't survive.

The dominant society devoted its efforts to the attempt to change the Indian into a white-Indian. No inhuman pressure to effect this change was overlooked. These pressures included starvation, incarceration and enforced education. Religious and healing customs were banished.

In spite of the years of oppression, the Indian and the Indian spirit survived. Not, however, without adverse effect. One of the major effects was the loss of cultured values and the concomitant loss of personal identity . . . The Indian was taught to be ashamed of being Indian and to emulate the non-Indian. In short, "white was right." For the Indian male, the only route to be successful, to be good, to be right, and to have an identity was to be as much like the white man as he could.[4]

Often it is said that the increase of violence against women is a result of various sociological factors such as oppression, racism, poverty, hopelessness, emasculation of men, and loss of male self-esteem as their own place within traditional society has been systematically destroyed by increasing urbanization, industrialization, and institutionalization, but seldom do we notice that for the past forty to fifty years, American popular media have depicted American Indian men as bloodthirsty savages devoted to treating women cruelly. While traditional Indian men seldom did any such thing—and in fact among most tribes abuse of women was simply unthinkable, as was abuse of children or the aged—the lie about "usual" male Indian behavior seems to have taken root and now bears its brutal and bitter fruit.

Image casting and image control constitute the central process that American Indian women must come to terms with, for on that control rests our sense of self, our claim to a past and to a future that we define and that we build. Images of Indians in media and educational materials profoundly influence how we act, how we relate to the world and to each other, and how we value ourselves. They also determine to a large extent how our men act toward us, toward our children, and toward each other. The popular American media image of Indian people as savages with no conscience, no compassion, and no sense of the value of human life and human dignity was hardly true of the tribes—however true it was of the invaders. But as Adolf Hitler noted a little over fifty years ago, if you tell a lie big enough and often enough, it will be believed. Evidently, while Americans and people all over the world have been led into a deep and unquestioned belief that American Indians are cruel savages, a number of American Indian men have been equally deluded into internalizing that image and acting on it. Media images, literary images, and artistic images, particularly those embedded in popular culture, must be changed before Indian women will see much relief from the violence that destroys so many lives.

To survive culturally, American Indian women must often fight the United States government, the tribal governments, women and men of their tribe or their urban community who are virulently misogynist or who are threatened by attempts to change the images foisted on us over the centuries by whites. The colonizers' revisions of our lives, values, and histories have devastated us at the most critical level of all—that of our own minds, our own sense of who we are.

Many women express strong opposition to those who would alter our life supports, steal our tribal lands, colonize our cultures and cultural expressions, and revise our very identities. We must strive to maintain tribal status; we must make certain that the tribes continue to be legally recognized entities, sovereign nations within the larger United States, and we must wage this struggle in many ways—political, educational, literary, artistic, individual, and communal. We are doing all we can: as mothers and grandmothers; as family members and tribal members; as professionals, workers, artists, shamans, leaders, chiefs, speakers, writers, and organizers, we daily demonstrate that we have no intention of disappearing, of being silent, or of quietly acquiescing in our extinction.

How the West Was Really Won

In the beginning were the people, the spirits, the gods; the four-leggeds, the two-leggeds, the wingeds, the crawlers, the burrowers, the plants, the trees, the rocks. There were the moon, the sun, the earth, the waters of earth and sky. There were the stars, the thunders, the mountains, the plains, the mesas and the hills. There was the Mystery. There were the Grandmothers, the Mothers, the clans, the people. At the end of the fifteenth century, Anglo-European time, the old world that the tribes, Nations, and Confederacies lived in began to be torn apart. At first the tear seemed small enough, and for various reasons we did not grasp the enormity of the threat; indeed, many tribes did not know there was a threat for another two to three hundred years.

The wars of conquest that began with the landing of Christopher Columbus on an isolated little island on the edge of the southeastern sea gained momentum until every tribe and every aspect of traditional life was swept up in it; during the centuries of those wars everything in our lives was affected and much was changed, even the earth, the waters, and the sky. We went down under wave after wave of settlement, each preceded, accompanied by, and followed by military engagements that were more often massacres of our people than declared wars. These wars, taken together, constitute the longest undeclared war neo-Americans have fought, and no end is in sight.

It is still being fought on reservations, in urban communities, along Indian-white frontiers (which occur wherever Indian and non-Indian interface); in Mexico and in Central America—Guatemala, El Salvador, Nicaragua, Honduras, and Costa Rica; in South America— Brazil, Argentina, Chile, Venezuela, Peru. In some areas we have been all but extinguished, as in the islands of the Caribbean, Canada, and the United States; in others we continue to survive in large numbers, though usually characterized as peasants and disguised as Hispanics by the Anglo-European/Hispanic media, scholars, officials, and political activists. Still we endure, and many of our old values, lifeways, and philosophies endure with us, for they, like us, are inextricably linked to the land, the sky, the waters, and the spirits of this Turtle Island, this Earth-Surface place, that the whites call "the New World."

From Gynecentric to Patriarchal

During the five hundred years of Anglo-European colonization, the tribes have seen a progressive shift from gynecentric, egalitarian, ritual-based social systems to secularized structures closely imitative of the European patriarchal system. During this time women (including lesbians) and gay men—along with traditional medicine people, holy people, shamans, and ritual leaders—have suffered severe loss of status, power, and leadership. That these groups have suffered concurrent degradation is not coincidental; the woman-based, woman-centered traditions of many precontact tribes were tightly bound to ritual, and ritual was based on spiritual understandings rather than on economic or political ones.

The genocide practiced against the tribes is aimed systematically at the dissolution of ritual tradition. In the past this has included prohibition of ceremonial practices throughout North and Meso-America, Christianization, enforced loss of languages, reeducation of tribal peoples through government-supported and Christian mission schools that Indian children have been forced to attend, renaming of the traditional ritual days as Christian feast days, missionization (incarceration) of tribal people, deprivation of language, severe disruption of cultures and economic and resource bases of those cultures, and the degradation of the status of women as central to the spiritual and ritual life of the tribes.

Along with the devaluation of women comes the devaluation of traditional spiritual leaders, female and male, and, largely because of their ritual power and status, the devaluation of lesbian and gay tribal members as leaders, shamans, healers, or ritual participants. Virtually all customary sexual customs among the tribes were changed—including marital, premarital, homosexual, and ritual sexual practices, along with childhood and adult indulgence in open sexuality, common in many tribes.

Colonization means the loss not only of language and the power of self-government but also of ritual status of all women and those males labeled "deviant" by the white Christian colonizers. The usual divisions of labor—generally gender-based (if you count homosexual men as women and dikes as men)—were altered, prohibited, or forced underground, from whence they have only recently begun to reemerge as the tribes find themselves engaged in a return to more traditional ways of life.

In considering gender-based roles, we must remember that while the roles themselves were fixed in most archaic American cultures, with divisions of "women's work" and "men's work," the individuals fit into these roles on the basis of proclivity, inclination, and temperament. Thus men who in contemporary European and American societies are designated gay or homosexual were gender-designated among many tribes as "women" in terms of their roles; women who in contemporary societies are designated as lesbians (actually, "dikes" is more accurate) were designated as men in tribal cultures. As an example, the Kaska of Canada would designate a daughter in a family that had only daughters as a boy. When she was small, around five, her parents would tie a pouch of dried bear ovaries to her belt. She would dress in male clothing and would function in the Kaska male role for the rest of her life. Interestingly, if a male attempted to make sexual advances to this male-designated person, he was liable to punishment, because the Kaska felt this violation would ruin the "dike's" luck in hunting.[1]

The Yuma had a tradition of gender designation based on dreams; a female who dreamed of weapons became a male for all practical purposes. In this the Yumas were similar to the neighboring Mohaves and Cocopah, except the gender-role designation was based on the choice of companions and play objects of a young person. In such systems a girl who chose to play with boys or with boys' objects such as a bow and arrow became a male functionary. Among the Mohave, another dream-culture people related to the Yuma, the hwame, a term roughly corresponding to "dike" in English, took a male name and was in all respects subject to ritual male taboos vis à vis females, such as avoidance of contact with a menstruating wife. The hwame's wife was not considered hwame but simply a woman.[2]

In addition to these tribes, others that display a positive acceptance of lesbianism include the Navajo (who considered lesbians an asset), the Mohave (who thought that from the inception of the world homosexuals were a natural and necessary part of society), the Quinault, the Apache, the Ojibwa, and the Eskimo.[3]

In her brilliant, comprehensive gay cultural history *Another Mother Tongue: Gay Words, Gay Worlds*, poet and writer Judy Grahn devotes a large chapter to the existence of lesbians and homosexuals as ritually and socially valued tribal members. Citing numerous sources including Jonathan Katz, Sue Ellen Jacobs, myself, Carolyn Neithammer, Arthur Evans, Edward Carpenter, Michael Wilken, John (Fire) Lame Deer, Hamilton Tyler, John Gunn, and various contemporary gay and lesbian American Indian poets and writers, Grahn writes a lengthy chronicle about the place gays held among many American Indian peoples. Grahn cites anthropologist Sue Ellen Jacobs as listing eighty-eight tribes whose recorded cultural attributes include references to gayness, with twenty of these including specific references to lesbianism. According to Jacobs, eleven tribes denied any homosexuality to anthropologists or other writers (which doesn't necessarily mean it wasn't openly sanctioned and practiced, acknowledged, or valued), and those denials came from tribes located in areas of heaviest, lengthiest, and most severely puritanical white encroachment. Among the eighty-eight tribes who admitted homosexuality among them and referred to it in positive ways are the Apache, Navajo, Winnebago, Cheyenne, Pima, Crow, Shoshoni, Paiute, Osage, Acoma, Zuñi, Sioux, Pawnee, Choctaw, Creek, Seminole, Illinois, Mohave, Shasta, Aleut, Sac and Fox, Iowa, Kansas, Yuma, Aztec, Tlingit, Maya, Naskapi, Ponca, Menomini, Maricopa, Klamath, Quinault, Yuki, Chilula, and Kamia—indicating the presence of lesbianism and homosexuality in every area of North America.[4]

Some of the native names for gays that Grahn lists include Alyha and Hwame (Mohave), Nadle (Navajo), Siange (Winnebago), Winkte and Adi-wa-lona (male) and Koshkalaka (female) (Lakota), Mingu-ga

(Omaha and Ponca), Ko'thlama (Zuñi), Wergern (Yurok), Bo-te (Crow), Kwerhame (lesbian) and Elxa (homosexual) (Yuma), and Joya (Chumash). About this last name, Grahn writes:

> Gay queens among the Indians of the Santa Barbara region were called "Jewel," and so the Spanish recorded it as "Joya" . . .
> The European soldiers, trappers, explorers, and settlers were contemptuous of Gay traditions in their own cultures, and several centuries of persecution under the Inquisition had taught them to deny all Gayness. The heaviest persecutions in Europe ran concurrent to the heaviest periods of colonization of the Indians in North America . . . Small wonder, perhaps, that Gay people were often the first Indians killed and that even when tribes were tolerated by the white people, their Gay people were mocked and persecuted to the point of changing their behavior for the sake of the safety of their people. Balboa, for instance, set wild dogs on the Gay medicine men of California tribes, killing them, the "Jewels" of their own people.[5]

Recent scholarly work reveals the universal or nearly universal presence of homosexuality and lesbianism among tribal peoples, the special respect and honor often accorded gay men and women, and the alteration in that status as a result of colonization of the continent by Anglo-Europeans. These studies demonstrate the process by which external conquest and colonization become internalized among the colonized with vivid clarity. Homophobia, which was rare (perhaps even absent entirely) among tribal peoples in the Americas, has steadily grown among them as they have traded traditional tribal values for Christian industrial ones.

Gay historian Walter Williams records particularly poignant stories about contemporary homosexuals in which colonization is clearly linked to homophobia and racist colonial attempts to eradicate tribal cultures. Citing numerous scholarly sources, Williams refers to homosexuality among the Maya, Ojibwa, various branches of the Sioux, the Sac and Fox, the Osage, unspecified California and Alaskan Indians, the Papago, Crow, Hopi, Navajo, Klamath, Winnebago, Yokuts, Zuñi, Iroquois, Cheyenne, Omaha, and Aleut.[6]

Among the many accounts Williams cites, the stark homophobia of the white recorders contrasts sharply with the easy acceptance the Indians accord the presence of gays among themselves. This is particularly notable in the earliest white reports; as colonization deepens its hold on tribal lifeways, the reported attitudes of Indians splits: some, usually the most traditional, continue to accord high respect to homosexuals, even to the present day. Of these, many, perhaps most, will not discuss the subject with non-Indians because they are unwilling to have institutions or practices that they value subjected to ridicule or contempt. They also may feel a strong need to protect the homosexuals and lesbians among them and the tribe as a whole from further life-threatening assaults which for too long have been directed against them.

Other Indians, more acculturated and highly Christianized, treat the presence of lesbianism or homosexuality among them with fear and loathing. They do not confine that loathing to homosexuality but direct it to other aspects of tribal ceremonial life, particularly when it has to do with sexuality. Thus a Hopi man despairs of his people, saying that there is nothing good in the old Hopi ways. This man, Kuanwikvaya, testified to U.S. officials: "There is nothing good in the Hopi religion. It is all full of adultery and immorality. I cannot tell all the dirt and filth that is in these ceremonies." Another Hopi man, Tuwaletstiwa, testified that before he accepted Christianity his life "was unspeakably evil . . . When a Hopi becomes a Christian he quits attending these dances. He knows the evil in them is so great."[7] These testimonies were taken in 1920, when U.S. officials suppressed the Hopi dances. The men's statements were used as "local witness" proof that the traditional ceremonies were properly banned.

These men eerily echo earlier white commentaries on the subject of homosexuality. Hubert Bancroft, a scholar of considerable stature on Native American subjects, characterizes the ritual institutions of homosexuality as "the most repugnant of all their practices" and "a shameful custom."[8]

Then there is George Catlin, the renowned painter and chronicler of what he took to be the "vanishing" Indian way of life. Catlin was invited to attend a feast given to honor Sac and Fox "berdaches" (*berdache* was the word of choice for gay males at the time Catlin wrote in the late nineteenth century—an unhappy choice as the term signifies Arab love boy or sex-slave boy and as such is entirely inapplicable to the homosexuality practiced among the Sac and Fox or other tribal peoples). Catlin remarked in summarizing his visit among the "berdache": "This is one of the most unaccountable and disgusting customs that I have ever met in Indian country." He continues, in the words used over and over by whites as a justification for the removal, assimilation, or destruction of native tribes: "For further account of [the berdache feast] I am constrained to refer the reader to the country where it is practiced, and where I should wish that it might be extinguished before it be more fully recorded."[9]

But the pattern of colonized psychology and social valuation among Indian people may be being reversed. Recently, Russell Means of the American Indian Movement—a man not always noted for his liberal attitudes toward women and other devalued individuals—said, in defense of homosexuals and their anciently valued place among the people: "The Indian looked upon these unique individuals as something special the Great Mystery created to teach us. These people had something special to tell us."[10] And the Oglala Sioux holy man John (Fire) Lame Deer said, "To us a man is what nature, or his dreams, make him. We accept him for what he wants to be. That's up to him . . . There are good men among the *winktes* and they have been given certain powers."[11]

It is significant, I think, that those who are homophobic are also very likely to be misogynist. Indeed, the latter often masquerade as the former. The colonizers' treatment of gays is analogous to their treatment of healers, holy people, dreamers, and other traditional leaders, foremost among whom have traditionally been the women—the matrons, clan mothers, dreamers, and makers of ritual and tribal life in the western hemisphere.

Before the coming of the white man, or long ago, so far, as the people say, the Grandmother(s) created the firmament, the earth, and all the spirit beings in it. She (or they) created, by thinking into being, the Women, or the Woman, from whom the people sprang. The Women thus thought into being also gave thought, and the people and all the orders of being in this world came into being, including the laws, the sciences, agriculture, householding, social institutions—everything. Long ago the peoples of this hemisphere knew that their power to live came to them from the Grandmother or Grandmothers (depending on the tribe) not only originally but continuously, even to the present. Many old mythologies and most ceremonial cycles (if taken within their entire cultural framework) reiterate and celebrate this central fact of tribal Native American existence. Many of the tribes retain this old knowledge—a knowledge that they have kept hidden from the whites and often from their own tribespeople but that they have preserved. Only recently have the women begun to raise our voices again, at the behest of the Grandmother(s), to tell the story as it is told and to lay claim to the ancient power that is vested in Woman since before time.

In a recent interview published in the West German feminist monthly *Emma*, three Native American representatives of a movement called Concerned Aboriginal Women discussed the present crisis among American Indians in Canada and the part the women are taking in their struggle to retain title to their lands. One of the women, identified as Vera, said: "You know, for such a long long time our men struggled and struggled, and things got worse. Then the grandmothers and mothers decided that now we must intervene! Among our people we have a tradition that the women make the decisions. Later we can go back to taking care of our children." Another woman, Judalon, continued: "The government corrupted our leaders and it took the women to realize it." The third woman, Dinah, added, "They've turned our men around the way they want them, so that they have lost their direction and no longer know where they should be going."

The interviewer asked the women why they sound like they want to "step back" to taking care of the children when German women are struggling to do more than housework and childrearing. German women "want to be able to participate in public decisions," the interviewer said. Judalon explained that Native American women have always participated in public decisions.

> For example, in my mother's tribe, the Mohawks, the women made all the decisions. In the Longhouse the clan mothers would gather and sit on one side. The chiefs would sit on the other side. On the other two sides, the rest of the people would sit and the current problem would be discussed. The clan mothers would decide what should happen, but the men would speak for them. The men never made decisions. It was that way in the tribe and also in a clan's household. The women were responsible and made the decisions.
>
> Everything has changed since we've had contact with the Europeans. First, our leaders were brainwashed. They became vain and thought that they alone could decide things . . . Today many Indian men behave like European men.

The other two women agree, noting that traditionally respect for women by Indian men was high and that all work was valued because it was all important. At this the interviewer asked about division of labor into gender roles, and the Iroquois women responded that work was generally divided along gender lines,

> but I think with us there were never such sharp divisions between these areas as with you. The men had to be able to cook since, for example, they were often away hunting or fighting. And there were also girl warriors. In some tribes there were also women leaders. Of course, there are great differences between the Indian nations, but most of them did not have this sharp division of roles. There were also girls who were raised as boys, if, for example, a family only had daughters. And these women would then marry other women. We even have special initiation rites for transvestites . . . In those families which lead a traditional lifestyle, it is still the case that the men have great respect for the women. And with the help of the spiritual movement, things have been changing over the last ten years. More and more Indians are returning to the traditional ways. The old people are teaching us.[12]

The way it is now is generally very different from the way it was; the devaluation of women that has accompanied Christianization and westernization is not a simple matter of loss of status. It also involves increases in violence against women by men, a phenomenon not experienced until recently and largely attributable to colonization and westernization.

Many people believe that Indian men have suffered more damage to their traditional status than have Indian women, but I think that belief is more a reflection of colonial attitudes toward the primacy of male experience than of historical fact. While women still play the traditional role of housekeeper, childbearer, and nurturer, they no longer enjoy the unquestioned positions of power, respect, and decision making on local and international levels that were not so long ago their accustomed functions. Only in some tribes do they still enjoy the medicine or shamanistic power they earlier possessed. No longer, except in backwoods pockets of resistance, do they speak with the power and authority of inviolable law.

It is true that colonization destroyed roles that had given men their sense of self-esteem and identity, but the significant roles lost were not those of hunter and warrior. Rather, colonization took away the security of office men once derived from their ritual and political relationship to women. Men's status in all tribes that use clan systems, and perhaps in others, came to them through the agency of women, who got their own status from the spirit people, particularly the Grandmother powers that uphold and energize the universe. But with the coming of the white man and his patriarchal system, the powers of the women were systematically undermined in countless ways, and this undermining was and is reinforced willingly by many of the men.

The history of the subjugation of women under the dominant patriarchal control of males is a long and largely ugly one, and it affects every tribe and Nation now as much as ever. It is synchronistic rather than coincidental that most of the Indian women known to the general non-Indian public have been convicted of playing into the white man's game and betraying the Indian; all have been accused of doing so because of sexual or romantic connections with white men, and all have been blamed by many Indians for white conquest. Patriarchy requires that powerful women be discredited so that its own system will seem to be the only one that reasonable or intelligent people can subscribe to.

The nature of the change in the images of women and gays among American Indians caused by patriarchal propaganda is historical, cultural, and political. In that change can be seen the history of patriarchy on this continent and, by extension, all over the world. As American Indian women emerge from the patriarchally imposed ignominy of the past centuries, the falsity of all the colonizers' stories about Native Americans, about spirituality, gayness, and femaleness, becomes increasingly apparent. And as we articulate a feminine analysis of the effects of colonization, we are more and more able to demonstrate that the colonizers' image of Indian women has, more than any other factor, led to the high incidence of rape and abuse of Indian women by Indian men. This violent behavior is tacitly approved of by the tribes through the refusal of tribal governments across the country and in urban Indian enclaves to address the issue and provide care, shelter, and relief for the women victims and competent, useful treatment for the offenders. The white and recently Indian image of powerful Indian women as traitors is another chapter in the patriarchal folktale that begins with Eve causing Adam's fall from grace into divine disgrace.

Women as Healers, Dreamers, and Shamans

I met Essie Parrish on a field trip with my students to the Kashia Pomo reservation at Stewart's Point, California, in 1974. The next year I met and heard a lecture by the Pomo dreamer and basketmaker

Mabel McCabe. The teachings of these two women provide clear information about the ancient ritual power of Indian women.

Mrs. McCabe spoke about the meaning of having a tradition, about how a woman becomes a basketmaker among her people—a process that is guided entirely by a spirit-teacher when the woman is of the proper age. It is not transmitted to her through human agency. For Mrs. McCabe, having a tradition means having a spirit-teacher or guide. That is the only way she used the term "tradition" and the only context in which she understood it. Pomo baskets hold psychic power, spirit power; so a basketmaker weaves a basket for a person at the direction of her spirit guide. Owning a basket should not be by purchase, but by gift.

Imagine how much spirit power of the tribes is locked away in museums or kept secured in white homes where their true significance goes unrecognized. Soul theft is a terrible crime, and while there are many museums and field workers who are concerned with this issue and are trying to restore the sacred objects to their owners, there are many more who are blissfully ignorant of the significance of their collecting instincts or the meaning of their possessions.

Essie Parrish, who died within the last few years, was the Dreamer of the Kashia Pomo. The Dreamer is the person responsible for the continued existence of the people as a psychic (that is, tribal) entity. It is through her dreams that the people have being; it is through her dreams that they find ways to function in whatever reality they find themselves. It is through her dreams that the women keep children safe in war, that healings are made possible, and that children are assured a safe passage through life.

Under the auspices of the University of California at Berkeley, Mrs. Parrish made several movies recording her dances and songs. In one of them, *Dream Dances of the Kashia Pomo*, she and others dance and display the dance costumes that are made under her direction, appliquéd with certain dream-charged designs that hold the power she brings from the spirit world. She tells about the role of the Dreamer, who is the mother of the people not because she gives physical birth (though Mrs. Parrish has done that) but because she gives them life through her power of dreaming—that is, she en-livens them. Actually, the power of giving physical birth is a consequence of the power of giving nonmaterial or, you might say, "astral" birth.

The Dreamer, then, is the center of psychic/spiritual unity of the people. She is the center, the hub of the wheel. It is by virtue of her gift, her ability, that the people live and are a people, connected to one another in ways more than mere language, culture, or proximity can assure.

The life force that is passed to the Dreamer from the nonmaterial planes is embodied in songs, dances, ritual objects, and garments that the women make. The songs are sung by the Dreamer or sometimes by the dancers. The drums or other accompaniment are played by men. In many tribes the singing is done only by men, corresponding, I think, to the Mohawk male function of speaker or agent of the women's decisions. In such dream systems, among them the Iroquois, the Pomo, the Maya, the Mohave, and many other Nations, decisions are made in ritual ways. That is, their rituals, customs, social institutions, foodstuffs, healing materials and methods, their "magic" or paranormal competencies, architecture, agriculture (or horticulture), land use, water use, food production methods, relationships to animals, plants, mountains, clouds, rain, lightning, thunder, earthquakes—anything and everything—come to them through dreams or vision-based concourse with the world of the spirit people, the divinities and deities, the Grandmothers, and the other exotic powers.

Even among Plains people, long considered the most male-oriented Indians, at least by the media and its precursors in popular culture, power was and is gained, accrued, mediated, and dispensed only through the grace and beneficence of female influence. Thus the Kiowa take their tribal realization, their psychic commonality, from their sacred Grandmother bundles; the Sioux and other Sun Dance people perform their rites (which are inextricably interwoven with feminine power) within the secure psychic power-generating and protective "battery" of the circle of Grandmothers, and the Sacred Pipe way of the Lakota comes to them from the spirit White Buffalo Woman.

In these and many other tribal systems, the oral tradition in its ceremonial and ritual aspects rests on female power; shamanism, which is accorded to certain persons, including gays and lesbians, derives from the power of dream/vision and the living presence of the Dreamer among the people.

In another film, *Pomo Shaman*, Mrs. Parrish demonstrates a healing ritual, in which she uses water and water power, captured and focused through her motions, words, and use of material water, to heal a patient. She demonstrates the means of healing, and in the short narrative segments, she repeats in English some of the ritual. It is about creation and creating and signifies the basic understanding the tribal peoples generally have about how sickness comes about and how its effects can be assuaged, relieved, and perhaps even removed.

The mental health practitioner Phyllis Old Dog Cross alludes to this belief when she quotes anthropologist Peggy Sanday: "'Where men are in harmony with their environment rape is usually absent.'"[13] That is, rape or other acts of political or power-based violence result from a disorder in the relationship between person and cosmos.

Traditional American Indian systems depended on basic concepts that are at present being reformulated and to some extent practiced by western feminists, including cooperation (but by that traditional Indians generally meant something other than noncompetitiveness or passivity), harmony (again, this did not necessarily mean absence of conflict), balance, kinship, and respect. Their material, social, and ritual systems were predicated on these essential values, which might be seen as objectives, parameters, norms, or principles depending on how they were being applied in a given situation. They did not rely on external social institutions such as schools, court, and prisons, kings, or other political rulers, but rather on internal institutions such as spirit-messengers, guides, teachers, or mentors; on tradition, ritual, dream and vision; on personal inclination (understood more in a geological sense than in a hedonistic one) and the leadership of those who had demonstrated competence with the foregoing characteristics.

Thus to traditional American Indians, social and personal life is governed by internal rather than external factors, and systems based on spiritual orders rather than on material ones are necessarily heavily oriented toward internal governing mechanisms.

Among traditionals the psychospiritual characteristics of the individual are channeled to blend harmoniously with those of the rest of the group. This channeling is done by applying custom, by sharing appropriate items from the oral tradition, and by helping and encouraging children in tribally approved endeavors that are matched to individual inclinations but that will provide useful skills, understandings, and abilities for the good of the entire group. The young person is trained in a number of ways, formal and informal, and by a number of individuals in the tribe. Traditionally, female children (or female surrogates) are trained by women, while male children (or male surrogates) are trained by men in learning their ritual roles within their social system. In some groups such as the Cherokee, however, shamans are typically trained along cross-gender rather than same gender lines.

Thus male shamans train female apprentices, and female shamans train male apprentices. Traditionally, proper behavior falls along gender lines, as did expectations, but gender is understood in a psychological or psychospiritual sense much more than in a physiological one.

Thus the high position held by women as a group and by certain women as individuals results from certain inclinations that the women are born with and that they demonstrate through temperament, interest, competence, spirit-direction, and guidance. Women are by the nature of feminine "vibration" graced with certain inclinations that make them powerful and capable in certain ways (all who have this temperament, ambience, or "vibration" are designated women and all who do not are not so designated). Their power includes bearing and rearing children (but in tribal life everyone is in some sense "raising" the children); cooking and similar forms of "woman's work"; decision making; dreaming and visioning; prophesying; divining, healing, locating people or things; harvesting, preserving, preparing, storing, or transporting food and healing stuffs; producing finished articles of clothing; making houses and laying them out in the proper village arrangement; making and using all sorts of technological equipment such as needles, scrapers, grinders, blenders, harvesters, diggers, fire makers, lathes, spindles, looms, knives, spoons, and ladles; locating and/or allocating virtually every resource used by the people. Guiding young women through the complex duties of womanhood must have taxed the creative, physical, psychic, and spiritual powers of all the women. In addition, they bore responsibility for preserving and using the oral tradition; making important tribal decisions about the life or death of captives and other outsiders; and overseeing ritual occasions, including making spiritual and physical provisions for ceremonies in cultures that devoted as much as two-thirds of their time to ritual/ceremonial pursuits. In short, the women did—and wherever possible still do—everything that maintains the life and stability of their tribal people. It is no wonder that Indian people in general insist that among them women are considered sacred. Nor, as perhaps you can see, is this an empty compliment in a society that depends for its life upon the sacred.

As shamans, the women in many tribes function in all ways that male shamans are known to. They perform healings, hunting ceremonies, vision quests and the guidance for them, acts of psychokinesis, teleportation, weather direction, and more. In the various tribes according to each one's customs, the shaman also creates certain artifacts—clothing, baskets, ornaments, objects to be worn in pouches or under skirts or sewed into belts. She officiates at burials, births, child naming and welcoming into this world, menstrual and pregnancy rituals and rites, psychic manipulation of animals, metamorphoses or transformations. She does much of this through dancing and chanting, and a large part of the method, symbols, significances, and effects of her shamanic efforts are recorded in the stories she tells, the songs she sings, and the knowledge she possesses. Much of this knowledge she transmits to others in ways that will be of use to them, and much of it she keeps to herself, teaches in formal settings to her apprentices, or shares with other shamans.

One of the primary functions of the shaman is her effect on tribal understandings of "women's roles," which in large part are traditional in Mrs. McCabe's sense of the word. It is the shaman's connection to the spirit world that Indian women writers reflect most strongly in our poetry and fiction. If there is any Indian woman's tradition that informs our work, it is the spiritual understanding of womanhood as an expression of spirit. That understanding is formed on the recognition that everything is alive, that the spirit people are part of our daily world, that all life lives in harmony and kinship with and to all other life, and that sickness of all kinds and of all orders comes about because of our resistance to surrendering to the complexity and multi-dimensionality of existence.

So we acknowledge that the violation of the Mothers' and Grandmothers' laws of kinship, respect, balance, and harmony brings about social, planetary, and personal illness and that healing is a matter of restoring the balance within ourselves and our communities. To this restoration of balance, of health, and wellness (wealth) we contribute our energies. For we are engaged in the work of reclaiming our minds, our gods, and our traditions. The sacred hoop cannot be restored unless and until its sacred center is recognized.

Who Is Your Mother?
Red Roots of
White Feminism

At Laguna Pueblo in New Mexico, "Who is your mother?" is an important question. At Laguna, one of several of the ancient Keres gynocratic societies of the region, your mother's identity is the key to your own identity. Among the Keres, every individual has a place within the universe—human and nonhuman—and that place is defined by clan membership. In turn, clan membership is dependent on matrilineal descent. Of course, your mother is not only that woman whose womb formed and released you—the term refers in every individual case to an entire generation of women whose psychic, and consequently physical, "shape" made the psychic existence of the following generation possible. But naming your own mother (or her equivalent) enables people to place you precisely within the universal web of your life, in each of its dimensions: cultural, spiritual, personal, and historical.

Among the Keres, "context" and "matrix" are equivalent terms, and both refer to approximately the same thing as knowing your derivation and place. Failure to know your mother, that is, your position and its attendant traditions, history, and place in the scheme of things, is failure to remember your significance, your reality, your right relationship to earth and society. It is the same as being lost—

isolated, abandoned, self-estranged, and alienated from your own life. This importance of tradition in the life of every member of the community is not confined to Keres Indians; all American Indian Nations place great value on traditionalism.

The Native American sense of the importance of continuity with one's cultural origins runs counter to contemporary American ideas: in many instances, the immigrants to America have been eager to cast off cultural ties, often seeing their antecedents as backward, restrictive, even shameful. Rejection of tradition constitutes one of the major features of American life, an attitude that reaches far back into American colonial history and that now is validated by virtually every cultural institution in the country. Feminist practice, at least in the cultural artifacts the community values most, follows this cultural trend as well.

The American idea that the best and the brightest should willingly reject and repudiate their origins leads to an allied idea—that history, like everything in the past, is of little value and should be forgotten as quickly as possible. This all too often causes us to reinvent the wheel continually. We find ourselves discovering our collective pasts over and over, having to retake ground already covered by women in the preceding decades and centuries. The Native American view, which highly values maintenance of traditional customs, values, and perspectives, might result in slower societal change and in quite a bit less social upheaval, but it has the advantage of providing a solid sense of identity and lowered levels of psychological and interpersonal conflict.

Contemporary Indian communities value individual members who are deeply connected to the traditional ways of their people, even after centuries of concerted and brutal effort on the part of the American government, the churches, and the corporate system to break the connections between individuals and their tribal world. In fact, in the view of the traditionals, rejection of one's culture—one's traditions, language, people—is the result of colonial oppression and is hardly to be applauded. They believe that the roots of oppression are to be found in the loss of tradition and memory because that loss is always accompanied by a loss of a positive sense of self. In short, Indians think it is important to remember, while Americans believe it is important to forget.

The traditional Indians' view can have a significant impact if it is expanded to mean that the sources of social, political, and philosophical thought in the Americas not only should be recognized and honored by Native Americans but should be embraced by American society. If American society judiciously modeled the traditions of the various Native Nations, the place of women in society would become central, the distribution of goods and power would be egalitarian, the elderly would be respected, honored, and protected as a primary social and cultural resource, the ideals of physical beauty would be considerably enlarged (to include "fat," strong-featured women, gray-haired, and wrinkled individuals, and others who in contemporary American culture are viewed as "ugly"). Additionally, the destruction of the biota, the life sphere, and the natural resources of the planet would be curtailed, and the spiritual nature of human and nonhuman life would become a primary organizing principle of human society. And if the traditional tribal systems that are emulated included pacifist ones, war would cease to be a major method of human problem solving.

Re-membering Connections and Histories

The belief that rejection of tradition and of history is a useful response to life is reflected in America's amazing loss of memory concerning its origins in the matrix and context of Native America. America does not seem to remember that it derived its wealth, its values, its food, much of its medicine, and a large part of its "dream" from Native America. It is ignorant of the genesis of its culture in this Native American land, and that ignorance helps to perpetuate the longstanding European and Middle Eastern monotheistic, hierarchical, patriarchal cultures' oppression of women, gays, and lesbians, people of color, working class, unemployed people, and the elderly. Hardly anyone in America speculates that the constitutional system of government might be as much a product of American Indian ideas and practices as of colonial American and Anglo-European revolutionary fervor.

Even though Indians are officially and informally ignored as intellectual movers and shapers in the United States, Britain, and Europe, they are peoples with ancient tenure on this soil. During the ages when tribal societies existed in the Americas largely untouched by patriarchal oppression, they developed elaborate systems of thought that included science, philosophy, and government based on a belief in the central importance of female energies, autonomy of individuals, cooperation, human dignity, human freedom, and egalitarian distribution of status, goods, and services. Respect for others, reverence for life, and, as a by-product, pacifism as a way of life; importance of kinship ties in the customary ordering of social interaction; a sense of the sacredness and mystery of existence; balance and harmony in relationships both sacred and secular were all features of life among the tribal confederacies and nations. And in those that lived by the largest number of these principles, gynarchy was the norm rather than the exception. Those systems are as yet unmatched in any contemporary industrial, agrarian, or postindustrial society on earth.

As we have seen in previous essays, there are many female gods recognized and honored by the tribes and Nations. Femaleness was highly valued, both respected and feared, and all social institutions reflected this attitude. Even modern sayings, such as the Cheyenne statement that a people is not conquered until the hearts of the women are on the ground, express the Indians' understanding that without the power of woman the people will not live, but with it, they will endure and prosper.

Indians did not confine this belief in the central importance of female energy to matters of worship. Among many of the tribes (perhaps as many as 70 percent of them in North America alone), this belief was reflected in all of their social institutions. The Iroquois Constitution or White Roots of Peace, also called the Great Law of the Iroquois, codified the Matrons' decision-making and economic power:

> The lineal descent of the people of the Five Fires [the Iroquois Nations] shall run in the female line. Women shall be considered the progenitors of the Nation. They shall own the land and the soil. Men and women shall follow the status of their mothers. (Article 44)
>
> The women heirs of the chieftainship titles of the League shall be called Oiner or Otinner [Noble] for all time to come. (Article 45)
>
> If a disobedient chief persists in his disobedience after three warnings [by his female relatives, by his male relatives, and by one of his fellow council members, in that order], the matter shall go to the council of War Chiefs. The Chiefs shall then take away the title of the erring chief *by order of the women in whom the title is vested.* When the chief is deposed, the women shall notify the chiefs of the League . . . and the chiefs of the League shall sanction the act. The women will then select another of their sons as a candidate and the chiefs shall elect him. (Article 19) (Emphasis mine)[1]

The Matrons held so much policy-making power traditionally that once, when their position was threatened they demanded its return, and consequently the power of women was fundamental in shaping the Iroquois Confederation sometime in the sixteenth or early seventeenth century. It was women

> who fought what may have been the first successful feminist rebellion in the New World. The year was 1600, or thereabouts, when these tribal feminists decided that they had had enough of unregulated warfare by their men. Lysistratas among the Indian women proclaimed a boycott on lovemaking and childbearing. Until the men conceded to them the power to decide upon war and peace, there would be no more warriors. Since the men believed that the women alone knew the secret of childbirth, the rebellion was instantly successful.
>
> In the Constitution of Deganawidah the founder of the Iroquois Confederation of Nations had said: "He caused the body of our mother, the woman, to be of great worth and honor. He purposed that she shall be endowed and entrusted with the birth and upbringing of men, and that she shall have the care of all that is planted by which life is sustained and supported and the power to breathe is fortified: *and moreover that the warriors shall be her assistants.*"
>
> The footnote of history was curiously supplied when Susan B. Anthony began her "Votes for Women" movement two and a half centuries later. Unknowingly the feminists chose to hold their founding convention of latter-day suffragettes in the town of Seneca [Falls], New York. The site was just a stone's throw from the old council house where the Iroquois women had plotted their feminist rebellion. (Emphasis mine)[2]

Beliefs, attitudes, and laws such as these became part of the vision of American feminists and of other human liberation movements around the world. Yet feminists too often believe that no one has ever experienced the kind of society that empowered women and made that empowerment the basis of its rules of civilization. The price the feminist community must pay because it is not aware of the recent presence of gynarchical societies on this continent is unnecessary confusion, division, and much lost time.

The Root of Oppression Is Loss of Memory

An odd thing occurs in the minds of Americans when Indian civilization is mentioned: little or nothing. As I write this, I am aware of how far removed my version of the roots of American feminism must seem to those steeped in either mainstream or radical versions of feminism's history. I am keenly aware of the lack of image Americans have about our continent's recent past. I am intensely conscious of popular notions of Indian women as beasts of burden, squaws, traitors, or, at best, vanished denizens of a long-lost wilderness. How odd, then, must my contention seem that the gynocratic tribes of the American continent provided the basis for all the dreams of liberation that characterize the modern world.

We as feminists must be aware of our history on this continent. We need to recognize that the same forces that devastated the gynarchies of Britain and the Continent also devastated the ancient African civilizations, and we must know that those same materialistic, antispiritual forces are presently engaged in wiping out the same gynarchical values, along with the peoples who adhere to them, in Latin America. I am convinced that those wars were and continue to be about the imposition of patriarchal civilization over the holistic, pacifist, and spirit-based gynarchies they supplant. To that end the wars of imperial conquest have not been solely or even mostly waged over the land and its resources, but they have been fought within the bodies, minds, and hearts of the people of the earth for dominion over them. I think this is the reason traditionals say we must remember our origins, our cultures, our histories, our mothers and grandmothers, for without that memory, which implies continuance rather than nostalgia, we are doomed to engulfment by a paradigm that is fundamentally inimical to the vitality, autonomy, and self-empowerment essential for satisfying, high-quality life.

The vision that impels feminists to action was the vision of the Grandmothers' society, the society that was captured in the words of the sixteenth-century explorer Peter Martyr nearly five hundred years ago. It is the same vision repeated over and over by radical thinkers of Europe and America, from François Villon to John Locke, from William Shakespeare to Thomas Jefferson, from Karl Marx to Friedrich Engels, from Benito Juarez to Martin Luther King, from Elizabeth Cady Stanton to Judy Grahn, from Harriet Tubman to Audre Lorde, from Emma Goldman to Bella Abzug, from Malinalli to Cherrie Moraga, and from Iyatiku to me. That vision as Martyr told it is of a country where there are "no soldiers, no gendarmes or police, no nobles, kings, regents, prefects, or judges, no prisons, no lawsuits . . . All are equal and free," or so Friedrich Engels recounts Martyr's words.[3]

Columbus wrote:

> Nor have I been able to learn whether they [the inhabitants of the islands he visited on his first journey to the New World] held personal property, for it seemed to me that whatever one had, they all took shares of . . . They are so ingenuous and free with all they have, that no one would believe it who has not seen it; of anything that they possess, if it be asked of them, they never say no; on the contrary, they invite you to share it and show as much love as if their hearts went with it.[4]

At least that's how the Native Caribbean people acted when the whites first came among them; American Indians are the despair of social workers, bosses, and missionaries even now because of their deeply ingrained tendency to spend all they have, mostly on others. In any case, as the historian William Brandon notes,

> the Indian *seemed* free, to European eyes, gloriously free, to the European soul shaped by centuries of toil and tyranny, and this impression operated profoundly on the process of history and the development of America. Something in the peculiar character of the Indian world gave an impression of classlessness, of propertylessness, and that in turn led to an impression, as H. H. Bancroft put it, of "humanity unrestrained . . . in the exercise of liberty absolute."[5]

A Feminist Heroine

Early in the women's suffrage movement, Eva Emery Dye, an Oregon suffragette, went looking for a heroine to embody her vision of feminism. She wanted a historical figure whose life would symbolize the strengthened power of women. She found Sacagawea (or Sacajawea) buried in the journals of Lewis and Clark. The Shoshoni teenager had traveled with the Lewis and Clark expedition, carrying her infant son, and on a small number of occasions acted as translator.[6]

Dye declared that Sacagawea, whose name is thought to mean Bird Woman, had been the guide to the historic expedition, and through Dye's work Sacagawea became enshrined in American memory as a moving force and friend of the whites, leading them in the settlement of western North America.[7]

But Native American roots of white feminism reach back beyond Sacagawea. The earliest white women on this continent were well acquainted with tribal women. They were neighbors to a number of tribes and often shared food, information, child care, and health care.

Of course little is made of these encounters in official histories of colonial America, the period from the Revolution to the Civil War, or on the ever-moving frontier. Nor, to my knowledge, has either the significance or incidence of intermarriage between Indian and white or between Indian and Black been explored. By and large, the study of Indian-white relations has been focused on government and treaty relations, warfare, missionization, and education. It has been almost entirely documented in terms of formal white Christian patriarchal impacts and assaults on Native Americans, though they are not often characterized as assaults but as "civilizing the savages." Particularly in organs of popular culture and miseducation, the focus has been on what whites imagine to be degradation of Indian women ("squaws"), their equally imagined love of white government and white conquest ("princesses"), and the horrifyingly misleading, fanciful tales of "bloodthirsty, backward primitives" assaulting white Christian settlers who were looking for life, liberty, and happiness in their chosen land.

But, regardless of official versions of relations between Indians and whites or other segments of the American population, the fact remains that great numbers of apparently "white" or "Black" Americans carry notable degrees of Indian blood. With that blood has come the culture of the Indian, informing the lifestyles, attitudes, and values of their descendents. Somewhere along the line—and often quite recently—an Indian woman was giving birth to and raising the children of a family both officially and informally designated as white or Black—not Indian. In view of this, it should be evident that one of the major enterprises of Indian women in America has been the transfer of Indian values and culture to as large and influential a segment of American immigrant populations as possible. Their success in this endeavor is amply demonstrated in the Indian values and social styles that increasingly characterize American life. Among these must be included "permissive" childrearing practices, for as noted in an earlier chapter ("When Women Throw Down Bundles"), imprisoning, torturing, caning, strapping, starving, or verbally abusing children was considered outrageous behavior. Native Americans did not believe that physical or psychological abuse of children would result in their edification. They did not believe that children are born in sin, are congenitally predisposed to evil, or that a good parent who wishes the child to gain salvation, achieve success, or earn the respect of her or his fellows can be helped to those ends by physical or emotional torture.

The early Americans saw the strongly protective attitude of the Indian people as a mark of their "savagery"—as they saw the Indian's habit of bathing frequently, their sexual openness, their liking for scant clothing, their raucous laughter at most things, their suspicion and derision of authoritarian structures, their quick pride, their genuine courtesy, their willingness to share what they had with others less fortunate than they, their egalitarianism, their ability to act as if various lifestyles were a normal part of living, and their granting that women were of equal or, in individual cases, of greater value than men.

Yet the very qualities that marked Indian life in the sixteenth century have, over the centuries since contact between the two worlds occurred, come to mark much of contemporary American life. And those qualities, which I believe have passed into white culture from Indian culture, are the very ones that fundamentalists, immigrants from Europe, the Middle East, and Asia often find the most reprehensible. Third- and fourth-generation Americans indulge in growing nudity, informality in social relations, egalitarianism, and the rearing of women who value autonomy, strength, freedom, and personal dignity—and who are often derided by European, Asian, and Middle Eastern men for those qualities. Contemporary Americans value leisure almost as much as tribal people do. They find themselves increasingly unable to accept child abuse as a reasonable way to nurture. They bathe more than any other industrial people on earth—much to the scorn of their white cousins across the Atlantic, and they sometimes enjoy a good laugh even at their own expense (though they still have a less developed sense of the ridiculous than one might wish).

Contemporary Americans find themselves more and more likely to adopt a "live and let live" attitude in matters of personal sexual and social styles. Two-thirds of their diet and a large share of their medications and medical treatments mirror or are directly derived from Native American sources. Indianization is not a simple concept, to be sure, and it is one that Americans often find themselves resisting; but it is a process that has taken place, regardless of American resistance to recognizing the source of many if not most of American's vaunted freedoms in our personal, family, social, and political arenas.

This is not to say that Americans have become Indian in every attitude, value, or social institution. Unfortunately, Americans have a way to go in learning how to live in the world in ways that improve the quality of life for each individual while doing minimal damage to the biota, but they have adapted certain basic qualities of perception and certain attitudes that are moving them in that direction.

An Indian-Focused Version of American History

American colonial ideas of self-government came as much from the colonists' observations of tribal governments as from their Protestant or Greco-Roman heritage. Neither Greece nor Rome had the kind of pluralistic democracy as that concept has been understood in the United States since Andrew Jackson, but the tribes, particularly the gynarchical tribal confederacies, did. It is true that the *oligarchic* form of government that colonial Americans established was originally based on Greco-Roman systems in a number of important ways, such as its restriction of citizenship to propertied white males over twenty-one years of age, but it was never a form that Americans as a whole have been entirely comfortable with. Politics and government in the United States during the Federalist period also reflected the English common law system as it had evolved under patriarchal feudalism and monarchy—hence the United States' retention of slavery and restriction of citizenship to propertied white males.

The Federalists did make one notable change in the feudal system from which their political system derived on its Anglo side. They rejected blooded aristocracy and monarchy. This idea came from the Protestant Revolt to be sure, but it was at least reinforced by colonial America's proximity to American Indian nonfeudal confederacies and their concourse with those confederacies over the two hundred years of the colonial era. It was this proximity and concourse that enabled the revolutionary theorists to "dream up" a system in which all local polities would contribute to and be protected by a central governing body responsible for implementing policies that bore on the common interest of all. It should also be noted that the Reformation followed Columbus's contact with the Americas and that his and Martyr's reports concerning Native Americans' free and easy egalitarianism were in circulation by the time the Reformation took hold.

The Iroquois federal system, like that of several in the vicinity of the American colonies, is remarkably similar to the organization of the federal system of the United States. It was made up of local, "state," and federal bodies composed of executive, legislative, and judicial branches. The Council of Matrons was the executive: it instituted and determined general policy. The village, tribal (several villages), and Confederate councils determined and implemented policies when they did not conflict with the broader Council's decisions or with theological precepts that ultimately determined policy at all levels. The judicial was composed of the men's councils and the Matron's council, who sat together to make decisions. Because the matrons were the ceremonial center of the system, they were also the prime policymakers.

Obviously, there are major differences between the structure of the contemporary American government and that of the Iroquois. Two of those differences were and are crucial to the process of just government. The Iroquois system is spirit-based, while that of the United States is secular, and the Iroquois Clan Matrons formed the executive. The female executive function was directly tied to the ritual nature of the Iroquois politic, for the executive was lodged in the hands of the Matrons of particular clans across village, tribe, and national lines. The executive office was hereditary, and only sons of eligible clans could serve, at the behest of the Matrons of their clans, on the councils at the three levels. Certain daughters inherited the office of Clan Matron through their clan affiliations. No one could impeach or disempower a Matron, though her violation of certain laws could result in her ineligibility for the Matron's council. For example, a woman who married *and took her husband's name* could not hold the title Matron.

American ideas of social justice came into sharp focus through the commentaries of Iroquois observers who traveled in France in the colonial period. These observers expressed horror at the great gap between the lifestyles of the wealthy and the poor, remarking to the French philosopher Montaigne, who would heavily influence the radical communities of Europe, England, and America, that "they had noticed that in Europe there seemed to be two moities, consisting of the rich 'full gorged' with wealth, and the poor, starving 'and bare with need and povertie.' The Indian tourists not only marveled at the division, but marveled that the poor endured 'such an injustice, and that they took not the others by the throte, or set fire on their house.'"[8] It must be noted that the urban poor eventually did just that in the French Revolution. The writings of Montaigne and of those he influenced provided the theoretical framework and the vision that propelled the struggle for liberty, justice, and equality on the Continent and later throughout the British empire.

The feminist idea of power as it ideally accrues to women stems from tribal sources. The central importance of the clan Matrons in the formulation and determination of domestic and foreign policy as well as in their primary role in the ritual and ceremonial life of their respective Nations was the single most important attribute of the Iroquois, as of the Cherokee and Muskogee, who traditionally inhabited the southern Atlantic region. The latter peoples were removed to what is now Oklahoma during the Jackson administration, but prior to the American Revolution they had regular and frequent communication with and impact on both the British colonizers and later the American people, including the African peoples brought here as slaves.

Ethnographer Lewis Henry Morgan wrote an account of Iroquoian matriarchal culture, published in 1877,[9] that heavily influenced Marx and the development of communism, particularly lending it the idea of the liberation of women from patriarchal dominance. The early socialists in Europe, especially in Russia, saw women's liberation as a central aspect of the socialist revolution. Indeed, the basic ideas of socialism, the egalitarian distribution of goods and power, the peaceful ordering of society, and the right of every member of society to participate in the work and benefits of that society, are ideas that pervade American Indian political thought and action. And it is through various channels—the informal but deeply effective Indianization of Europeans, and christianizing Africans, the social and political theory of the confederacies feuding and then intertwining with European dreams of liberty and justice, and, more recently, the work of Morgan and the writings of Marx and Engels—that the age-old gynarchical systems of egalitarian government found their way into contemporary feminist theory.

When Eva Emery Dye discovered Sacagawea and honored her as the guiding spirit of American womanhood, she may have been wrong in bare historical fact, but she was quite accurate in terms of deeper truth. The statues that have been erected depicting Sacagawea as a Matron in her prime signify an understanding in the American mind, however unconscious, that the source of just government, of right ordering of social relationships, the dream of "liberty and justice for all" can be gained only by following the Indian Matrons' guidance. For, as Dr. Anna Howard Shaw said of Sacagawea at the National American Woman's Suffrage Association in 1905:

Forerunner of civilization, great leader of men, patient and motherly woman, we bow our hearts to do you honor! . . . May we the daughters of an alien race . . . learn the lessons of calm endurance, of patient persistence and unfaltering courage exemplified in your life, in our efforts to lead men through the Pass of justice, which goes over the mountains of prejudice and conservatism to the broad land of the perfect freedom of a true republic; one in which men and women together shall in perfect equality solve the problems of a nation that knows no caste, no race, no sex in opportunity, in responsibility or in justice! May 'the eternal womanly' ever lead us on![10]

Kochinnenako in Academe: Three Approaches to Interpreting a Keres Indian Tale

I became engaged in studying feminist thought and theory when I was first studying and teaching American Indian literature in the early 1970s. Over the ensuing fifteen years, my own stances toward both feminist and American Indian life and thought have intertwined as they have unfolded. I have always included feminist content and perspectives in my teaching of American Indian subjects, though at first the mating was uneasy at best. My determination that both areas were interdependent and mutually significant to a balanced pedagogy of American Indian studies led me to grow into an approach to both that is best described as tribal-feminism or feminist-tribalism. Both terms are applicable: if I am dealing with feminism, I approach it from a strongly tribal posture, and when I am dealing with American Indian literature, history, culture, or philosophy I approach it from a strongly feminist one.

A feminist approach to the study and teaching of American Indian life and thought is essential because the area has been dominated by paternalistic, male-dominant modes of consciousness since the first writings about American Indians in the fifteenth century. This male bias has seriously skewed our understanding of tribal life and philosophy, distorting it in ways that are sometimes obvious but are most often invisible.

Often what appears to be a misinterpretation caused by racial differences is a distortion based on sexual politics. When the patriarchal paradigm that characterizes western thinking is applied to gynecentric tribal modes, it transforms the ideas, significances, and raw data into something that is not only unrecognizable to the tribes but entirely incongruent with their philosophies and theories. We know that materials and interpretations amassed by the white intellectual establishment are in error, but we have not pinpointed the major sources of that error. I believe that a fundamental source has been male bias and that feminist theory, when judiciously applied to the field, makes the error correctible, freeing the data for reinterpretation that is at least congruent with a tribal perceptual mode.

To demonstrate the interconnections between tribal and feminist approaches as I use them in my work, I have developed an analysis of a traditional Kochinnenako, or Yellow Woman story of the Laguna-Acoma Keres, as recast by my mother's uncle John M. Gunn in his book *Schat Chen*.[1] My analysis utilizes three approaches and demonstrates the relationship of context to meaning, illuminating three consciousness styles and providing students with a traditionally tribal, nonracist, feminist understanding of traditional and contemporary American Indian life.

Some Theoretical Considerations

Analyzing tribal cultural systems from a mainstream feminist point of view allows an otherwise overlooked insight into the complex interplay of factors that have led to the systematic loosening of tribal ties, the disruption of tribal cohesion and complexity, and the growing disequilibrium of cultures that were anciently based on a belief in balance, relationship, and the centrality of women, particularly elder women. A feminist approach reveals not only the exploitation and oppression of the tribes by whites and white government but also areas of oppression within the tribes and the sources and nature of that oppression. To a large extent, such an analysis can provide strategies for ameliorating the effects of patriarchal colonialism, enabling many of the tribes to reclaim their ancient gynarchical,* egalitarian, and sacred traditions.

*In a system where all persons in power are called Mother Chief and where the supreme deity is female, and social organization is matrilocal, matrifocal, and matrilineal, gynarchy is happening. However, it does not imply domination of men by women as patriarchy implies domination by ruling class males of all aspects of a society.

At the present time, American Indians in general are not comfortable with feminist analysis or action within the reservation or urban Indian enclaves. Many Indian women are uncomfortable with feminism because they perceive it (correctly) as white-dominated. They (not so correctly) believe it is concerned with issues that have little bearing on their own lives. They are also uncomfortable with it because they have been reared in an anglophobic world that views white society with fear and hostility. But because of their fear of and bitterness toward whites and their consequent unwillingness to examine the dynamics of white socialization, American Indian women often overlook the central areas of damage done to tribal tradition by white Christian and secular patriarchal dominance. Militant and "progressive" American Indian men are even more likely to quarrel with feminism; they have benefited in certain ways from white male-centeredness, and while those benefits are of real danger to the tribes, the individual rewards are compelling.

It is within the context of growing violence against women and the concomitant lowering of our status among Native Americans that I teach and write. Certainly I could not locate the mechanisms of colonization that have led to the virulent rise of woman-hating among American Indian men (and, to a certain extent, among many of the women) without a secure and determined feminism. Just as certainly, feminist theory applied to my literary studies clarifies a number of issues for me, including the patriarchal bias that has been systematically imposed on traditional literary materials and the mechanism by which that bias has affected contemporary American Indian life, thought, and culture.

The oral tradition is more than a record of a people's culture. It is the creative source of their collective and individual selves. When that wellspring of identity is tampered with, the sense of self is also tampered with; and when that tampering includes the sexist and classist assumptions of the white world within the body of an Indian tradition, serious consequences necessarily ensue.

The oral tradition is a living body. It is in continuous flux, which enables it to accommodate itself to the real circumstances of a people's lives. That is its strength, but it is also its weakness, for when a people finds itself living within a racist, classist, and sexist reality, the oral tradition will reflect those values and will thus shape the people's consciousness to include and accept racism, classism and sexism, and they will incorporate that change, hardly noticing the shift. If the oral tradition is altered in certain subtle, fundamental ways, if elements alien to it are introduced so that its internal coherence is disturbed, it becomes the major instrument of colonization and oppression.

Such alterations have occurred and are still occurring. Those who translate or "render" narratives make certain crucial changes, many unconscious. The cultural bias of the translator inevitably shapes his or her perception of the materials being translated, often in ways that he or she is unaware of. Culture is fundamentally a shaper of perception, after all, and perception is shaped by culture in many subtle ways. In short, it's hard to see the forest when you're a tree. To a great extent, changes in materials translated from a tribal to a western language are a result of the vast difference in languages; certain ideas and concepts that are implicit in the structure of an Indian language are not possible in English. Language embodies the unspoken assumptions and orientations of the culture it belongs to. So while the problem is one of translation, it is not simply one of word equivalence. The differences are perceptual and contextual as much as verbal.

Sometimes the shifts are contextual; indeed, both the context and content usually are shifted, sometimes subtly, sometimes blatantly. The net effect is a shifting of the whole axis of the culture. When shifts of language and context are coupled with the almost infinite changes occasioned by Christianization, secularization, economic dislocation from subsistence to industrial modes, destruction of the wilderness and associated damage to the biota, much that is changed goes unnoticed or unremarked by the people being changed. This is not to suggest that Native Americans are unaware of the enormity of the change they have been forced to undergo by the several centuries of white presence, but much of that change is at deep and subtle levels that are not easily noted or resisted.

John Gunn received the story I am using here from a Keres-speaking informant and translated it himself. The story, which he titles "Sh-ah-cock and Miochin or the Battle of the Seasons," is in reality a narrative version of a ritual. The ritual brings about the change of season and of moiety among the Keres. Gunn doesn't mention this, perhaps because he was interested in stories and not in religion or perhaps because his informant did not mention the connection to him.

What is interesting about his rendering is his use of European, classist, conflict-centered patriarchal assumptions as plotting devices. These interpolations dislocate the significance of the tale and subtly alter the ideational context of woman-centered, largely pacifist people whose ritual story this is. I have developed three critiques of the tale as it appears in his book, using feminist and tribal understandings to discuss the various meanings of the story when it is read from three different perspectives.

In the first reading, I apply tribal understanding to the story. In the second, I apply the sort of feminist perspective I applied to traditional stories, historical events, traditional culture, and contemporary literature when I began developing a feminist perspective. The third reading applies what I call a feminist-tribal perspective. Each analysis is somewhat less detailed than it might be; but as I am interested in describing modes of perception and their impact on our understanding of cultural artifacts (and by extension our understanding of people who come from different cultural contexts than our own) rather than critiquing a story, they are adequate.

Yellow Woman Stories

The Keres of Laguna and Acoma Pueblos in New Mexico have stories that are called Yellow Woman stories. The themes and to a large extent the motifs of these stories are always female-centered, always told from Yellow Woman's point of view. Some older recorded versions of Yellow Woman tales (as in Gunn) make Yellow Woman the daughter of the hocheni. Gunn translates *hocheni* as "ruler." But Keres notions of the hocheni's function and position are as cacique or Mother Chief, which differ greatly from Anglo-European ideas of rulership. However, for Gunn to render *hocheni* as "ruler" is congruent with the European folktale tradition.[2]

Kochinnenako, Yellow Woman, is in some sense a name that means Woman-Woman because among the Keres, yellow is the color for women (as pink and red are among Anglo-European Americans), and it is the color ascribed to the Northwest. Keres women paint their faces yellow on certain ceremonial occasions and are so painted at death so that the guardian at the gate of the spirit world, Naiya Iyatiku (Mother Corn Woman), will recognize that the newly arrived person is a woman. It is also the name of a particular Irriaku, Corn Mother (sacred corn-ear bundle), and Yellow Woman stories in their original form detail rituals in which the Irriaku figures prominently.

Yellow Woman stories are about all sorts of things—abduction, meeting with happy powerful spirits, birth of twins, getting power from the spirit worlds and returning it to the people, refusing to marry, weaving, grinding corn, getting water, outsmarting witches, eluding or escaping from malintentioned spirits, and more. Yellow Woman's sisters are often in the stories (Blue, White, and Red Corn) as is Grandmother Spider and her helper Spider Boy, the Sun God or one of his aspects, Yellow Woman's twin sons, witches, magicians, gamblers, and mothers-in-law.

Many Yellow Woman tales highlight her alienation from the people: she lives with her grandmother at the edge of the village, for example, or she is in some way atypical, maybe a woman who refuses to marry, one who is known for some particular special talent, or one who is very quick-witted and resourceful. In many ways Kochinnenako is a role model, though she possesses some behaviors that are not likely to occur in many of the women who hear her stories. She is, one might say, the Spirit of Woman.

The stories do not necessarily imply that difference is punishable; on the contrary, it is often her very difference that makes her special adventures possible, and these adventures often have happy outcomes for Kochinnenako and for her people. This is significant among a people who value conformity and propriety above almost anything. It suggests that the behavior of women, at least at certain times or under certain circumstances, must be improper or nonconformist for the greater good of the whole. Not that all the stories are graced with a happy ending. Some come to a tragic conclusion, sometimes resulting from someone's inability to follow the rules or perform a ritual in the proper way.

Other Kochinnenako stories are about her centrality to the harmony, balance, and prosperity of the tribe. "Sh-ah-cock and Miochin" is one of these stories. John Gunn prefaces the narrative with the comment that while the story is about a battle, war stories are rarely told by the Keres because they are not "a war like people" and "very rarely refer to their exploits in war."

Sh-ah-cock and Miochin or the Battle of the Seasons

In the Kush-kut-ret-u-nah-tit (white village of the north) was once a ruler by the name of Hut-cha-mun Ki-uk (the broken prayer stick), one of whose daughters, Ko-chin-ne-nako, became the bride of Sh-ah-cock (the spirit of winter), a person of very violent temper. He always manifested his presence by blizzards of snow or sleet or by freezing cold, and on account of his alliance with the ruler's daughter, he was most of the time in the vicinity of Kush-kut-ret, and as these manifestations continued from month to month and year to year, the people of Kush-kut-ret found that their crops would not mature, and finally they were compelled to subsist on the leaves of the cactus.

On one occasion Ko-chin-ne-nako had wandered a long way from home in search of the cactus and had gathered quite a bundle and was preparing to carry home by singeing off the thorns, when on looking up she found herself confronted by a very bold but handsome young man. His attire attracted her gaze at once. He wore a shirt of yellow woven from the silks of corn, a belt made from the broad green blades of the same plant, a tall pointed hat made from the same kind of material and from the top which waved a yellow corn tassel. He wore green leggings woven from kow-e-nuh, the green stringy moss that forms in springs and ponds. His moccasins were beautifully embroidered with flowers and butterflies. In his hand he carried an ear of green corn.

His whole appearance proclaimed him a stranger and as Ko-chin-ne-nako gaped in wonder, he spoke to her in a very pleasing voice asking her what she was doing. She told him that on account of the cold and drouth, the people of Kush-kut-ret were forced to eat the leaves of the cactus to keep from starving.

"Here," said the young man, handing her the ear of green corn. "Eat this and I will go and bring more that you may take home with you."

He left her and soon disappeared going towards the south. In a short time he returned bringing with him a big load of green corn. Ko-chin-ne-nako asked him where he had gathered corn and if it grew near by. "No," he replied, "it is from my home far away to the south, where the corn grows and the flowers bloom all the year around. Would you not like to accompany me back to my country?" Ko-chin-ne-nako replied that his home must be very beautiful, but that she could not go with him because she was the wife of Sh-ah-cock. And then she told him of her alliance with the Spirit of Winter, and admitted that her husband was very cold and disagreeable and that she did not love him. The strange young man urged her to go with him to the warm land of the south, saying that he did not fear Sh-ah-cock. But Ko-chin-ne-nako would not consent. So the stranger directed her to return to her home with the corn he had brought and cautioned her not to throw away any of the husks out of the door. Upon leaving he said to her, "you must meet me at this place tomorrow. I will bring more corn for you."

Ko-chin-ne-nako had not proceeded far on her homeward way ere she met her sisters who, having become uneasy because of her long absence, had come in search of her. They were greatly surprised at seeing her with an armful of corn instead of cactus. Ko-chin-ne-nako told them the whole story of how she had obtained it, and thereby only added wonderment to their surprise. They helped her to carry the corn home; and there she again had to tell her story to her father and mother.

When she had described the stranger even from his peaked hat to his butterfly moccasins, and had told them that she was to meet him again on the day following, Hut-cha-mun Ki-uk, the father, exclaimed:

"It is Mi-o-chin!"

"It is Mi-o-chin! It is Mi-o-chin!," echoed the mother. "Tomorrow you must bring him home with you."

The next day Ko-chin-ne-nako went again to the spot where she had met Mi-o-chin, for it was indeed Mi-o-chin, the Spirit of Summer. He was already there, awaiting her coming. With him he had brought a huge bundle of corn.

Ko-chin-ne-nako pressed upon him the invitation of her parents to accompany her home, so together they carried the corn to Kush-kut-ret. When it had been distributed there was sufficient to feed all the people of the city. Amid great rejoicing and thanksgiving, Mi-o-chin was welcomed at the Hotchin's (ruler's) house.

In the evening, as was his custom, Sh-ah-cock, the Spirit of the Winter, returned to his home. He came in a blinding storm of snow and hail and sleet, for he was in a boisterous mood. On approaching the city, he felt within his bones that Mi-o-chin was there, so he called in a loud and blustering voice:

"Ha! Mi-o-chin, are you here?"

For answer, Mi-o-chin advanced to meet him.

Then Sh-ah-cock, beholding him, called again,

"Ha! Mi-o-chin, I will destroy you."

"Ha! Sh-ah-cock, I will destroy you," replied Mi-o-chin, still advancing.

Sh-ah-cock paused, irresolute. He was covered from head to foot with frost (skah). Icycles [sic] (ya-pet-tu-ne) draped him round. The fierce, cold wind proceeded from his nostrils.

As Mi-o-chin drew near, the wintry wind changed to a warm

229

summer breeze. The frost and icycles melted and displayed beneath them, the dry, bleached bulrushes (ska-ra-ru-ka) in which Sh-ah-cock was clad.

Seeing that he was doomed to defeat, Sh-ah-cock cried out:

"I will not fight you now, for we cannot try our powers. We will make ready, and in four days from this time, we will meet here and fight for supremacy. The victor shall claim Ko-chin-ne-nako for his wife."

With this, Sh-ah-cock withdrew in rage. The wind again roared and shook the very houses; but the people were warm within them, for Mi-o-chin was with them.

The next day Mi-o-chin left Kush Kutret for his home in the south. Arriving there, he began to make his preparations to meet Sh-ah-cock in battle.

First he sent an eagle as a messenger to his friend, Ya-chun-ne-ne-moot (kind of shaley rock that becomes very hot in the fire), who lived in the west, requesting him to come and help to battle Sh-ah-cock. Then he called together the birds and the four legged animals—all those that live in sunny climes. For his advance guard and shield he selected the bat (pickikke), as its tough skin would best resist the sleet and hail that Sh-ah-cock would hurl at him.

Meantime Sh-ah-cock had gone to his home in the north to make his preparations for battle. To his aid he called all the winter birds and all of the four legged animals of the wintry climates. For his advance guard and shield he selected Shro-ak-ah (a magpie).

When these formidable forces had been mustered by the rivals, they advanced, Mi-o-chin from the south and Sh-ah-cock from the north, in battle array.

Ya-chun-ne-ne-moot kindled his fires and piled great heaps of resinous fuel upon them until volumes of steam and smoke ascended, forming enormous clouds that hurried forward toward Kush-kut-ret and the battle ground. Upon these clouds rode Mi-o-chin, the Spirit of Summer, and his vast army. All the animals of the army, encountering the smoke from Ya-chun-ne-ne-moot's fires, were colored by the smoke so that, from that day, the animals from the south have been black or brown in color.

Sh-ah-cock and his army came out of the north in a howling blizzard and borne forward on black storm clouds driven by a freezing wintry wind. As he came on, the lakes and rivers over which he passed were frozen and the air was filled with blinding sleet.

When the combatants drew near to Kush-kut-ret, they advanced with fearful rapidity. Their arrival upon the field was marked by fierce and terrific strife.

Flashes of lightning darted from Mi-o-chin's clouds. Striking the animals of Sh-ah-cock, they singed the hair upon them, and turned it white, so that, from that day, the animals from the north have worn a covering of white or have white markings upon them.

From the south, the black clouds still rolled upward, the thunder spoke again and again. Clouds of smoke and vapor rushed onward, melting the snow and ice weapons of Sh-ah-cock and compelling him, at length, to retire from the field. Mi-o-chin, assured of victory, pursued him. To save himself from total defeat and destruction, Sh-ah-cock called for armistice.

This being granted on the part of Mi-o-chin, the rivals met at Kush-kut-ret to arrange the terms of the treaty. Sh-ah-cock acknowledged himself defeated. He consented to give up Ko-chin-ne-nako to Mi-o-chin. This concession was received with rejoicing by Ko-chin-ne-nako and all the people of Kush-kut-ret.

It was then agreed between the late combatants that, for all time thereafter, Mi-o-chin was to rule at Kush-kut-ret during one-half of the year, and Sh-ah-cock was to rule during the remaining half, and that neither should molest the other.[3]

John Gunn's version has a formal plot structure that makes the account seem to be a narrative. But had he translated it directly from the Keres, even in "narrative" form, as in a storytelling session, its ritual nature would have been clearer.

I can only surmise about how the account might go if it were done that way, basing my ideas on renderings of Keres rituals in narrative forms I am acquainted with. But a direct translation from the Keres would have sounded more like the following than like Gunn's rendition of it:

Long ago. Eh. There in the North. Yellow Woman. Up northward she went. Then she picked burrs and cactus. Then here went Summer. From the south he came. Above there he arrived. Thus spoke Summer. "Are you here? How is it going?" said Summer. "Did you come here?" thus said Yellow Woman. Then answered Yellow Woman. "I pick these poor things because I am hungry." "Why do you not eat corn and melons?" asked Summer. Then he gave her some corn and melons. "Take it!" Then thus spoke

Yellow Woman, "It is good. Let us go. To my house I take you." "Is not your husband there?" "No. He went hunting deer. Today at night he will come back."

Then in the north they arrived. In the west they went down. Arrived then they in the east. "Are you here?" Remembering Prayer Sticks said. "Yes" Summer said. "How is it going?" Summer said. Then he said, "Your daughter Yellow Woman, she brought me here." "Eh. That is good." Thus spoke Remembering Prayer Sticks.

The story would continue, with many of the elements contained in Gunn's version but organized along the axis of directions, movement of the participants, their maternal relationships to each other (daughter, mother, mother chief, etc.), and events sketched in only as they pertained to directions and the division of the year into its ritual/ ceremonial segments, one belonging to the Kurena (summer supernaturals or powers who are connected to the summer people or clans) and the other belonging to the Kashare, perhaps in conjunction with the Kopishtaya, the Spirits.

Summer, Miochin, is the Shiwana who lives on the south mountain, and Sh-ah-cock is the Shiwana who lives on the north mountain.[4] It is interesting to note that the Kurena wear three eagle feathers and ctc'otika' feathers (white striped) on their heads, bells, and woman's dress and carry a reed flute, which perhaps is connected with Iyatiku's sister, Istoakoa, Reed Woman.

A Keres Interpretation

When a traditional Keres reads the tale of Kochinnenako, she listens with certain information about her people in mind: she knows, for example, that Hutchamun Kiuk (properly it means Remembering Prayer Sticks, though Gunn translates it as Broken Prayer Sticks)[5] refers to the ritual (sacred) identity of the cacique and that the story is a narrative version of a ceremony related to the planting of corn. She knows that Lagunas and Acomas don't have rulers in the Anglo-European sense of monarchs, lords, and such (though they do, in recent times, have elected governors, but that's another matter, and that a person's social status is determined by her mother's clan and position in it rather than by her relationship to the cacique as his daughter.

(Actually, in various accounts, the cacique refers to Yellow Woman as his mother, so the designation of her as his daughter is troublesome unless one is aware that relationships in the context of their ritual significance are being delineated here.)

In any case, our hypothetical Keres reader also knows that the story is about a ritual that takes place every year and that the battle imagery refers to events that take place during the ritual; she is also aware that Kochinnenako's will, as expressed in her attraction to Miochin, is a central element of the ritual. She knows further that the ritual is partly about the coming of summer and partly about the ritual relationship and exchange of primacy between the two divisions of the tribe, that the ritual described in the narrative is enacted by men, dressed as Miochin and Sh-ah-cock, and that Yellow Woman in her Corn Mother aspect is the center of this and other sacred rites of the Kurena, though in this ritual she may also be danced by a Kurena mask dancer. (Gunn includes a drawing of this figure, made by a Laguna, and titled "Ko-chin-ne-nako—In the Mask Dances.")

The various birds and animals along with the forces such as warm air, fire, heat, sleet, and ice are represented in the ritual; Hutchamun Kiuk, the timekeeper or officer who keeps track of the ritual calendar (which is intrinsically related to the solstices and equinoxes), plays a central role in the ritual. The presence of Kochinnenako and Hutchamun Kiuk and the Shiwana Miochin and Sh-ah-cock means something sacred is going on for the Keres.

The ritual transfers the focus of power, or the ritual axis, held in turn by two moieties whose constitution reflects the earth's bilateral division between summer and winter, from the winter to the summer people. Each moiety's right to power is confirmed by and reflective of the seasons, as it is reflective of and supported by the equinoxes. The power is achieved through the Iyani (ritual empowerment) of female Power,[6] embodied in Kochinnenako as mask dancer and/or Irriaku. Without her empowering mediatorship among the south and north *Shiwana*, the *cacique*, and the village, the season and the moiety cannot change, and balance cannot be maintained.

Unchanging supremacy of one moiety/season over the other is unnatural and therefore undesirable because unilateral dominance of one aspect of existence and of society over another is not reflective of or supported by reality at meteorological or spiritual levels. Sh-ah-cock, is the Winter Spirit or Winter Cloud, a *Shiwana* (one of several categories of supernaturals), and as such is cold and connected to sleet, snow, ice, and hunger. He is not portrayed as cold because he is a source of unmitigated evil (or of evil at all, for that matter).

Half of the people (not numerically but mystically, so to speak) are Winter, and in that sense are Sh-ah-cock; and while this aspect of the group psyche may seem unlovely when its time is over, that same half is lovely indeed in the proper season. Similarly, Miochin will also age—that is, pass his time—and will then give way for his "rival," which is also his complement. Thus balance and harmony are preserved for the village through exchange of dominance, and thus each portion of the community takes responsibility in turn for the prosperity and well-being of the people.

A Keres is of course aware that balance and harmony are two primary assumptions of Keres society and will not approach the narrative wondering whether the handsome Miochin will win the hand of the unhappy wife and triumph over the enemy, thereby heroically saving the people from disaster. The triumph of handsome youth over ugly age or of virile liberality over withered tyranny doesn't make sense in a Keres context because such views contradict central Keres values.

A traditional Keres is satisfied by the story because it reaffirms a Keres sense of rightness, of propriety. It is a tale that affirms ritual understandings, and the Keres reader can visualize the ritual itself when reading Gunn's story. Such a reader is likely to be puzzled by the references to rulers and by the tone of heroic romance but will be reasonably satisfied by the account because in spite of its westernized changes, it still ends happily with the orderly transfer of focality between the moieties and seasons accomplished in seasonal splendor as winter in New Mexico blusters and sleets its way north and summer sings and warms its way home. In the end, the primary Keres values of harmony, balance, and the centrality of woman to maintain them have been validated, and the fundamental Keres principal of proper order is celebrated and affirmed once again.

A Modern Feminist Interpretation

A non-Keres feminist, reading this tale, is likely to wrongly suppose that this narrative is about the importance of men and the use of a passive female figure as a pawn in their bid for power. And, given the way Gunn renders the story, a modern feminist would have good reason to make such an inference. As Gunn recounts it, the story opens in classic patriarchal style and implies certain patriarchal complications: that Kochinnenako has married a man who is violent and destructive. She is the ruler's daughter, which might suggest that the traditional Keres are concerned with the abuses of power of the wealthy. This in turn suggests that the traditional Keres social system, like the traditional Anglo-European ones, suffer from oppressive class structures in which the rich and powerful bring misery to the people, who in the tale are reduced to bare subsistence seemingly as a result of Kochinnenako's unfortunate alliance. A reader making the usual assumptions western readers make when enjoying folk tales will think she is reading a sort of Robin Hood story, replete with a lovely maid Marian, an evil Sheriff, and a green-clad agent of social justice with the Indian name Miochin.

Given the usual assumptions that underlie European folktales, the Western romantic view of the Indian, and the usual antipatriarchal bias that characterizes feminist analysis, a feminist reader might assume that Kochinnenako has been compelled to make an unhappy match by her father the ruler, who must be gaining some power from the alliance. Besides, his name is given as Broken Prayer Stick, which might be taken to mean that he is an unholy man, remiss in his religious duties and weak spiritually.

Gunn's tale does not clarify these issues. Instead it proceeds in a way best calculated to confirm a feminist's interpretation of the tale as only another example of the low status of women in tribal cultures. In accordance with this entrenched American myth, Gunn makes it clear that Kochinnenako is not happy in her marriage; she thinks Sh-ah-cock is "cold and disagreeable, and she cannot love him." Certainly, contemporary American women will read that to mean that Sh-ah-cock is an emotionally uncaring, perhaps cruel husband and that Kochinnenako is forced to accept a life bereft of warmth and love. A feminist reader might imagine that Kochinnenako, like many women, has been socialized into submission. So obedient is she, it seems, so lacking in spirit and independence, that she doesn't seize her chance to escape a bad situation, preferring instead to remain obedient to the patriarchal institution of marriage. As it turns out (in Gunn's tale), Kochinnenako is delivered from the clutches of her violent and unwanted mate by the timely intervention of a much more pleasant man, the hero.

A radical feminist is likely to read the story for its content vis à vis racism and resistance to oppression. From a radical perspective, it seems politically significant that Sh-ah-cock is white. That is, winter is white. Snow is white. Blizzards are white. Clearly, while the story does not give much support to concepts of a people's struggles, it could be construed to mean that the oppressor is designated white in the story because the Keres are engaged in serious combat with white colonial power and, given the significance of storytelling in tribal cultures, are chronicling that struggle in this tale. Read this way, it would seem to acknowledge the right and duty of the people in overthrowing the hated white dictator, who by this account possesses the power of life and death over them.

Briefly, in this context, the story can be read as a tale about the nature of white oppression of Indian people, and Kochinnenako then becomes something of a revolutionary fighter through her collusion with the rebel Miochin in the overthrow of the tyrant Sh-ah-cock. In this reading, the tale becomes a cry for liberation and a direct command to women to aid in the people's struggle to overthrow the colonial powers that drain them of life and strength, deprive them of their rightful prosperity, and threaten them with extinction. An activist teacher could use this tale to instruct women in their obligation to the revolutionary struggle. The daughter, her sisters, and the mother are, after all, implicated in the attempt to bring peace and prosperity to the people; indeed, they are central to it. Such a teacher could, by so using the story, appear to be incorporating culturally diverse materials in the classroom while at the same time exploiting the romantic and moral appeal Native Americans have for other Americans.

When read as a battle narrative, the story as Gunn renders it makes clear that the superiority of Miochin rests as much in his commitment to the welfare of the people as in his military prowess and that because his attempt to free the people is backed up by their invitation to him to come and liberate them, he is successful. Because of his success he is entitled to the hand of the ruler's daughter, Kochinne-nako, one of the traditional Old World spoils of victory. Similarly, Sh-ah-cock is defeated not only because he is violent and oppressive but because the people, like Kochinnenako, find that they cannot love him.

A radical lesbian separatist might find herself uncomfortable with the story even though it is so clearly correct in identifying the enemy as white and violent. But the overthrow of the tyrant is placed squarely in the hands of another male figure, Miochin. This rescue is likely to be viewed with a jaundiced eye by many feminists (though more romantic women might be satisfied with it, since it's a story about an Indian woman of long ago), as Kochinnenako has to await the coming of a handsome stranger for her salvation, and her fate is decided by her father and the more salutary suitor Miochin. No one asks Kochinnenako what she wants to do; the reader is informed that her marriage is not to her liking when she admits to Miochin that she is unhappy. Nevertheless, Kochinnenako acts like any passive, dependent woman who is exploited by the males in her life, who get what they want regardless of her own needs or desires.

Some readers (like myself) might find themselves wondering hopefully whether Miochin isn't really female, disguised by males as one of them in order to buttress their position of relative power. After all, this figure is dressed in yellow and green, the colors of corn, a plant always associated with Woman. Kochinnenako and her sisters are all Corn Women and her mother is, presumably, the head of the Corn Clan; and the Earth Mother of the Keres, Iyatiku, is Corn Woman herself. Alas, I haven't yet found evidence to support such a wishful notion, except that the mask dancer who impersonates Kochinnenako is male, dressed female, which is sort of the obverse side of the wish.

A Feminist-Tribal Interpretation

The feminist interpretation I have sketched—which is a fair representation of one of my early readings from what I took to be a feminist perspective—proceeds from two unspoken assumptions: that women are essentially powerless and that conflict is basic to human existence. The first is a fundamental feminist position, while the second is basic to Anglo-European thought; neither, however, is characteristic of Keres thought. To a modern feminist, marriage is an institution developed to establish and maintain male supremacy; because she is the ruler's daughter, Kochinnenako's choice of a husband determines which male will hold power over the people and who will inherit the throne.[7]

When Western assumptions are applied to tribal narratives, they become mildly confusing and moderately annoying from any perspective.[8] Western assumptions about the nature of human society (and thus of literature) when contextualizing a tribal story or ritual must necessarily leave certain elements unclear. If the battle between Summer Spirit and Winter Spirit is about the triumph of warmth, generosity, and kindness over coldness, miserliness, and cruelty, supremacy of the good over the bad, why does the hero grant his antagonist rights over the village and Kochinnenako for half of each year?

The contexts of Anglo-European and Keres Indian life differ so greatly in virtually every assumption about the nature of reality, society, ethics, female roles, and the sacred importance of seasonal change that simply telling a Keres tale within an Anglo-European narrative context creates a dizzying series of false impressions and unanswerable (perhaps even unposable) questions.

For instance, marriage among traditional Keres is not particularly related to marriage among Anglo-European Americans. As I explain in greater detail in a later essay, paternity is not an issue among traditional Keres people; a child belongs to its mother's clan, not in the sense that she or he is owned by the clan, but in the sense that she or he belongs within it. Another basic difference is the attitude toward conflict; the Keres can best be described as a conflict-phobic people, while Euro-American culture is conflict-centered. So while the orderly and proper annual transference of power from Winter to Summer people through the agency of the Keres central female figure is the major theme of the narrative from a Keres perspective, the triumph of good over evil becomes its major theme when it is retold by a white man.

Essentially what happens is that Summer (a mask dancer dressed as Miochin) asks Kochinnenako permission, in a ritual manner, to enter the village. She (who is either a mask dancer dressed as Yellow Woman, or a Yellow Corn Irriaku) follows a ritual order of responses and actions that enable Summer to enter. The narrative specifies the acts she must perform, the words she must say, and those that are prohibited, such as the command that she not "throw any of the husks out of the door." This command establishes both the identity of Miochin and constitutes his declaration of his ritual intention and his ritual relationship to Kochinnenako.

Agency is Kochinnenako's ritual role here; it is through her ritual agency that the orderly, harmonious transfer of primacy between the Summer and Winter people is accomplished. This transfer takes place at the time of the year that Winter goes north and Summer comes to the pueblo from the south, the time when the sun moves north along the line it makes with the edge of the sun's house as ascertained by the hocheni calendar keeper who determines the proper solar and astronomical times for various ceremonies. Thus, in the proper time, Kochinnenako empowers Summer to enter the village. Kochinnenako's careful observance of the ritual requirements together with the proper conduct of her sisters, her mother, the priests (symbolized by the title Hutchamun Kiuk, whom Gunn identifies as the ruler and Yellow Woman's father, though he could as properly—more properly, actually—be called her mother), the animals and birds, the weather, and the people at last brings summer to the village, ending the winter and the famine that accompanies winter's end.

A feminist who is conscious of tribal thought and practice will know that the real story of Sh-ah-cock and Miochin underscores the central role that woman plays in the orderly life of the people. Reading Gunn's version, she will be aware of the vast gulf between the Lagunas and John Gunn in their understanding of the role of women in a traditional gynecentric society such as that of the western Keres. Knowing that the central role of woman is harmonizing spiritual relationships between the people and the rest of the universe by empowering ritual activities, she will be able to read the story for its western colonial content, aware that Gunn's version reveals more about American consciousness when it meets tribal thought than it reveals about the tribe. When the story is analyzed within the context to which it rightly belongs, its feminist content becomes clear, as do the various purposes to which industrialized patriarchal people can put a tribal story.

If she is familiar with the ritual color code of this particular group of Native Americans, a feminist will know that white is the color of Shipap, the place where the four rivers of life come together and where our Mother Iyatiku lives. Thus she will know that it is appropriate that the Spirit of Woman's Power/Being (Yellow Woman) be "married" (that is, ritually connected in energy-transferring gestalts) first with Winter who is the power signified by the color white, which informs clouds, the Mountain Tse-pina, Shipap, originating Power, Koshare, the north and northwest, and that half of the year, and then with Summer, whose color powers are yellow and green, which inform Kurena, sunrise, the growing and ripening time of Mother Earth, and whose direction is south and southeast and that portion of the year.

A feminist will know that the story is about how the Mother Corn Iyatiku's "daughter," that is, her essence in one of its aspects, comes to live as Remembering Prayer Sticks' daughter first with the Winter people and then with the Summer people, and so on.

The net effect of Gunn's rendition of the story is the unhappy wedding of the woman-centered tradition of the western Keres to patriarchal Anglo-European tradition and thus the dislocation of the central position of Keres women by their assumption under the rule of the men. When one understands that the hocheni is the person who tells the time and prays for all the people, even the white people, and that the Hutchamun Kiuk is the ruler only in the sense that the Constitution of the United States is the ruler of the citizens and government of the United States, then the Keres organization of women, men, spirit folk, equinoxes, seasons, and clouds into a balanced and integral dynamic will be seen reflected in the narrative. Knowing this, a feminist will also be able to see how the interpolations of patriarchal thinking distort all the relationships in the story and, by extension, how such impositions of patriarchy on gynocracy disorder harmonious social and spiritual relationships.

A careful feminist-tribal analysis of Gunn's rendition of a story that would be better titled "The Transfer of Ianyi (ritual power, sacred power) from Winter to Summer" will provide a tribally conscious feminist with an interesting example of how colonization works, however consciously or unconsciously to misinform both the colonized and the colonizer. She will be able to note the process by which the victim of the translation process, the Keres woman who reads the tale, is misinformed because she reads Gunn's book. Even though she knows that something odd is happening in the tale, she is not likely to apply sophisticated feminist analysis to the rendition; in the absence of real knowledge of the colonizing process of story-changing, she is all too likely to find bits of the Gunn tale sticking in her mind and subtly altering her perception of herself, her role in her society, and her relationship to the larger world.

The hazard to male Keres readers is, of course, equally great. They are likely to imagine that the proper relationship of women to men is subservience. And it is because of such a shockingly untraditional modern interpretation, brought on as much by reading Gunn as by other, perhaps more obvious societal mechanisms, that the relationships between men and women are so severely disordered at Laguna that wife-abuse, rape, and battery of women there has reached frightening levels in recent years.

Political Implications of Narrative Structure

The changes Gunn has made in the narrative are not only changes in content; they are structural as well. One useful social function of traditional tribal literature is its tendency to distribute value evenly among various elements, providing a model or pattern for egalitarian structuring of society as well as literature. However, egalitarian structures in either literature or society are not easily "read" by hierarchically inclined westerners.

Still, the tendency to equal distribution of value among all elements in a field, whether the field is social, spiritual, or aesthetic (and the distinction is moot when tribal materials are under discussion), is an integral part of tribal consciousness and is reflected in tribal social and aesthetic systems all over the Americas. In this structural framework, no single element is foregrounded, leaving the others to supply "background." Thus, properly speaking, there are no heroes, no villains, no chorus, no setting (in the sense of inert ground against which dramas are played out). There are no minor characters, and foreground slips along from one focal point to another until all the pertinent elements in the ritual conversation have had their say.

In tribal literatures, the timing of the foregrounding of various elements is dependent on the purpose the narrative is intended to serve. Tribal art functions something like a forest in which all elements coexist, where each is integral to the being of the others. Depending on the season, the interplay of various life forms, the state of the overall biosphere and psychosphere, and the woman's reason for being there, certain plants will leap into focus on certain occasions. For example, when tribal women on the eastern seaboard went out to gather sassafras, what they noticed, what stood out sharply in their attention, were the sassafras plants. But when they went out to get maple sugar, maples became foregrounded. But the foregrounding of sassafras or maple in no way lessens the value of the other plants or other features of the forest. When a woman goes after maple syrup, she is aware of the other plant forms that are also present.

In the same way, a story that is intended to convey the importance of the Grandmother Spirits will focus on grandmothers in their interaction with grandchildren and will convey little information about uncles. Traditional tales will make a number of points, and a number of elements will be present, all of which will bear some relationship to the subject of the story. Within the time the storyteller has alloted to the story, and depending on the interests and needs of her audience at the time of the storytelling, each of these elements will receive its proper due.

Traditional American Indian stories work dynamically among clusters of loosely interconnected circles. The focus of the action shifts from one character to another as the story unfolds. There is no "point of view" as the term is generally understood, unless the action itself, the story's purpose, can be termed "point of view." But as the old tales are translated and rendered in English, the western notion of proper fictional form takes over the tribal narrative. Soon there appear to be heroes, point of view, conflict, crisis, and resolution, and as western tastes in story crafting are imposed on the narrative structure of the ritual story, the result is a western story with Indian characters. Mournfully, the new form often becomes confused with the archaic form by the very people whose tradition has been re-formed.

The story Gunn calls "Sh-ah-cock and Mi-o-chin or The Battle of the Seasons" might be better termed "How Kochinnenako Balanced the World," though even then the title would be misleading to American readers, for they would see Kochinnenako as the heroine, the foreground of the story. They would see her as the central figure of the action, and of course that would be wrong. There is no central figure in the tale, though there is a central point. The point is concerned with the proper process of a shift in focus, not the resolution of a conflict. Kochinnenako's part in the process is agency, not heroics; even in Gunn's version, she does nothing heroic. A situation presents itself in the proper time, and Yellow Woman acts in accordance with the dictates of timing, using proper ritual as her mode. But the people cannot go from Winter into Summer without conscious acceptance of Miochin, and Yellow Woman's invitation to him, an acceptance that is encouraged and supported by all involved, constitutes a tribal act.

The "battle" between Summer and Winter is an accurate description of seasonal change in central New Mexico during the spring. This comes through in the Gunn rendition, but because the story is focused on conflict rather than on balance, the meteorological facts and their intrinsic relationship to human ritual are obscured. Only a non-Indian mind, accustomed to interpreting events in terms of battle, struggle, and conflict, would assume that the process of transfer had to occur through a battle replete with protagonist, antagonist, a cast of thousands, and a pretty girl as the prize. For who but an industrialized patriarch would think that winter can be vanquished? Winter and Summer enjoy a relationship based on complementarity, mutuality, and this is the moral significance of the tale.

Tribal Narratives and Women's Lives

Reading American Indian traditional stories and songs is not an easy task. Adequate comprehension requires that the reader be aware that Indians never think like whites and that any typeset version of traditional materials is distorting.

In many ways, literary conventions, as well as the conventions of literacy, militate against an understanding of traditional tribal materials. Western technological-industrialized minds cannot adequately interpret tribal materials because they are generally trained to perceive their entire world in ways that are alien to tribal understandings.

This problem is not exclusive to tribal literature. It is one that all ethnic writers who write out of a tribal or folk tradition face, and one that is also shared by women writers, who, after all, inhabit a separate folk tradition. Much of women's culture bears marked resemblance to tribal culture. The perceptual modes that women, even those of us who are literate, industrialized, and reared within masculinist academic traditions, habitually engage in more closely resemble inclusive-field perception than excluding foreground-background perceptions.

Women's traditional occupations, their arts and crafts, and their literature and philosophies are more often accretive than linear, more achronological than chronological, and more dependent on harmonious relationships of all elements within a field of perception than western culture in general is thought to be. Indeed, the patchwork quilt is the best material example I can think of to describe the plot and process of a traditional tribal narrative, and quilting is a non-Indian woman's art, one that Indian women have taken to avidly and that they display in their ceremonies, rituals, and social gatherings as well as in their homes.

It is the nature of woman's existence to be and to create background. This fact, viewed with unhappiness by many feminists, is of ultimate importance in a tribal context. Certainly no art object is bereft of background. Certainly the contents and tone of one's background will largely determine the direction and meaning of one's life and, therefore, the meaning and effect of one's performance in any given sphere of activity.

Westerners have for a long time discounted the importance of background. The earth herself, which is our most inclusive background, is dealt with summarily as a source of food, metals, water, and profit, while the fact that she is the fundamental agent of all planetary life is blithely ignored. Similarly, women's activities—cooking, planting, harvesting, preservation, storage, homebuilding, decorating, maintaining, doctoring, nursing, soothing, and healing, along with the bearing, nurturing, and rearing of children—are devalued as blithely.

An antibackground bias is bound to have social costs that have so far remained unexplored, but elite attitudes toward workers, nonwhite races, and women are all part of the price we pay for overvaluing the foreground.

In the western mind, shadows highlight the foreground. In contrast, in the tribal view the mutual relationships among shadows and light in all their varying degrees of intensity create a living web of definition and depth, and significance arises from their interplay. Traditional and contemporary tribal arts and crafts testify powerfully to the importance of balance among all elements in tribal perception, aesthetics, and social systems.

Traditional peoples perceive their world in a unified-field fashion that is very different from the single-focus perception that generally characterizes western masculinist, monotheistic modes of perception. Because of this, tribal cultures are consistently misperceived and misrepresented by nontribal folklorists, ethnographers, artists, writers, and social workers. A number of scholars have recently addressed this issue, but they have had little success because the demands of type and of analysis are, after all, linear and fixed, while the requirements of tribal literatures are accretive and fluid. The one is unidimensional, monolithic, excluding, and chronological while the other is multidimensional, achronological, and including.

How one teaches or writes about the one perspective in terms of the other is problematic. This essay itself is a pale representation of a tribal understanding of the Kochinnenako tale. I am acutely aware that much of what I have said is likely to be understood in ways I did not intend, and I am also aware of how much I did not say that probably needed to be said if the real story of the transfer of responsibility from one segment of the tribe to the other is to be made clear.

In the end, the tale I have analyzed is not about Kochinnenako or Sh-ah-cock and Miochin. It is about the change of seasons and it is about the centrality of woman as agent and empowerer of that change. It is about how a people engage themselves as a people within the spiritual cosmos and in an ordered and proper way that bestows the dignity of each upon all with careful respect, folkish humor, and ceremonial delight. It is about how everyone is part of the background that shapes the meaning and value of each person's life. It is about propriety, mutuality, and the dynamics of socioenvironmental change.

Hwame, Koshkalaka, and the Rest: Lesbians in American Indian Cultures

The lesbian is to the American Indian what the Indian is to the American—invisible. According to ethnographers' accounts, among the tribes there were women warriors, women leaders, women shamans, women husbands, but whether any of these were lesbians is seldom mentioned. On the few occasions lesbianism is referred to, it is with regard to a specific individual who is noted because she is a lesbian. This fosters the impression of uniform heterosexuality among Indian women except for a very few who deviate from that norm. It is an impression that is false.

In all the hundreds, perhaps thousands, of books and articles about American Indians that I have read while pursuing my studies or preparing for the variety of courses in American Indian studies that I have taught, I have encountered no reference to lesbians except one.[1] That one was contained in a novel by Fred Manfred, *The Manly-Hearted Woman*,[2] and though its protagonist dresses as a man and rejects her feminine role and though she marries a woman, the writer is very explicit: she and her wife do not share sexual intimacies, a possibility that seems beyond the writer's ability to envision. Indeed, the protagonist eventually falls in love with a rather strange young warrior who possesses enormous sexual prowess (given him by spirit power and a curious genetic circumstance). After the warrior's death the manly hearted woman divorces her wife and returns to woman's garb and occupation, discarding the spirit stone that has determined her life to that point. It seems that heterosexual love conquers all—even ritual tradition, custom, and spirit command.

Direct references to lesbians or lesbianism among American Indians are even more sparse than those about homosexual men (usually called hermaphrodites or berdache or, less often, transvestites), occurring almost outside the body of information about tribal life or included in ways that underscore white attitudes about tribes, Indians, and homosexuality. Consequently, much of my discussion of lesbians is necessarily conjectural, based on secure knowledge of American Indian social systems and customs that I have gathered from formal study, personal experience, and personally communicated information from other Indians as well as from my own knowledge of lesbian culture and practice.

My idea in this essay is to explore lesbianism within a larger social and spiritual tribal context as contrasted with its occurrence as an individual aberration that might show up on occasion but that has nothing to do with tribal life in general. Because tribal civilizations (like all others) function in entire gestalts and because they are based on the life-enhancing interconnectedness of all things, it is my contention that gayness, whether female or male, traditionally functions positively within tribal groups.

Certainly, the chances that aboriginal American women formed affectional alliances are enormous. Many tribes had marked tendency to encourage virginity or some version of chastity among pubescent women; this tendency rarely affected the sexual habits of married women, however, and it referred to intercourse with males. Nothing is said, to my knowledge, about sexual liaisons between women, except indirectly. It is equally likely that such relationships were practiced with social sanction, though no one is presently talking about this. The history of Native America is selective; and those matters pertaining to women that might contradict a western patriarchal world-view are carefully selected out.

Some suggestions about how things were in "time immemorial," as the old folks refer to pre-contact times, have managed to find their way into contemporary literature about American Indians. Many tribes have recorded stories concerning daughters born to spirit women who were dwelling alone on earth. These daughters then would become the mothers of entire tribes. In one such tale, First Mother was "born of the dew of the leaf of the beautiful plant."[3] Such tales point to a time prior to the advent of patriarchy. While historical and archeological evidence suggests that this time predated European contact in some regions of the western hemisphere, the change in cultural orientation was still proceeding. The tribes became more male-oriented and more male-dominated as acculturation accelerated. As this process continued, less and less was likely to be said by American Indians about lesbians among them. Indeed, less and less about women in any position other than that sanctioned by missionaries was likely to be recorded.

There are a number of understandings about the entire issue that will be important in my discussion of American Indian women, heterosexual or lesbian. It is my contention and belief that those two groups were not nearly as separate as modern lesbian and straight women are. My belief is based on my understanding of the cultures and social systems in which women lived. These societies were tribal, and tribal consciousness, with its attendant social structures, differs enormously from that of the contemporary western world.

This difference requires new understanding of a number of concepts. The concept of family, the concept of community, the concept of women, the concept of bonding and belonging, and the concept of power were all distinctly understood in a tribal matrix; and those concepts were/are very different from those current in modern America.

Women and Family in Tribal Societies

Among American Indians, Spirit-related persons are perceived as more closely linked than blood-related persons. Understanding this primary difference between American Indian values and modern Euro-Anglo-American Judeo-Christian values is critical to understanding Indian familial structures and the context in which lesbians functioned. For American Indian people, the primary value was relationship to the Spirit world. All else was determined by the essential nature of this understanding. Spirits, gods and goddesses, metaphysical/occult forces, and the right means of relating to them determined the tribes' every institution, every custom, every endeavor and pastime. This was not peculiar to inhabitants of the western hemisphere, incidentally; it was at one time the primary value of all tribal people on earth.

Relationship to the Spirit world has been of primary value to tribal people, but not to those who have studied them. Folklorists and ethnographers have other values that permeate their work and their understandings, so that most of what they have recorded or concluded about American Indians is simply wrong. Countless examples could illustrate this basic misunderstanding, but let me share just one, culled from the work of one of the most influential anthropologists, Bronislaw Malinowski. His massive study of the Keres Pueblo Acoma presumably qualified him as an authority on mother-right society in North America. In *Sex, Culture, and Myth* Malinowski wrote: "Patrilocal households are 'united households,' while 'split households' are the exclusive phenomena of matrilocal mother-right cultures."[4] While acknowledging that economic considerations alone do not determine the structure of marriage patterns, Malinowski fails to recognize marriage as a construct founded on laws derived from conversations with Spirits. The primary unit for a tribe is not, as he suggests, the household; even the term is misleading, because a tribal "household" includes a number of individuals who are clan rather than blood relatives. For nontribal people, "household" typically means a unit composed of a father, mother, and offspring—though contemporary living arrangements often deviate from that stereotyped conception. A tribal household might encompass assorted blood-kin, medicine society "kin," adoptees, servants, and visitors who have a clan or supernatural claim on membership although they are biologically unrelated to the rest of the household. Writing about tribal societies in Oceania, Malinowski wrote: "Throughout Oceania a network of obligations unites the members of the community and overrules the economic autonomy of the household."[5] To a tribal person, the very notion of the household's autonomy appears to be nonsensical. To exemplify his view of tribal practices, Malinowski cites the Trobriand Islanders' requirement that a man give approximately half of his produce to his sister(s) and another portion to other relatives, thus using only the remainder for "his own household" which, Malinowski concedes, is largely supported by the wife's brother(s) and other relatives. I mention this example from a tribe that is not American Indian because Malinowski himself encourages generalization: "Economic obligations," he continues, which "cut across the closed unity of the household could be quoted from every single tribe of which we have adequate information."[6]

Malinowski and other researchers have dismissed the household as an economic unit but have continued to perceive households from the viewpoint of the nuclear family—father, mother(s), and offspring. He remains within the accepted, biased European understanding of "household" when he states:

> The most important examples [of split households] come from the communities organised in extreme mother-right, where husband and wife are in most matters members of different households, and their mutual economic contributions show the character of gifts rather than of mutual maintenance.[7]

The case of matrifocal-matrilocal households seems extreme only when one defines "household" in terms that do not allow for various styles of bonding. Malinowski believes that this "extreme mother-right" method of housing people is exceptional. He does concede that it results from conditions found in high-level cultures rather than in "primitive" ones[8]—which is an extremely interesting observation. But in making it, he again relies on some assumptions that are not justified by available evidence.

If "household" signifies housing and food-provision systems, then the living arrangements of American Indians pose numerous problems, the matter of father-right versus mother-right being only one. In fact, Indians were inclined to live wherever they found themselves, if living signifies where you stash your belongings, where you take your meals, or where you sleep. Throughout North America, men were inclined to have little personal paraphernalia, to eat wherever they were when mealtime came, and to sleep in whatever spot was convenient when they were tired. Clan, band, and medicine-society affiliations had a primary bearing on these arrangements, as did the across-the-board separation of the sexes practiced formally or informally by most tribes.

Malinowski's view assumes that households may take various forms but that in any case they are unified to the extent that they may be spoken of as "mine" by a male who is husband to a woman and claims to be the father of her children. The "extreme" case of the "split household" occurs when a man who is identified as a woman's husband does not contribute to her economic life except by giving presents. This notion of "household" is quite removed from any held by tribal people with which I am familiar. Even among contemporary American Indians, a male who is identified as the husband of the lady of the house may not be (and often is not) the father of her children. But according to Malinowski, "The most important fact about such extreme matriarchal conditions [as among the Pueblo and several other groups cited] is that even there the principle of social legitimacy holds good; that though the father is domestically and economically almost superfluous, he is legally indispensable and the main bond of union between such matrilineal and matrilocal consorts is parenthood."⁹

Carefully examined, the foregoing observation makes no sense; even if it did, it suggests that although fatherhood is irrelevant in the home or office, a male remains indispensable because his presence (which may be very infrequent) confers legitimacy on something. Indeed.

Analyses like those of Malinowski can be explained only by the distorting function of cultural bias. A Pueblo husband is important because husbands are important. But I have known many "husbands" who had several "wives" and could claim that a number of women (who might or might not be claimed as wives) were the mothers of their children. And this remains the case despite some two to five hundred years of Christian influence. As an old Laguna woman has said in reference to these matters in the long ago, "We were very careless about such things then."

Actually, the legitimacy of motherhood was determined by its very existence. A woman who gave birth was a mother as long as she had a living child, and the source of a household's legitimacy was its very existence. American Indians were and are mystical, but they were and are a very practical people.

While there can be little question about the fact that most women married, perhaps several times, it is important to remember that tribal marriages often bore little resemblance to western concepts of that institution. Much that has been written about marriage as practiced among American Indians is wrong.

Among many tribes divorce was an easy matter for both women and men, and movement of individuals from one household to another was fluid and essentially unconstrained. There are many exceptions to this, for the tribes were distinct social groups; but many had patterns that did not use sexual constraint as a means of social control. Within such systems, individual action was believed to be directed by Spirits (through dreams, visions, direct encounter, or possession of power objects such as stones, shells, masks, or fetishes). In this context it is quite possible that lesbianism was practiced rather commonly, as long as the individuals cooperated with the larger social customs.

Women were generally constrained to have children, but in many tribes, childbearing meant empowerment. It was the passport to maturity and inclusion in woman-culture. An important point is that women who did not have children because of constitutional, personal, or Spirit-directed disinclination had other ways to experience Spirit instruction and stabilization, to exercise power, and to be mothers.

"Family" did not mean what is usually meant by that term in the modern western world. One's family might have been defined in biological terms as those to whom one was blood kin. More often it was defined by other considerations; spiritual kinship was at least as important a factor as "blood." Membership in a certain clan related one to many people in very close ways, though the biological connection might be so distant as to be practically nonexistent. This facet of familial ordering has been much obscured by the presence of white Christian influence and its New Testament insistence that the term "family" refers to mother, father, and children, and those others who are directly related to mother and father. In this construct, all persons who can point to common direct-line ancestors are in some sense related, though the individual's distance from that ancestor will determine the "degree" of relationship to other descendants of that ancestor.

Among many American Indians, family is a matter of clan membership. If clan membership is determined by your mother, and if your father has a number of wives, you are not related to the children of his other wives unless they themselves happen to be related to your mother. So half-siblings in the white way might be unrelated in an Indian way. Or in some tribes, the children of your mother's sister might be considered siblings, while those of your father's brother would be the equivalent of cousins. These distinctions should demonstrate that the concept of family can mean something very different to an Indian than it does to a non-Indian.

In gynecentric systems, a unified household is one in which the relationships among women and their descendants and sisters are ordered; a split household is one in which this is not the case. A community, then, is an ordering of sister relationships that determine who can depend on whom for what. Male relationships are ordered in accordance with the maternal principle; a male's spiritual and economic placement and the attendant responsibilities are determined by his membership in the community of sisterhood. A new acquaintance in town might be asked, "Who is your mother?" The answer identifies the person and determines the ensuing relationship between the questioner and the newcomer.

Again, community in the non-Indian modern world tends to mean people who occupy a definable geographical area or who share a culture (lifestyle) or occupation. It can extend to include people who share an important common interest—political, avocational, or spiritual. But "community" in the American Indian world can mean those who are of a similar clan and Spirit; those who are encompassed by a particular Spirit-being are members of a community. In fact, this was the meaning most often given to the concept in traditional tribal cultures. So it was not impossible that members of a community could have been a number of women who "belonged" to a given medicine society or who were alike in that they shared consciousness of a certain Spirit.

Women and Power

Any discussion of the status of women in general and of lesbians in particular cannot hope for accuracy if one misunderstands women's power in tribal societies. Indeed, in a recent random sampling of general ethnographies of several groups, I have noted that all matters of female life in the group under discussion can be found under the heading "Woman." This heading is divided into marriage, childbearing, childrearing, housekeeping, and, perhaps, menstruation. The discussions are neatly ordered according to middle-class white views about where women fit into social schemes, but they contain a number of false implications, not the least of which is that men don't marry, have children, or participate in childrearing.

It is clear, I think, that the ground we are exploring here is obscure: women in general have not been taken seriously by ethnographers or folklorists, and explorations that have been done have largely been distorted by the preconceptions engendered by a patriarchal world-view, in which lesbians are said not to exist and women are perceived as oppressed, burdened, powerless, and peripheral to interesting accounts of human affairs except in that they have babies.

In her discussion of the "universal" devaluation of women, Sherry Ortner cites the Crow, a matrilineal American Indian tribe that places women in high status. Crow Women, according to Ortner, were nevertheless required to ride "inferior" horses during menstruation and were prohibited from participating in ceremonies during their periods. She cites anthropologist Robert Lowie as stating that menstruation was seen as "a source of contamination, for [women] were not allowed to approach either a wounded man or men starting on a war party," and as a "threat to warfare, one of the most valued institutions of the tribe, one that is central to their [the tribe's] definition."[10] She interprets this evidence as proving that the Crow believed women inferior to men, even though many other aspects of their social structure and ritual life deny this assertion. But I think the vital question is why she interprets the evidence to demonstrate female inferiority and to mean that traditionally low status was woman's lot among them. She does not suggest that the present-day status of women among them might be attributable to the impact of colonization because she is attempting to prove that women have always and everywhere been oppressed by men. I contend that women have held a great deal of power in ritual cultures and that evidence supporting this contention is at least as massive as the evidence of our ignominy.

Ortner's conclusion that menstruation was perceived as dirty and contaminating by tribal people and that they saw it in the same light in which it was viewed by patriarchal peoples is simply wrong. Tribal people view menstruation as a "medicine" of such power that it can cause the death of certain people, such as men on the eve of combat, or pregnant women. Menstruating (or any other) Crow women do not go near a particularly sacred medicine bundle, and menstruating women are not allowed among warriors getting ready for battle, or those who have been wounded, because women are perceived to be possessed of a singular power, most vital during menstruation, puberty, and pregnancy, that weakens men's powers—physical, spiritual, or magical. The Crow and many other American Indians do not perceive signs of womanness as contamination; rather they view them as so powerful that other "medicines" may be canceled by the very presence of that power.

The Oglala Holy Man John (Fire) Lame Deer has commented that the Oglalas do not view menstruation, which they call isnati ("dwelling alone"), as "something unclean or to be ashamed of." Rather it was something sacred; a girl's first period was greeted by celebration. "But," he continues, "we thought that menstruation had a strange power that could bring harm under some circumstances. This power could work in some cases against the girl, in other cases against somebody else."[11]

Lois Paul has found similar attitudes in the context of a peasant culture. In her essay "Work and Sex in a Guatemalan Village," she discusses the power that menstruation, pregnancy, and menarche are believed to possess. She notes the belief of the peasant Pedranos in Guatemala that menstruating women can seriously impair a man's health or even kill him by stepping over him or putting menstrual blood in his food.[12]

Power among tribal people is not perceived as political or economic, though status and material possessions can and often do derive from it. Power is conceived of as being supernatural and paranormal. It is a matter of spirit involvement and destiny. Woman's power comes automatically, by virtue of her femaleness, her natural and necessary fecundity, and her personal acquaintance with blood. The Arapaho felt that dying in war and dying in childbirth were of the same level of spiritual accomplishment. In fact, there are suggestions in the literature on ritualism and tribal ceremony that warriors and male initiates into medicine societies gain their supernatural powers by imitating ritually the processes that women undergo naturally.

The power of women can be controlled and directed only by other women who possess power that is equal in magnitude but that is focused and under their control. A woman who is older is more cognizant of what that power entails, the kinds of destruction it can cause, and the ways in which it can be directed and used for good. Thus pubescent women are placed under the care of older women and are trained in manners and customs of modesty so that their powers will not result in harm to themselves or the larger community. Usually, a woman who has borne a child becomes an initiate into the mysteries of womanhood, and if she develops virtues and abilities beyond those automatically conferred on her by nature, she becomes a medicine woman. Often, the medicine woman knows of her destiny in early childhood; such children are watched very carefully so that they will be able to develop in the way ordained for them by the Spirits. Often these children are identified by excessive "sickliness," which leads them to be more reflective than other children and which often necessitates the added vigilance of adults around them.

Eventually, these people will enter into their true profession. How and when they do so will vary from tribe to tribe, but they will probably be well into their maturity before they will be able to practice. The Spirit or Spirits who teach and guide them in their medicine work will not appear for them until they have stabilized. Their health will usually improve, and their hormone-enzyme fluctuations will be regularized. Very often this stabilization will occur in the process of childbearing and nursing; this is one reason why women usually are not fully accepted as part of the woman's community until after the birth of a first child. Maternity was a concept that went far beyond the simple biological sense of the word. It was the prepotent power, the basic right to control and distribute goods, because it was the primary means of producing them. And it was the perfect sign of right spirit-human relationship. Among some modern American Indians this principle is still accepted. The Keres, for example, still recognize the Deity as female, and She is known as Thought Woman, for it is understood that the primary creative force is Thought.

Lesbians and Tribal Life

Simple reason dictates that lesbians did exist widely in tribal cultures, for they exist now. Because they were tribal people, the terms on which they existed must have been suited to the terms of tribal existence. The concepts of tribal cultures and of modern, western cultures are so dissimilar as to make ludicrous attempts to relate the long-ago women who dealt exclusively with women on sexual-emotional and spiritual bases to modern women who have in common an erotic attraction for other women.

This is not to make light of the modern lesbian but rather to convey some sense of the enormity of the cultural gulf that we must come to terms with when examining any phenomenon related to the American Indian. The modern lesbian sees herself as distinct from "society." She may be prone to believe herself somehow out of sync with "normal" women and often suffers great anguish at perceived differences. And while many modern lesbians have come to see themselves as singular but not sick, many of us are not that secure in our self-assessment. Certainly, however we come to terms with our sexuality, we are not in the position of our American Indian foresister who could find safety and security in her bond with another woman because it was perceived to be destined and nurtured by nonhuman entities, as were all Indian pursuits, and was therefore acceptable and respectable (albeit occasionally terrifying) to others in her tribe.

Spheres of influence and activity in American Indian cultures were largely divided between the sexes: there were women—goddesses, spirit-women, mothers, sisters, grandmothers, aunties, shamans, healers, prophets, and daughters; and there were men—gods, fathers, uncles, shamans, healers, diviners, brothers, and sons. What went on in one group was often unknown to the other.

There were points of confluence, of course, such as in matters pertaining to mundane survival. Family-band-clan groups interacted in living arrangements, in the procural or production of food, weaponry, clothing, and living space, and in political function. Men and women came together at certain times to perform social and ceremonial rituals or to undertake massive tasks such as hunts, harvests, or wars. They performed certain reciprocal tasks for one another. But in terms of any real sense of community, there were women and there were men.

Yet women who shared their lives with women did follow the usual custom of marrying. The duration of marriage and the bonding style of marriage differed among tribes. Many peoples practiced serial monogamy; others acknowledged the marriage bond but engaged in sexual activities outside of it. Women's adultery was not viewed with any particular alarm in most tribes, although some tribes did severely punish a woman who "transgressed" the marriage bonds, at least after they had some contact with Christian religious concepts.

But overall women spent a great deal of time together, outside the company of men. They had a whole array of women's rituals, only some of which were related to menstruation or childbearing. Together they spent weeks in menstrual huts; together women tilled their fields, harvested wild foods and herbs, ground grains, prepared skins, smoked or dried foodstuffs, and just visited. Women spent long periods together in their homes and lodges while the men stayed in men's houses or in the woods or were out on hunting or fishing expeditions. Young women were often separated from the larger groups for periods of months or years, as were young men. In such circumstances, lesbianism and homosexuality were probably commonplace. Indeed, same-sex relationships may have been the norm for primary pair-bonding. Families did not consist of nuclear units in any sense. There were clans and bands or villages, but the primary personal unit tended to include members of one's own sex rather than members of the opposite sex. It is questionable whether these practices would be identified as Lesbian by the politically radical lesbian community of today; for while sex between women probably occurred regularly, women also regularly married and raised children, often adopting children if they did not have any.

We should not see relationships among Indian women as being motivated primarily by opportunity. Lesbianism must be viewed in the context of the spiritual orientation of tribal life. It may be possible to distinguish between those women who took advantage of the abundant opportunities to form erotic bonds with other women and those women whose relationships with women were as much a matter of Spirit-direction as of personal preference (though the two were one in some senses).

It might be that some American Indian women could be seen as "dykes," while some could be seen as "lesbians," if one thinks of "dyke" as one who bonds with women to further some Spirit and supernatural directive and "lesbian" as a woman who is emotionally and physically intimate with other women. (The two groups would not have been mutually exclusive.)

The dyke (we might also call her a "ceremonial lesbian") was likely to have been a medicine woman in a special sense. She probably was a participant in the Spirit (intelligence, force field) of an Entity or Deity who was particularly close to earth during the Goddess period (though that Deity is still present in the lives of some American Indian women who practice Her ceremonies and participate actively and knowingly in Her reality). Signs of this Deity remain scattered all over the continent: Snake Mound in Ohio is probably one. La Virgin de Guadalupe is another. There are all sorts of petroglyphs, edifices, and stories concerning some aspect of Her, and Her signs are preserved in much of the lore and literature of many tribes.

Essentially a woman's spiritual way is dependent on the kind of power she possesses, the kind of Spirit to whom she is attached, and the tribe to which she belongs. She is required to follow the lead of Spirits and to carry out the tasks they assign her. For a description of one such rite, Fr. Bernard Haile's translation and notes on the Navajo Beautyway/Night chant is instructive. Such stories abound in the lore and literature of the American Indian people.[13] They all point to a serious event that results in the death of the protagonist, her visit to the Spirit realms from which she finally returns, transformed and powerful. After such events, she no longer belongs to her tribe or family, but to the Spirit teacher who instructed her. This makes her seem "strange" to many of her folk, and, indeed, she may be accused of witchcraft, though that is more likely to be charged at present than it was in the past. A dyke's initiation takes the same course as a male's: she is required to pass grueling physical tests, to lose her mundane persona, and to transform her soul and mind into other forms. (I might note here that among American Indians men are often accused of the same thing. Tales of evil sorcerers abound; in fact, in my reading, they seriously outnumber the tales about sorceresses.)

The Lakota have a word for some of these women, *koskalaka*, which is translated as "young man" or "woman who doesn't want to marry," in our terms, "dyke." These women are said to be the daughters (the followers/practitioners) of a Spirit/Divinity who links two women together making them one in Her power. They do a dance in which a rope is twined between them and coiled to form a "rope baby." The exact purpose or result of this dance is not mentioned, but its significance is clear. In a culture that values children and women because they bear them, two women who don't want to marry (a man) become united by the power of the Deity and their union is validated by the creation of a rope baby. That is, the rope baby signifies the potency of their union in terms that are comprehensible to their society, which therefore legitimizes it.

It is clear that the koskalaka are perceived as powerful, as are their presumed male counterparts, the *winkte*. But their power does not constitute the right "to determine [their] own and others' actions."[14] Rather, it consists of the ability to manipulate physical and nonphysical reality toward certain ends. When this power is used to determine others' actions, it at least borders on black magic or sorcery.

To clarify the nature of the power I am talking about, we can consider what Lame Deer says about the *winkte*. Lame Deer is inclined to speak rather directly and tends not to romanticize either the concept of power as it is understood and practiced by his people or the *winkte* as a person who has certain abilities that make him special.

He says that a *winkte* is a person who is a half-man and half-woman, perhaps even a hermaphrodite with both male and female organs. In the old days, *winktes* dressed like women and lived as women. Lame Deer admits that though the Lakotas thought people are what nature, or dreams, make them, still men weren't happy to see their sons running around with *winktes*. Still, he says that there are good men among the *winktes* and that they have special powers. He took Richard Erdoes (who was transcribing his conversation for their book *Lame Deer: Seeker of Visions*) with him to a bar to interview a *winkte*. He asked the man to tell him all about *winktes*, and the *winkte* told Lame Deer that "a *winkte* has a gift of prophecy and that he himself could predict the weather." The Lakota go to a *winkte* for a secret name, and such names carry great power, though they are often off-color. "You don't let a stranger know [the secret name]," the *winkte* told them. "He would kid you about it."[15] A *winkte*'s power to name often wins the *winkte* great fame and usually a fine gift as well.

The power referred to here is magical, mysterious, and sacred. That does not mean that its possessors are to be regarded as a priestly pious people, for this is hardly the case. But it does mean that those who possess "medicine power," women and men, are to be treated with a certain cautious respect.

It is interesting to note that the story—one of the few reliable accounts of persons whose sexual orientation differs from the heterosexual—concerns a male, a *winkte*. The stories about *koskalaka* are yet to be told. It seems to me that this suppression is a result of a series of coincidental factors: the historical events connected with the conquest of Native America; the influence of Christianity and the attendant brutal suppression of medicine people and medicine practices; the patriarchal suppression of all references to power held by women; Christian notions of proper sexual behavior; and, recently, an attempt on the part of a number of American Indian men to suppress knowledge among their own people (and among Europeans and Americans) of the traditional place of woman as powerful medicine people and leaders in their own right, accompanied by a dismissal of women as central to tribal ritual life.[16]

Under the reign of the patriarchy, the medicine-dyke has become anathema; her presence has been hidden under the power-destroying blanket of complete silence. We must not allow this silence to prevent us from discovering and reclaiming who we have been and who we are. We must not forget the true Source of our being, nor her powerfulness, and we must not allow ourselves to be deluded by patriarchal perceptions of power that rob us of our true power, regardless of how many feathers those perceptions are cloaked in. As Indian women, as lesbians, we must make the effort to understand clearly what is at stake, and this means that we must reject all beliefs that work against ourselves, however much we have come to cherish them as we have lived among the patriarchs.

Womanculture is unregulated by males and is misperceived by ethnographers. Perhaps this is so because it is felt—at least among ethnographers' tribal informants—that it is wise to let "sleeping dogs lie." There may also be fear of what power might be unleashed if the facts about American Indian lesbianism were discussed directly. A story that has recently come to my attention might best clarify this statement.

Two white lesbians, feminists and social activists, were determined to expand their activities beyond the lesbian and feminist communities and to this end became involved in an ecological movement that centered on American Indian concerns. In pursuit of this course, they invited a Sioux medicine man to join them and arranged to pick him up from the small rural town he was visiting. When he saw them, he accused them of being lesbians and became very angry. He abused them verbally, in serious and obscene terms. They left him where he was and returned home, angry and confused.

A certain amount of their confusion was a result of their misperception of Indians and of this particular medicine man. I have friends in the primarily white lesbian community who seem to think that Indian men, particularly medicine men, are a breed apart who are "naturally just." Like other Americans, Indians are inclined to act in ways that are consistent with their picture of the world, and, in this particular Indian's picture, the world was not big enough for lesbians. The women didn't announce their sexual preference to him, by the way; but he knew a *koskalaka* when he saw one and reacted accordingly.

A friend who knew the women involved asked me about this encounter. She couldn't understand why the medicine man acted the way he had. I suspect that he was afraid of the lesbian's power, and I told her that. Another American Indian woman to whom I recounted the story had the same reaction. *Koskalaka* have singular power, and this medicine man was undoubtedly aware of it. The power of the *koskalaka* can (potentially, at least) override that of men, even very powerful medicine men such as the one in my story. I know this particular man, and he is quite powerful as a medicine man.

Not so long ago, the American Indians were clearly aware of the power that women possessed. Even now there are those among traditionals who know the medicine power of women. This is why a clear understanding of the supernatural forces and their potential in our lives is necessary. More than an interesting tour through primitive exotica is to be gained.

Before we worry about collecting more material from aborigines, before we join forces with those who are in a position to destroy us, and before we decide, like Sherry Ortner, that belief in ancient matriarchal civilization is an irrational concept born of conjecture and wish, let us adjust our perspective to match that of our foresisters. Then, when we search the memories and lore of tribal peoples, we might be able to see what eons and all kinds of institutions have conspired to hide from our eyes.

The evidence is all around us. It remains for us to *dis*cover what it means.

Stealing the Thunder: Future Visions for American Indian Women, Tribes, and Literary Studies

Strange things begin to happen when the focus in American Indian literary studies is shifted from a male to a female axis. One of the major results of the shift is that the materials become centered on continuance rather than on extinction. This is true for both traditional tribal literatures and contemporary poetry, fiction, and other writings such as autobiography, journals, "as-told-to" narratives and mixed-genre works. The shift from pessimism to optimism, from despair to hope is so dramatic that one wonders if the focus on male traditions and history that has characterized the whole field of American Indian literature and lore was not part of the plot to exterminate Native American tribal peoples and cultures and to extinguish their aboriginal title to land, resources, and moral primacy of the Americas.

Of course, plots or conspiracies do not characterize American politics or scholarship, as we all know. But popular ideas about American Indians—warriors, chiefs, colorful befeathered veterans of the wars of progress, colonialism, imperialism, or whatever one wants to call it, brave noble, dying but brave braves—hauntingly pervade the American mind, and behind them lurks the image of the hostile, bloodthirsty savage, the redskin who howls out of the wilderness intent on the total destruction of innocent Christian families trying to build a nation founded in liberty, justice, and moral truth.

However he is viewed—sympathetically or with suspicion and terror—the Indian is always *he*. Certainly *she* never rides tall and noble in the saddle, face framed in savage splendor with plundered feathers of great fighting birds. *She* never parlays in powwow council with the white man, offering the peace pipe/calumet to the gods, asking that the proceedings be blessed by heathen powers. *She* never dies at Sand Creek or Wounded Knee. *She* is not the old shaman who gives advice to the young and sends them to the mountains to find their vision; *she* does not have the visions that tell of a nation's destruction. *She* does not stand on the top of a bluff weeping for the broken hoop of the nation. *She* is not revered in the memory of Americans as shaman, warrior-chief, peacemaker.

In the annals of American Indian literary lore there has been no female Red Cloud, Sealth, Logan, Black Elk, Lame Deer, or Rolling Thunder to bear literary witness to the shamanistic traditions of American Indians; there has been no female Sitting Bull, no Crazy Horse, no Handsome Lake, no Wovoka, no Sweet Medicine. And because there have been no great and noble women in that essentially literary cultural memory called tradition, there is no sense of the part that women have played in tribal life either in the past or today.

But let us suppose that among the true heroes were and are many women. Suppose the names of Molly Brant, Magnus, Pocahontas, Sacagawea, Malinalli, Nancy Ward, Sara Winnemucca, and scores of others were the names that came to mind when we thought of the noble and sacred past of the tribes. Suppose that when we heard the tribal deities referred to we thought of Thought Woman, Sky Woman, Cihuacoatl, Selu—that theirs was the name of god, the Great Spirit. Let us for a moment imagine that all the great deeds and noble philosophies, all the earth-centeredness, egalitarianism, medicine systems of sacred power, all the life ways and values of the Native Americans from the northern barrens to Tierra del Fuego, are woman-inspired and woman-maintained. Let us imagine this truth and see how it affects our understanding of American Indian literature. Enabling Americans to imagine, to recognize, and to acknowledge that truth is what my scholarly and creative work has been about for almost fifteen years, and the implications of that shift in perception are at least as exciting as the second coming would be.

What I have done, am doing—putting women at the center of the tribal universe—is not particularly revolutionary, though it has entailed groping around in a false dark created by the massive revisionism of tribal life and thought that characterizes American literary scholarship in the field, a revisionism that has trickled down into tribal attitudes and thought and therefore into what the tribes have preserved in their oral traditions. But I am from a gynocratic tribal society, and so I have been aided by my background in locating material that points to the truth about the nature of the tribes prior to Anglo-European invasion and conquest.

My tribe, the Keres Pueblo Indians of the Southwest, put women at the center of their society long ago. Of course, they don't say *they* did it, they say *She* did it. That She is Thought, Memory, Instinct, Tradition, and Medicine or Sacred Power; that She is ritual, ceremony, food, and shelter; that She is the ways by which these are developed—the bringer of them and the teacher of them and the creator of them. Where I come from, the people believe traditionally that nothing can happen that She does not think into being, and because they believe this they say that the Woman is the Supreme Being, the Great Spirit, the Great Mystery, the All-Being. This WomanGod, Thought/Thinking Woman they call Spider Grandmother, acknowledging her potency as creator, as Dream/Vision being, as She Who Weaves existence on all material and supermaterial planes into being.

This is not extraliterary material I am discussing; it is the heart of the literary impulse. For literature comes out of tradition, and traditionally in the gynocratic tribal world, woman is at the center of existence. That means that for writers such as Leslie Marmon Silko, Carol Lee Sanchez, Paula Gunn Allen, Simon J. Ortiz, N. Scott Momaday, Janet Campbell Hale, D'Arcy McNickle, James Welch, Beth Brant, Joy Harjo, Linda Hogan, Wendy Rose, Maurice Kenny, Elizabeth Cook-Lynn, Diane Burns, Gerald Vizenor, Geary Hobsen, nila northSun, Mary TallMountain, Ray Young Bear, and many more, the centrality of the feminine power of universal being is crucial to their work and to the study and teaching of it.

These writers are not all Keres, though the first four named are, but they are all Indians. Many of them come from clearly woman-centered or gynocratic tribal societies and others, those who hail from northern or southern Plains tribes or northern Algonkian tribes, have powerful female deities and female-centered social and spiritual structures. As we move into the 1990s and my lone voice is joined by the growing multitude of women's voices across the country and within the profession of writing and of literary scholarship, the facts of tribal gynocracy or powerful woman-focused traditions will impact more and more decisively on the study and teaching of American Indian literature as well as on other areas of American Indian life.

The impact will develop along the following lines:

·· Women writers will have more and more accessibility to female traditions from which to write and think and will be more greatly empowered to use these resources. In turn this increase in woman-focused literature will generate growing understanding of the real nature of pre-Columbian tribal life. The idea of Indian in the contemporary public mind will shift from warrior/brave/hunter/chief to grandmother/mother/Peacemaker/farmer. It also means that central "Indian" symbols such as feathers, wampum, war bonnets, war paint, bows and arrows, and tomahawks will be replaced by corn meal and corn pollen, corn mothers, metates, grinding stones, hoes, plows, pottery and basket designs, and the like, and the understanding of the tribal traditions as warrior-oriented will shift to an understanding of them as peace-oriented. For the tribes were largely peaceful, and peace was upheld by the presence of powerful women shamans and women's councils. That all housing, most food production and preparation, most medicine, and ritual was and is done by or through the empowering agency of women and that the tribes as a whole never viewed women as objects of scorn or contempt, fit only to bear burdens and do all the work, will become common knowledge. The emphasis on "special" beings like sachems, "priests," and chiefs will shift to an emphasis on the whole of the tribe, the whole of the tribal cosmos—for such was and is the focus of traditional American Indian life and such was the basis of gynocracy and tribal belief in the prowess of women.

·· Male writers will not be able to simply "plug into" existing popular notions about Indians but will be forced to write and think more creatively, more accurately, and more honestly about their tribes, their lives, and their histories.

·· Critics who are interested in either traditional or contemporary American Indian literature will have to dig more deeply into existing materials on Indian women to be able to illuminate the works they hope to explicate or teach. In the process, they will locate "lost," buried, and hidden materials about women in tribal traditions, providing an ever-widening pool of lore and symbols for writers to draw upon.

· · At the very least, critical understanding of the cultural traditions of American Indians will shift rather smartly as a result of the shift from male to female focus in tribal America. This by itself will result in a net gain for the Indian people because as long as they are seen as braves and warriors the fiction that they were conquered in a fair and just war will be upheld. It is in the interest of the United States—along with the other political entities in the western hemisphere to maintain that foolish and tragic deception, and thus the focus has long been on Indian as noble or savage warrior who, as it happens, lost the war to superior military competence. The truth is more compelling: the tribes did not fight off the invaders to any great extent. Generally they gave way to them; generally they fed and clothed and doctored them; generally they shared their knowledge about everything from how to plant corn and tobacco to how to treat polio victims to how to cross the continent with them. Generally Chief Joseph, Sitting Bull, Crazy Horse, and the rest are historical anomalies. Generally, according to D'Arcy McNickle, the Indian historian, anthropologist, and novelist, at least 70 percent of the tribes were pacifist, and the tribes that lived in peacefulness as a way of life were always woman-centered, always gynecentric, always agricultural, always "sedentary," and always the children of egalitarian, peace-minded, ritual, and dream/vision-centered female gods. The people conquered in the invasion of the Americas by Europe were woman-focused people.

· · All the interpretations and conclusions scholars in the fields of folklore, ethnology, and contemporary literary studies will have to be altered, all the evidence reexamined, and all the materials chosen for exemplification of tribal life—which at present reveal more about academic male bias than about the traditions and peoples they purport to depict—will have to be redone. This is because the shift in focus from a male to a female axis recontextualizes the entire field.

For clarity here I must note that literary studies in the field of American Indian studies is not purely literary in the sense that the discipline is pursued in the west. We critics of Indian literature must be cultural, historical, and political as well as literary scholars because neither traditional peoples (and their literatures) nor contemporary poets and writers can write outside a cultural, historical, and political context. Factual contextualization of the tribal and contemporary literary materials of Indian people is central to the pursuit of literary studies in the field, and when a critic such as myself—or a poet and writer such as myself and scores of others—moves the focus from male to female traditions, recontextualizing the materials on and about American Indian life and thought, the huge changes I have described necessarily must occur in the whole field.

• • Finally, the most important implication of the shift in focus is the one with which I began these essays: the traditions of the women have, since time immemorial, been centered on continuance, just as those of the men have been centered on transitoriness. The most frequently occurring male themes and symbols from the oral tradition have been feathers, smoke, lightning bolts (sheet lightning is female), risk, and wandering. These symbols are all related in some way to the idea of the transitoriness of life and its wonders. The Kiowa death song (a male tradition that was widespread among Plains tribes) says, "I die, but you live forever; beautiful Earth you alone remain; wonderful Earth, you remain forever," telling the difference in the two traditions, male and female.

The male principle is transitory; it dies and is reconstituted. The female principle, which is immanent in hard substances (like the earth, minerals, crystals, and stones), wood, and water, is permanent; it remains. Male is breath, air, wind, and projectile point; female controls, creates, and "owns" breath, air and wind, bird and feather, and the hard substance from which the projectile point is shaped. Female is earth, sun, moon, sky, water in its multitudinous forms and its ever-generating cycle, corn, mother of the deer, mother of the gods, bringer of fire and light, and fire itself (which is why the women are its keepers among many if not most groups). He is what comes and goes, she is what continues, what stays.

When we shift our attention from the male, the transitory, to the female, the enduring, we realize that the Indians are not doomed to extinction but rather are fated to endure. What a redemptive, empowering realization that is! As the Cheyenne long have insisted, no people is broken until the heart of its women is on the ground. Then they are broken. Then will they die.

The plot that we all know doesn't exist has been contrived to convince Indians and everyone else that Indians are doomed to extinction, to throw to the ground every woman's heart. It has been carried out by the simple process of subjecting our cultures, lives, traditions, rituals, philosophies, and customs to Christian patriarchal scrutiny, seeing only the male in them, putting male bias into systems that never had it, interpreting rituals, customs, philosophies, and attitudes in male-biased terms, and generally creating out of whole cloth the present male-dominating view about the tribes and their significance.

Women's rituals, ceremonies, traditions, customs, attitudes, values, activities, philosophies, ceremonial and social positions, histories, medicine societies, and shamanistic identities—that is, all the oral tradition that is in every sense and on every level the literature of the tribes—have been largely ignored by folklorists, ethnographers, and literary critics in the field of American Indian studies. These traditions have *never* been described or examined in terms of their proper, that is, woman-focused, context. Actually, it is primarily the context that has been ignored—vanished, disappeared, buried under tons of scholarly materials selected and erected to hide the centrality of women in tribal society, tribal literature, and tribal hearts and minds. The data has been studiously recorded, then filed. Sometimes it surfaces in print, distorted almost out of recognition by the wholesale revision of the context in which it occurs. In the Keres way, context is female and it is God, because it is the source and generator of meaning. A vanished context is the same as a meaningless pile of data, and it is the same as a vanished source of meaning, a vanished God. Destroying the context parallels the destruction of women; in this case it also parallels the destruction of a race. It amounts to Deicide.

In this way the hearts of the women have been forced to the ground because the power of imagination, of image, which is the fundamental power of literature, is the power to determine a people's fate. By the simple expedient of shifting the view back to its original and rightful position, the whole picture changes, and it becomes clear that our heart is in the sky. We understand that woman is the sun and the earth: she is grandmother; she is mother; she is Thought, Wisdom, Dream, Reason, Tradition, Memory, Deity, and Life itself. Nos Vemos.

 Notes

Grandmother of the Sun:
Ritual Gynocracy in Native America

1. Anthony Purley, "Keres Pueblo Concepts of Deity," *American Indian Culture and Research Journal*, vol. 1, no. 1 (Fall 1974), p. 29. The passage cited is Purley's literal translation from the Keres Indian language of a portion of the Thought Woman story. Purley is a native-speaker Laguna Pueblo Keres. Shipapu is the underworld where the dead go, where the Great Mother in her various aspects and guises lives, and from whence she confers to the caciques the authority to govern. Shi wana are the rain cloud spirits. They come from Shipapu by way of southeastern or southwestern wind currents. They are the dead, or the ancestors, who are obliged to bring rain to the pueblo in the proper season. Cha-yah-ni (cheani) are medicine men or holy people. The word may also have the connotation of medicine or ritual power. Kopishtaya or Kupistaya is the Laguna word for Spirits; it, like its allied terms katsina or koshare, is a collective noun.

2. Purley, "Keres Pueblo Concepts," pp. 30–31.

3. Hamilton A. Tyler, *Pueblo Gods and Myths*, Civilization of the American Indian Series (Norman: University of Oklahoma Press, 1964), p. 37. Evidently, Huruing Wuhti has other transformative abilities as well. Under pressure from patriarchal politics, she can change her gender, her name, and even her spiritual nature, as this passage from Tyler suggests:

> Something of the vastness of the changes in concepts which have taken place can be seen if we recall a statement quoted earlier. There a man of our generation

mentions that the roads to the village are closed "to clear the spiritual highway which leads from there to the rising sun. This is a road over which they walk to offer their prayers to the Great Spirit." It will be recalled that the closing of the roads was in actuality part of an All Souls ceremony for the dead, and in it, Masau'u [the major supernatural of this fourth world and of death, but in no way a creator-god] who has now become the Great Spirit, was most certainly connected with the dead and the underworld, rather than with the sun. The new arrangement is not made out of the whole cloth, however, as the idea is old, but it belonged to the initiation of a new village chieftain. Since the town chief was supposed to be on good terms with the cloud-people, or spirits of the dead, a Kwan man closes the ceremony with these words: "Now I make you a chief and now I give you a good path to lead us to the Sun. Now you are our father."

From now on we will hear very little of death, or even of fertility, and much of a sky god who is a supreme being. In the *Hopi Hearings* . . . , old and new attitudes are combined. Simon Scott, whose name hides a Hopi, at one point says: "This supreme being who is over all of us is here with us and listening to all of us in this meeting and will be with us until this meeting is adjourned." Despite the Christian tone, the statement is not far removed conceptually from the remark Stephen quoted, but some days later the same Hopi leader added a few ideas: "It is the Executive Supreme Being who created the world and created a human for a holy purpose. It is this Executive Supreme who made two humans. One has a white flesh and the other is red." Since he was referring to Masau'u, the latter statement contains something quite new: as every Hopi knows, the world was created by Huruing Wuhti, Hard Beings Woman, and in all the accounts we have heard there is no suggestion that Masau'u was the creator, either of the world or of mankind. Furthermore, the god has been changed by the competition of white politics as well as white religion. Our Chief Executive must have been an appealing idea, both in phrasing and thought content (p. 82).

4. Tyler, *Pueblo Gods*, p. 93.

5. For one version of this myth, see "The Woman Who Fell from the Sky: A Seneca Account," *Literature of the American Indian*, ed. Thomas E. Sanders and Walter W. Peek (New York: Glencoe, 1973), pp. 41–43. Cf. "Creation Story: A Mohawk Account," in the *1982 Akwesasne Notes Calendar* (Mohawk via Roosevelt, N.Y.: Akwesasne Notes, 1982).

6. Tyler, *Pueblo Gods*, p. 93.

7. Purley, "Keres Pueblo Concepts," p. 31.

8. Purley, "Keres Pueblo Concepts," p. 31.

9. Fr. Noël Dumarest, *Memoirs: Notes of Cochiti, New Mexico*, vol. 6, no. 3 (Lancaster: American Anthropological Association, 1919), p. 227. Cited in Tyler, *Pueblo Gods*, p. 91.

10. John G. Neihardt, *Black Elk Speaks* (Lincoln: University of Nebraska Press, 1961), and Joseph Epes Brown, *The Sacred Pipe* (Baltimore: Penguin, 1971), p. 44.

11. Alice Baldeagle, personal correspondence, May 8, 1978.

12. See Franz Boas, *Keresan Texts* (New York: Publications of the American Ethnological Society, 1928), especially "P'acaya'Nyi," vol. 8, pt. 1, pp. 13–16.

According to Elsie Clews Parsons, who gives an account of a healing done by one of the katsina organizations, the she'kine, the healer, sets up at the altar, color-coded for the ritual and graced with Irriaku, and uses a crystal to locate the heart of the patient, which has been stolen by someone wishing evil on the patient. Holding a bear's paw, the healer rushes out of the house in pursuit of the heart, and when it is found, the war captains take it. At this juncture, the healer loses consciousness and is revived by female relatives. Mentioned by Boas, *Keresan Texts*, pp. 118–122.

13. Mathew W. Stirling, "Origin Myth of the Acoma and Other Records," *Bureau of American Ethnology Bulletin* 135 (Washington, D.C., 1932), p. 32.

14. See the story "The Cacique Who Visited the Dead" in *Tales of the Cochiti Indians*, ed. Ruth Benedict (Albuquerque: University of New Mexico Press, 1981), pp. 30–31; cf. Benedict, p. 255.

15. Anthony Purley, like Franz Boas, believes that the trend to refer to Uretsete as male is a late development and may reflect a Keres gesture to white tastes in deity. Uretsete is not always male, even in present-day narratives or sacred myths, but changes gender midstream, as it were.

16. For more on this, see Fred Eggan, *Social Organization of the Western Pueblos* (Chicago: University of Chicago Press, 1950), pp. 283–284; Boas, *Keresan Texts*, p. 94; Elsie Clews Parsons, *Notes on Ceremonialism at Laguna*, Anthropological Papers of the American Museum of Natural History 19, pt. 4 (New York: Kraus, n.d.), pp. 109–112, and Tyler, *Pueblo Gods*, p. 106.

17. Boas, *Keresan Texts*, p. 285, says that war captains are the representatives of Ma'sewe and O'yo'yo'we. He adds, "It seems therefore twin heroes must be considered helpers and assistants of all these supernatural beings and that they are types rather than individuals. In the pueblo the twin heroes are represented by the war captains, the 'out of town chiefs.' They are in charge of all public functions. They take care of the shamans, accompany them on their ceremonial visit to Mt. Taylor; they attend curing ceremonials; they are in charge of the rabbit hunt; they make prayer-sticks for hunters and sacrifice for them; they act as town criers; they take part in the ceremonial dance of the warriors (op'i)" (p. 286).

18. Boas writes, "The head religious officer, the so called cacique, is called Tyi'amun'i ho:tc'am u nyo, the chief leader, because he led the people from the place of Emergence. In tales he is always called *ho·tc'anyi ha'tcam'uy k'ayo·k'ai* (chief prayer stick holding), that is, 'always remembering the prayer sticks.' (In the beginning I misheard *k'ayo'ka* for *k'ayo'kai*. The former means 'broken'). The cacique may belong to any clan. The office has been extinct for a long time [at Laguna]. The last caciques are still remembered . . . The cacique does no everyday labor. He makes prayer-sticks, carries them up the hill near the village, north, west, south, east in this order, and prays for the people. He may not be a shaman but he must know how to pray. He must be serious-minded and must not have a quick temper . . . The people attend to the cacique's field and the women cook for him . . . In tales the cacique is the only one who is allowed to make prayer-sticks for the katsina . . . In many cases he himself appears as a town crier, giving notice to the people of his orders" (pp. 288–289).

19. John M. Gunn, *Schat Chen* (Albuquerque, N. Mex.: Albright and Anderson, 1917), p. 218.

20. Natalie Curtis, recorder and editor, *The Indians' Book: Songs and Legends of the American Indians* (New York: Dover, 1950), p. 6.

21. Curtis, *Indians' Book*, p. 4.

22. Curtis, *Indians' Book*, p. 5.

23. Curtis, *Indians' Book*, p. 6.

24. Matilda Coxe Stevenson, "The Sia," *Eleventh Annual Report, 1889–90*, Bureau of American Ethnology (Washington, D.C., 1894), p. 39.

25. Sylvanus G. Morley and Delia Goetz, *Popul Vuh: The Sacred Book of the Ancient Quiche Maya*, from the translation of Adrian Recinos (Norman: University of Oklahoma Press, 1950), p. 82.

26. Morley and Goetz, *Popul Vuh*, p. 82.

27. Stirling, "Origin Myth of the Acoma," pl. 10, fig. 2, and 121n.

28. William Brandon, *The Last Americans: The Indian in American Culture* (New York: McGraw-Hill, 1974), p. 52.

29. Stevenson, "Sia," pp. 40–41.

30. Kay Turner, "Contemporary Feminist Rituals," in *The Politics of Women's Spirituality: Essays on the Rise of Spiritual Power Within the Feminist Movement*, ed. Charlene Spretnak (New York: Anchor, 1982), p. 228.

31. Boas, *Keresan Texts*, pp. 64–65.

32. Boas, *Keresan Texts*, pp. 56–75.

33. Boas, *Keresan Texts*, p. 62.

When Women Throw Down Bundles:
Strong Women Make Strong Nations

1. Stan Steiner, *The New Indians* (New York: Dell, Delta Books, 1968), p. 224. Steiner's chapter on Indian women, "Changing Women," is an important contribution to our understanding of the shift in women's positions under colonization. It should be read by those interested in learning about contemporary processes of patriarchalization and tribal resistance or acquiescence to it.

2. Carolyn Foreman, *Indian Women Chiefs* (Washington, D.C.: Zenger Publishing Co., 1976), p. 7.

3. John P. Brown, *Old Frontiers* (Kingsport, Tenn.: State of Wisconsin, State Historical Society, Draper Manuscripts, 1938), p. 20. Cited in Foreman, *Indian Women Chiefs*, p. 7.

4. Foreman, *Indian Women Chiefs*, p. 9.

5. See William Brandon, *The Last Americans: The Indian in American Culture* (New York: McGraw-Hill, 1974), p. 214, for more detail. Also see "Red Roots of White Feminism" in Part 3 of this volume.

6. The terms *gynecentric* and *egalitarianism* are not mutually exclusive; in fact, I doubt that egalitarianism is possible without gynecentrism at its base.

7. See Elisa-Buenaventura-Posso and Susan E. Brown, "Forced Transition from Egalitarianism to Male Dominance: The Bari of Colombia," in *Women and Colonization: Anthropological Perspectives*, eds. Mona Etienne and Eleanor Leacock (New York: Praeger, 1980), pp. 109–134, for an informative discussion

of contemporary attempts to force the last remaining traditional group of Bari to shift their social structure to authoritarian male dominance.

8. Foreman, *Indian Women Chiefs*, p. 32. *Squaw* is not a derogatory word in its own language. Like the Anglo-Saxon "forbidden" word *cunt*, which is mostly used as an insult to women, *squaw* means "queen" or "lady," as will be seen in the following discussion. The fact that it has been taken to mean something less is only another example of patriarchal dominance, under which the proudest names come to be seen as the most degrading epithets, which the conquered and the conquerer alike are forbidden to use without the risk of sounding racist.

9. Robert Steven Grumet, "Sunksquaws, Shamans, and Tradeswomen: Middle Atlantic Coastal Algonkian Women During the 17th and 18th Centuries," in Etienne and Leacock, *Women and Colonization*, p. 49. In his note to this passage, Grumet comments that Regina Flannery ("An Analysis of Coastal Algonquian Culture," *Catholic University Anthropological Series*, no. 7 [1939], p. 145) "listed women's inheritance of chiefly rank among the Massachusett, Natick, Caconnet, Martha's Vineyard (Wampanoag), Narragansett, Western Niantic, Scaticook, Piscataway, and Powhatan groups" (p. 60n).

10. Grumet, "Sunksquaws," p. 60.

11. Grumet, "Sunksquaws," p. 50.

12. Grumet, "Sunksquaws," p. 50.

13. Grumet, "Sunksquaws," p. 50.

14. Grumet, "Sunksquaws," p. 51.

15. Grumet, "Sunksquaws," pp. 51–52.

16. Grumet, "Sunksquaws," pp. 51–52.

17. Grumet, "Sunksquaws," pp. 52–53.

18. Lieutenant Henry Timberlake, *Lieut. Henry Timberlake's Memoirs* (Marietta, Ga., 1948), p. 94 and n. 56. Cited in Foreman, *Indian Women Chiefs*, p. 76.

19. Timberlake, *Memoirs*, p. 94 and n. 56. Cited in Foreman, *Indian Women Chiefs*, p. 77.

20. Colonel James D. Wofford, whose name is frequently spelled Wafford, cited in Foreman, *Indian Women Chiefs*, p. 85.

21. Foreman, *Indian Women Chiefs*, p. 79.

22. Eleanor Leacock, "Montaignais Women and the Jesuit Program for Colonization," in Etienne and Leacock, *Women and Colonization*, p. 27. She is citing R. G. Thwaites, ed., *The Jesuit Relations and Allied Documents*, 71 vols. (Cleveland: Burrows Brothers Co., 1906), 2:77.

23. Leacock, "Montaignais Women," p. 27. Le Jeune's remarks from Thwaites, *Jesuit Relations*, 6:233.

24. Leacock, "Montaignais Women," p. 27. Thwaites, *Jesuit Relations*, 12:169.

25. Leacock, "Montaignais Women," p. 28. Thwaites, *Jesuit Relations*, 5:197.

26. Leacock, "Montaignais Women," p. 30. Thwaites, *Jesuit Relations*, 16:165.

27. Leacock, "Montaignais Women," p. 30. Thwaites, *Jesuit Relations*, 6:243.

28. Leacock, "Montaignais Women," pp. 40–41.

The Sacred Hoop: A Contemporary Perspective

1. *Mythic:* 1. narratives that deal with metaphysical, spiritual, and cosmic occurrences that recount the spiritual past and the "mysteries" of the tribe; 2. sacred story. The *Word* in its cosmic, creative sense. This usage follows the literary meaning rather than the common or vernacular meaning of "fictive" or "not real narrative dealing with primitive, irrational explanations of the world." 3. translational.

2. Hyemehosts Storm, *Seven Arrows* (New York: Harper and Row, 1972), p. 4.

3. John G. Neihardt, *Black Elk Speaks* (Lincoln: University of Nebraska Press, 1961), p. 35.

4. Frederick Turner III, Introduction, *Geronimo: His Own Story*, by Geronimo, ed. S. M. Barrett (New York: Ballantine, 1978), p. 7.

5. D'Arcy McNickle, *Native American Tribalism: Indian Survivals and Renewals* (New York: Oxford University Press, 1973), pp. 12–13.

6. Alice Marriott and Carol K. Rachlin, *American Indian Mythology* (New York: New American Library, 1972), p. 39.

7. Marriott and Rachlin, *American Indian Mythology*, p. 39.

8. Natalie B. Curtis, *The Indians' Book: Songs and Legends of the American Indians* (New York: Dover, 1968), pp. 8, 7.

9. From a prayer of the Night Chant of the Navajo people.

10. I am making this inference from the account of the appearance of White Buffalo Cow Woman to Kablaya as recounted by Black Elk in *The Sacred Pipe: Black Elk's Account of the Seven Rites of the Oglala Sioux*, ed. Joseph Eyes Brown (Baltimore: Penguin, 1971), pp. 67–100.

11. T. Kroeber and Robert F. Heizer, *Almost Ancestors: The First Californians*, ed. F. David Hales (San Francisco: Sierra Club, 1968), pp. 28–30.

12. Margot Astrov, *American Indian Prose and Poetry* (New York: Capricorn, 1962), p. 12.

13. Curtis, *Indians' Book*, p. 356. I have reproduced this part of the chant in its entirety, although the Curtis version has only one stanza with a note regarding the proper form.

14. Astrov, *American Indian Prose*, p. 12.

15. Astrov, *American Indian Prose*, p. 50.

16. Astrov, *American Indian Prose*, p. 50.

17. John (Fire) Lame Deer and Richard Erdoes, *Lame Deer: Seeker of Visions* (New York: Touchstone, 1972), pp. 108–109.

18. Crazy Dog Society song of the Kiowa people. This version appears in Alice Marriott, *Kiowa Years: A Study in Culture Impact* (New York: Macmillan, 1968), p. 118.

19. Lame Deer and Erdoes, *Lame Deer*, p. 115.

20. Sigmund Freud, *Totem and Taboo*, trans. James Strachey (New York: Norton, 1952), p. 14.

21. Lame Deer and Erdoes, *Lame Deer*, p. 115.

22. Lame Deer and Erdoes, *Lame Deer*, p. 112.

23. '49 songs were sung (danced) just before a war party went out. They are widely enjoyed today after a powwow has officially ended after midnight. One '49 song goes like this:

When the dance is ended sweetheart
I will take you home.
He-ya he-he-ya
He-ya he-he-ya.

24. Curtis, *Indians' Book*, p. x.

Whose Dream Is This Anyway? Remythologizing and Self-definition in Contemporary American Indian Fiction

1. A. LaVonne Brown Ruoff, "Western Native American Writers: The Early Period," in *Literary History of the American West*, ed. Thomas J. Lyon et al., forthcoming.

2. See Hamilton A. Tyler's recounting of the Salt Woman tradition in *Pueblo Gods and Myths* (Norman: University of Oklahoma Press, 1964), pp. 213–218. Another tale that bears striking thematic similarities to *Ceremony* (New York: Viking, 1977) is the Hopi story of Tayo, a boy who brought the rain back to Hopi after a severe drought, as recounted in G. M. Mullett, *Spider Woman Stories* (Tucson: University of Arizona Press, 1979), pp. 7–43.

3. For a recent comprehensive discussion of myth criticism and the present idea that "rites share their symbolic nature with art, but their peculiar satisfaction lies in the experience of community," see Richard F. Hardin, "'Ritual' in Recent Criticism: The Elusive Sense of Community," *PMLA* 98 (1983), pp. 846–862.

4. Mourning Dove (Humishuma), *Cogewea, the Half-Blood: A Depiction of the Great Montana Cattle Range, by Hum-ishu-ma, "Mourning Dove,"* . . . *Given Through Sho-pow-tan*, with notes and bibliographical sketch by Lucullus Virgil McWhorter (1927; reprint, Lincoln: University of Nebraska Press, Basic Books, 1981). All references in this paper are to the reprint edition.

5. Ruoff, "Western Native American Writers."

6. D'Arcy McNickle, *The Surrounded* (1936; reprint, Albuquerque: University of New Mexico Press, 1978). All references are to the reprint edition. D'Arcy McNickle, *Wind from an Enemy Sky* (New York: Harper and Row, 1968; New York: Signet, 1969). All references are to the Signet edition.

7. I am indebted to poet Judy Grahn for insights about male rituals that led to this understanding of male ritual elements in the recent novels of American Indian men.

8. N. Scott Momaday, *House Made of Dawn* (New York: Harper and Row, 1968; New York: Signet, 1969). All references are to the Signet edition.

9. Killing the albino was "the most natural thing in the world . . . They must know that he would kill the white man again, if he had the chance . . . For he would know what the white man was, and he would kill him if he could" (p. 95). Cf. pages 76–79, in which the albino is described in ways that allude to his snakelike qualities. Among the Pueblos, witches often transform themselves into snakes and are known as witches because of that ability.

10. James Welch, *Winter in the Blood* (New York: Harper and Row, 1979).

11. William Thackery, "Crying for Pity in *Winter in the Blood*," *MELUS*, vol. 1, no. 7 (1980), pp. 61–78.

12. Leslie Marmon Silko, *Ceremony* (New York, 1977); Gerald Vizenor, *The Darkness in Saint Louis Bearheart* (Saint Paul, Minn.: Truck Press, 1978).

13. Paula Gunn Allen, *The Woman Who Owned the Shadows* (San Francisco: Spinsters Ink, 1983).

14. Based on Keres uses of the number four in its esoteric relation to women and its universal use as a sacred number among Native Americans, I believe that *four* is a categorical symbol-statement about the primacy of female power in tribal ritual life.

Something Sacred Going on Out There: Myth and Vision in American Indian Literature

1. *Random House Dictionary of the English Language*, unabridged (New York: Random House, 1966).

2. Walter W. Skeat, *An Etymological Dictionary of the English Language*, 4th rev. ed. (Oxford: Oxford University Press, 1978), pp. 755–756.

3. Rollo May, *Love and Will* (New York: Random House, 1966), p. 107.

4. Thomas Mann, "Freud and the Future," in Henry A. Murray, ed., *Myth and Mythmakers* (New York: George Braziller, 1960), p. 373.

5. Harry Levin, "Some Meanings of Myth" in Murray, *Myth*, p. 106.

6. John Stands-in-Timber and Margot Liberty, *Cheyenne Memories* (Lincoln: University of Nebraska Press, 1972), p. 27.

7. Stands-in-Timber and Liberty, *Cheyenne Memories*, p. 36.

8. Stands-in-Timber and Liberty, *Cheyenne Memories*, p. 39.

9. Stands-in-Timber and Liberty, *Cheyenne Memories*, pp. 39–41.

10. See John (Fire) Lame Deer and Richard Erdoes, *Lame Deer: Seeker of Visions* (New York: Touchstone, 1972); Black Elk and Joseph Epes Brown, *The Sacred Pipe* (Baltimore: Penguin, 1971), p. 44, for details on inipi and hanblecheya.

11. John G. Neihardt, *Black Elk Speaks* (Lincoln: University of Nebraska Press, 1961).

12. Sitting Bull had a vision before the Battle of the Greasy Grass (Little Big Horn) that foretold Custer's defeat. Yet histories, sometimes mentioning the vision as an example of primitive superstition, I suppose, generally lay the defeat to the

"overwhelming" numbers of warriors Custer fought and to ambush tactics. The facts of the matter are quite different, as an earnest student of military strategy can discover: as many Indians as some reports estimate couldn't have watered their horses or found sufficient game to feed themselves, let alone ambush Yellow Hair.

13. Neihardt, *Black Elk Speaks*, p. 22.

14. Neihardt, *Black Elk Speaks*, p. 22.

15. Neihardt, *Black Elk Speaks*, p. 92. There are explanations of the ritual significance of the directions in a number of sources. Hamilton A. Tyler, *Pueblo Gods and Myths* (Norman: University of Oklahoma Press, 1964), is a good source. Few adequate accounts of Indian religions or philosophy can be complete without some discussion of this.

16. Neihardt, *Black Elk Speaks*, pp. 25–26.

17. Neihardt, *Black Elk Speaks*, p. 30.

18. Neihardt, *Black Elk Speaks*, p. 26.

19. Neihardt, *Black Elk Speaks*, pp. 26–29.

20. Neihardt, *Black Elk Speaks*, pp. 29–30.

21. Neihardt, *Black Elk Speaks*, pp. 39–40.

22. Neihardt, *Black Elk Speaks*, pp. 40, 43.

23. Neihardt, *Black Elk Speaks*, p. 40.

24. Neihardt, *Black Elk Speaks*, p. 40.

25. Neihardt, *Black Elk Speaks*, p. 35. I have included all the lines of the songs, as proper, though Neihardt only indicates where the repetitions go.

26. Neihardt, *Black Elk Speaks*, p. 44.

27. Neihardt, *Black Elk Speaks*, pp. 163–165.

28. Neihardt, *Black Elk Speaks*, p. 165.

29. Neihardt, *Black Elk Speaks*, pp. 166–180.

30. Neihardt, *Black Elk Speaks*, p. 180.

31. Neihardt, *Black Elk Speaks*, see pp. 174–179 for entire relevant passage.

32. Neihardt, *Black Elk Speaks*, pp. 178–179.

33. Neihardt, *Black Elk Speaks*, pp. 234–251. See also Stands-in-Timber and Liberty, *Cheyenne Memories*, Natalie Curtis, ed., *The Indians' Book* (New York: Dover, 1968), and especially James Mooney, *The Ghost Dance Religion and the Great Sioux Outbreak of 1890* (Chicago: University of Chicago Press, 1965).

34. Neihardt, *Black Elk Speaks*, p. 169.

35. Neihardt, *Black Elk Speaks*, pp. 42, 43, 44.

36. May, *Love and Will*, p. 124.

A Stranger in My Own Life: Alienation in American Indian Poetry and Prose

1. Peter Martyr, *The History of Travayle in the West and East Indies, etc.* (London, 1555), fragmentary translation by Richard Eden, in William Brandon, *The Last Americans: The Indian in American Culture* (New York: McGraw-Hill, 1974), p. 291.

2. nila northSun, "the Way and the way things are," in *Diet Pepsi and Nacho Cheese* (Fallon, Nev.: Duck Down Press, 1977), p. 13.

3. Jeff Saunders, "I Came Far Today," in *Four Indian Poets*, ed. John R. Milton (Vermillion, S.D.: Dakota Press, 1974), p. 61.

4. Simon J. Ortiz, "Toward Spider Springs," in *Going for the Rain* (New York: Harper and Row, 1976), p. 25.

5. nila northSun, "my cousin the shadow," in *Diet Pepsi*, p. 35.

6. Marnie Walsh, "Vickie Loans-Arrow, 1971," in *A Taste of the Knife* (Boise: Ahsahte Press, 1976), pp. 10–11. Cf. *The Remembered Earth*, ed. Geary Hobsen (Albuquerque: University of New Mexico Press, 1980), pp. 367–68.

7. James Welch, "Winter Indian," unpublished manuscript, 1971.

8. Welch, "Blackfeet, Blood and Peigan Hunters," in *Riding the Earthboy 40*, rev. ed. (New York: Harper and Row, 1976), p. 36.

9. Walsh, "Vickie Loans-Arrow," pp. 4–6.

10. N. Scott Momaday, *House Made of Dawn* (New York: Signet, 1969), pp. 78–79.

11. Momaday, *House*, p. 64.

12. Leslie Marmon Silko, *Ceremony* (New York: Viking, 1977). The term *cousin-brother* is used at Laguna to describe the relationship between maternal cousins who are more like siblings than cousins in their kinship system.

13. Silko, *Ceremony*, p. 30.

14. James Welch, *Winter in the Blood* (New York: Harper and Row, 1974), p. 172.

15. Welch, *Winter*, p. 172.

16. James Welch, *The Death of Jim Loney* (New York: Harper and Row, 1979), p. 91.

17. Welch, *Death*, p. 91.

18. Welch, *Death*, p. 91.

19. Welch, *Death*, p. 89.

20. Welch, *Death*, p. 167.

21. Welch, *Death*, p. 167.

The Ceremonial Motion of Indian Time: Long Ago, So Far

1. N. Scott Momaday, *House Made of Dawn* (New York: Harper and Row, 1968; New York: Signet, 1969). All references are to the Signet edition.

2. Paula Gunn Allen, "Hoop Dancer," in *Shadow Country* (Los Angeles: University of California and Native American Center, 1982).

3. Leslie Marmon Silko, *Ceremony* (New York: Viking, 1977).

4. Paula Gunn Allen, *The Woman Who Owned the Shadows* (San Francisco: Spinsters Ink, 1983).

Answering the Deer: Genocide and Continuance in the Poetry of American Indian Women

1. Linda Hogan, "Blessing," in *Calling Myself Home* (New York: Greenfield Review Press, 1978), p. 27. Also in *The Remembered Earth*, ed. Geary Hobsen (Albuquerque, N. Mex.: Red Earth Press, 1979; reissued Albuquerque: University of New Mexico Press, 1981), p. 55.

2. Mary Randle TallMountain, "The Last Wolf," in *There Is No Word for Goodbye* (Marvin, S.D.: Blue Cloud Quarterly, 1981), p. 15.

3. Wendy Rose, "I Expected My Skin to Ripen," in *Lost Copper* (Morongo Indian Reservation, Canning, Calif.: Malki Museum Press, 1980), p. 219.

4. Rose, "I Expected," p. 219.

5. Leslie Marmon Silko, "Toe'osh: A Laguna Coyote Story," in *Storyteller* (New York: Viking, 1981), p. 237. Also in *The Third Woman: Minority Women Writers of the United States*, ed. Dexter Fisher (Boston: Houghton Mifflin, 1980), p. 94.

6. Elizabeth Cook-Lynn, "Contradiction," in *Then Badger Said This* (New York: Vantage Press, 1977), p. 12. Also in Fisher, *Third Woman*, p. 104.

7. nila northSun, "moving camp too far," in *Diet Pepsi and Nacho Cheese* (Fallon, Nev.: Duck Down Press, 1977), p. 14. Also in Hobsen, *Remembered Earth*, p. 380.

8. Joy Harjo, "3 AM," in *The Last Song* (Las Cruces, N. Mex.: Puerto del Sol Press, 1975), and in *What Moon Drove Me to This* (Berkeley, Calif.: Reed and Cannon, 1979), p. 43. Also in Hobsen, *Remembered Earth*, p. 380.

9. Roberta Hill Whiteman, "Leap in the Dark," in Fisher, *Third Woman*, pp. 123–124. Reprinted, *Star Quilt* (Minneapolis: Holy Cow! Press, 1984), pp. 13–15.

10. Hill Whiteman, "Leap," pp. 123–124.

11. Linda Hogan, "Morning: The World in the Lake," unpublished manuscript, 1981. Revised version published in *Seeing Through the Sun* (Amherst: University of Massachusetts Press, 1985), p. 56.

12. Paula Gunn Allen, from "Transformations," revised version in manuscript; original in *Starchild* (Marvin, S.D.: Blue Cloud Quarterly, 1981).

This Wilderness in My Blood: Spiritual Foundations of the Poetry of Five American Indian Women

1. Joy Harjo, interview with Paula Gunn Allen, Phoenix, Ariz., October 1981.

2. Harjo, interview, 1981.

3. Harjo, interview, 1981.

4. Joy Harjo, "Moonlight," Strawberry Press Post Card Series (Brooklyn, N.Y.: Strawberry Press, 1980).

5. Linda Hogan, interview with Paula Gunn Allen, Idledale, Col., June 1982.

6. Hogan, interview, 1982.

7. Hogan, interview, 1982.

8. Hogan, journal excerpt, unpublished, 1979.

9. Hogan, journal excerpt, unpublished, 1981.

10. Hogan, journal excerpt, April 17, 1981.

11. Linda Hogan, "The Women Speaking," in *Daughters, I Love You* (Denver, Col.: Loretto Heights College, 1981), p. 15.

12. Mary Randle TallMountain, "The Figure in Clay," in *There Is No Word for Goodbye* (Marvin, S.D.: Blue Cloud Quarterly, 1982).

13. Wendy Rose, "Affirmative Action, Berkeley, 1977," unpublished manuscript.

14. Carol Lee Sanchez, interview with Paula Gunn Allen, May 1982.

15. Sanchez, interview with Paula Gunn Allen, May 1982.

16. Carol Lee Sanchez, "the Song, the Dance, the Poem," unpublished manuscript.

Angry Women Are Building: Issues and Struggles Facing American Indian Women Today

1. It is likely, say some researchers, that fetal alcohol syndrome, which is serious among many Indian groups, will be so serious among the White Mountain Apache and the Pine Ridge Sioux that if present trends continue, by the year 2000 some people estimate that almost one half of all children born on those reservations will in some way be affected by FAS. (Michael Dorris, Native American Studies, Dartmouth College, private conversation. Dorris has done extensive research into the syndrome as it affects native populations in the United States as well as in New Zealand.)

2. Phyllis Old Dog Cross, "Sexual Abuse, a New Threat to the Native American Woman: An Overview," *Listening Post: A Periodical of the Mental Health Programs of Indian Health Services*, vol. 6, no. 2 (April 1982), p. 18.

3. Old Dog Cross, p. 18.

4. Old Dog Cross, p. 20.

How the West Was Really Won

1. Carolyn Neithammer, *Daughters of the Earth* (New York: Collier, 1977), p. 231. It must be said that Neithammer is as homophobic in her reporting on lesbianism as she is racist in her accounts of tribal views of womanhood. In her three-page treatment, she begins with accounts of positive valuing of lesbians, then moves to tolerance of lesbianism, and ends the section with a rousing tale of how the good villagers of a heterosexist Eskimo village routed the evil lesbian and her lover and forced them to give up their unconventional lifestyle and return to the

ways of their village. Sadly, her book is often the main title featured on the Native American Women shelf at women's bookstores across the country.

2. Neithammer, *Daughters*, pp. 231–234.

3. In an unpublished paper, Evelyn Blackwood cites Kaj Birket-Smith's *The Chugach Eskimo* (Copenhagen: National Museum, 1953) on the interesting point that evidently only the Chugash Eskimo and the Navajo literally perceive the berdache as "half-man/half-woman," which, Blackwood says, is not a common perception. "Sexuality, Gender and Mode of Production: The Case of Native American Female Homosexuality (Berdache)," unpublished manuscript, 1983.

4. Judy Grahn, *Another Mother Tongue: Gay Words, Gay Worlds* (Boston: Beacon Press, 1984), pp. 55–56.

5. Grahn, *Another Mother Tongue*, pp. 55–56.

6. Walter Williams, "American Indian Responses to the Suppression of the Homosexual Berdache Tradition," presented at the Organization of American Historians convention, Spring 1983.

7. Martin Duberman, ed., "Documents in Hopi Indian Sexuality," *Radical History Review* 20 (Spring 1979), pp. 109, 112, 113.

8. Hubert Howe Bancroft, *The Native Races of the Pacific States of North America*, vol. 1 (New York: Appleton, 1875), p. 82.

9. George Catlin, *Illustrations of the Manners, Customs, and Conditions of the North American Indians, with Letters and Notes*, 10th ed. (London: Henry Bohn, 1866), 2:214–215. Cited in Jonathon Katz, *Gay American History, Lesbians and Gay Men in the U.S.A.* (New York: Crowell, 1976), p. 302.

10. Russell Means, Interview, *Penthouse Magazine* (April 1981), p. 138.

11. John (Fire) Lame Deer and Richard Erdoes, *Lame Deer: Seeker of Visions* (New York: Simon and Schuster, 1972), p. 149.

12. Interview in *Emma* (June 1982). Reprinted in *Connexions: An International Women's Quarterly*, no. 8 (Spring 1983) pp. 6–8.

13. Phyllis Old Dog Cross, "Sexual Abuse, a New Threat to the Native American Woman: An Overview," *Listening Post: A Periodical of the Mental Health Programs, Indian Health Service*, vol. 4, no. 2 (April 1982), p. 22.

Who Is Your Mother?
Red Roots of White Feminism

1. The White Roots of Peace, cited in *The Third Woman: Minority Women Writers of the United States*, ed. Dexter Fisher (Boston: Houghton Mifflin, 1980), p. 577. Cf. Thomas Sanders and William Peek, eds., *Literature of the American Indian* (New York: Glencoe Press, 1973), pp. 208–239. Sanders and Peek refer to the document as "The Law of the Great Peace."

2. Stan Steiner, *The New Indians* (New York: Dell, 1968), pp. 219–220.

3. William Brandon, *The Last Americans: The Indian in American Culture* (New York: McGraw-Hill, 1974), p. 294.

4. Brandon, *Last Americans*, p. 6.

5. Brandon, *Last Americans*, pp. 7–8. The entire chapter "American Indians and American History" (pp. 1–23) is pertinent to the discussion.

6. Ella E. Clark and Margot Evans, *Sacagawea of the Lewis and Clark Expedition* (Berkeley: University of California Press, 1979), pp. 93–98. Clark details the fascinating, infuriating, and very funny scholarly escapade of how our suffragette foremothers created a feminist hero from the scant references to the teenage Shoshoni wife of the expedition's official translator, Pierre Charbonneau.

7. The implications of this maneuver did not go unnoticed by either whites or Indians, for the statues of the idealized Shoshoni woman, the Native American matron Sacagawea, suggest that American tenure on American land, indeed, the right to be on this land, is given to whites by her. While that implication is not overt, it certainly is suggested in the image of her that the sculptor chose: a tall, heavy woman, standing erect, nobly pointing the way westward with upraised hand. The impression is furthered by the habit of media and scholar of referring to her as "the guide." Largely because of the popularization of the circumstances of Sacagawea's participation in the famed Lewis and Clark expedition, Indian people have viewed her as a traitor to her people, likening her to Malinalli (La Malinche, who acted as interpreter for Cortés and bore him a son) and Pocahontas, that unhappy girl who married John Rolfe (not John Smith) and died in England after bearing him a son. Actually none of these women engaged in traitorous behavior. Sacagawea led a long life, was called Porivo (Chief Woman) by the Commanches, among whom she lived for more than twenty years, and in her old age engaged her considerable skill at speaking and manipulating white bureaucracy to help in assuring her Shoshoni people decent reservation holdings.

A full discussion is impossible here but an examination of American child-rearing practices, societal attitudes toward women and exhibited by women (when compared to the same in Old World cultures) as well as the foodstuffs, medicinal materials, countercultural and alternative cultural systems, and the deeply Indian values these reflect should demonstrate the truth about informal acculturation and cross-cultural connections in the Americas.

8. Brandon, *Last Americans*, p. 6.

9. Lewis Henry Morgan, *Ancient Society or Researches in the Lines of Human Progress from Savagery Through Barbarism to Civilization* (New York, 1877).

10. Clark and Evans, *Sacagawea*, p. 96.

Kochinnenako in Academe: Three Approaches to Interpreting a Keres Indian Tale

1. John M. Gunn, *Schat Chen: History, Traditions and Narratives of the Queres Indians of Laguna and Acoma* (Albuquerque, N. Mex.: Albright and Anderson, 1917; reprint, New York: AMS, 1977). Gunn, my mother's uncle, lived among the Lagunas all his adult life. He spoke Laguna (Keres) and gathered information in somewhat informal ways while sitting in the sun visiting with older

people. He married Meta Atseye, my great-grandmother, years after her husband (John Gunn's brother) died and may have taken much of his information from her stories or explanations of Laguna ceremonial events. She had a way of "translating" terms and concepts from Keres into English and from a Laguna conceptual framework into an American one, as she understood it. For example, she used to refer to the Navajo people as "gypsies," probably because they traveled in covered wagons and the women wear long, full skirts and head scarves and both men and women wear a great deal of jewelry.

2. His use of the term may reflect the use by his informants, who were often educated in Carlisle or Menaul Indian schools, in their attempt to find an equivalent term that Gunn could understand to signify the deep respect and reverence accorded the hocheni tyi'a'muni. Or he might have selected the term because he was writing a book for an anonymous non-Keres audience, which included himself. Since he spoke Laguna Keres, I think he was doing the translations himself, and his renderings of words (and contexts) was likely influenced by the way Lagunas themselves rendered local terms into English. I doubt, however, that he was conscious of the extent to which his renderings reflected European traditions and simultaneously distorted Laguna-Acoma ones.

Gunn was deeply aware of the importance and intelligence of the Keresan tradition, but he was also unable to grant it independent existence. His major impulse was to link the western Keres with the Sumerians, to in some strange way demonstrate the justice of his assessment of their intelligence. An unpublished manuscript in my possession written by John Gunn after *Schat Chen* is devoted to his researches and speculations into this idea.

3. Gunn, *Schat Chen*, pp. 217–222.

4. Franz Boas, *Keresan Texts*, Publications of the American Ethnological Society, vol. 8, pt. 1 (New York: American Ethnological Society, 1928), writes, "The second and the fourth of the shiwana appear in the tale of summer and winter . . . Summer wears a shirt of buckskin with squash ornaments, shoes like moss to which parrot feathers are tied. His face is painted with red mica and flowers are tied on to it . . . Winter wears a shirt of icicles and his shoes are like ice. His shirt is shiny and to its end are tied turkey feathers and eagle feathers" (p. 284).

5. Boas, *Keresan Texts*, p. 288. Boas says he made the same mistake at first, having misheard the word they used.

6. When my sister Carol Lee Sanchez spoke to her university Women's Studies class about the position of centrality women hold in our Keres tradition, one young woman, a self-identified radical feminist, was outraged. She insisted that Sanchez and other Laguna women had been brainwashed into believing that we had power over our lives. After all, she knew that no woman anywhere has ever had that kind of power; her feminist studies had made that fact quite plain to her. The kind of cultural chauvinism that has been promulgated by well-intentioned but culturally entranced feminists can lead to serious misunderstandings such as this and in the process become a new racism based on what becomes the feminist canon. Not that feminists can be faulted entirely on this—they are, after all, reflecting the research and interpretation done in a patriarchal context, by male-

biased researchers and scholars, most of whom would avidly support the young radical feminist's strenuous position. It's too bad, though, that feminists fall into the patriarchal trap!

7. For a detailed exposition of what this dynamic consists of, see Adrienne Rich, "Compulsory Heterosexuality and Lesbian Existence," *Signs: Journal of Women in Culture and Society*, vol. 5, no. 4 (Summer 1980). Reprinted in 1982 as a pamphlet with an updated forward, Antelope Publications, 1612 St. Paul, Denver, CO 80206.

8. Elaine Jahner, a specialist in Lakota language and oral literature, has suggested that the western obsession with western plot in narrative structure led early informant George Sword to construct narratives in the western fashion and tell them as Lakota traditional stories. Research has shown that Sword's stories are not recognized as Lakota traditional stories by Lakotas themselves; but the tribal narratives that are so recognized are loosely structured and do not exhibit the reliance on central theme or character that is so dear to the hearts of western collectors. As time has gone by, the Sword stories have become a sort of model for later Lakota storytellers who, out of a desire to convey the tribal tales to western collectors have changed the old structures to ones more pleasing to American and European ears. Personal conversations with Elaine Jahner.

Education in western schools, exposure to mass media, and the need to function in a white-dominated world have subtly but perhaps permanently altered the narrative structures of the old tales and, with them, the tribal conceptual modes of tribal people. The shift has been away from associative, synchronistic, event-centered narrative and thought to a linear, foreground-centered one. Concurrently, tribal social organization and interpersonal relations have taken a turn toward authoritarian, patriarchal, linear, and misogynist modes—hence the rise of violence against women, an unthinkable event in older, more circular, and tribal times.

Hwame, Koshkalaka, and the Rest: Lesbians in American Indian Cultures

1. I have read accounts that mention American Indian lesbians taken from a variety of sources, but those are all in publications that focus on gays and/or lesbians rather than on Native Americans.

2. Frederick Manfred, *The Manly-Hearted Woman* (New York: Bantam, 1978).

3. Natalie Curtis, *The Indians' Book* (New York: Dover, 1950), p. 4.

4. Bronislaw Malinowski, *Sex, Culture, and Myth* (New York: Harcourt, Brace & World, 1962), p. 12.

5. Malinowski, *Sex, Culture, and Myth*, p. 12.

6. Malinowski, *Sex, Culture, and Myth*, p. 12.

7. Malinowski, *Sex, Culture, and Myth*, p. 13.

8. Malinowski, *Sex, Culture, and Myth*, p. 13.

9. Malinowski, *Sex, Culture, and Myth*, p. 13.

10. Sherry B. Ortner, "Is Female to Male as Nature Is to Culture?" in *Woman, Culture and Society*, ed. Michelle Zimbalist Rosaldo and Louise Lamphere (Stanford: Stanford University Press, 1974), p. 70.

11. John (Fire) Lame Deer and Richard Erdoes, *Lame Deer, Seeker of Visions: The Life of a Sioux Medicine Man* (New York: Simon and Schuster, 1972), pp. 148–149.

12. Lois Paul, "Work and Sex in a Guatemalan Village," in Rosaldo and Lamphere, *Woman, Culture and Society*, pp. 293–298. Paul's article discusses these concepts in the framework of a peasant culture, that is, one that exists in a pastoral, agriculture-centered environment and whose social structure is based on perceived relationship to the land. This type of culture occupies a niche that might be thought of as halfway between industrial urban society and tribal, ritual society.

13. See John Bierhorst, ed., *Four Masterworks of American Indian Literature: Quetzalcoatl/The Ritual of Concolence/Cuceb/The Night Chant* (New York: Farrar, Straus and Giroux, 1974). Fr. Bernard Haile's work is included in Leland C. Wyman, ed., *Beautyway: A Navajo Ceremonial*, Bollingen Series, 53 (New York: Pantheon, 1975).

14. As it is accurately put by Jane Fishburne Collier in "Women in Politics," in Rosaldo and Lamphere, *Woman, Culture and Society*, p. 90.

15. Lame Deer, *Lame Deer, Seeker of Visions*, p. 150.

16. Joan Bamburger, "The Myths of Matriarchy: Why Men Rule in Primitive Society," in Rosaldo and Lamphere, *Woman, Culture and Society*, pp. 260–271.

 Selected
Bibliography

Autobiographies and Biographies

Andrews, Lynn V. *Medicine Woman.* San Francisco: Harper and Row, 1981. Paperback reprint. San Francisco: Harper and Row, 1982.
————. *Flight of the Seventh Moon.* San Francisco: Harper and Row, 1984.
Black Elk (Lakota). *Black Elk Speaks.* Recorded and edited by John G. Neihardt. 1932. Reprint. Lincoln: University of Nebraska Press, 1961; New York: Pocketbooks, 1961.
Blowsnake, Sam (Big Winnebago; Crashing Thunder) (Winnebago). *The Autobiography of a Winnebago.* Edited by Paul Radin. 1920. Reprint. New York: Dover, 1963.
Brant, Beth (Mohawk). *Mohawk Trail.* Ithaca, N.Y.: Firebrand Books, 1985.
Cameron, Anne. *Daughters of Copper Woman.* Vancouver, B.C.: Press Gang, 1981. A tribal biography about Nootka Women.
Campbell, Maria (Metis). *Halfbreed.* Lincoln: University of Nebraska Press, 1973.
Lame Deer, John (Fire) (Lakota), and Richard Erdoes. *Lame Deer: Seeker of Visions: The Life of a Sioux Medicine Man.* New York: Simon and Schuster, 1972. One of the best.
Momaday, N. Scott (Kiowa). *The Way to Rainy Mountain.* Albuquerque: University of New Mexico Press, 1969. Paperback reprint. New York: Ballantine, 1979.
Mountain Wolf Woman (Winnebago). *Mountain Wolf Woman, Sister of Crashing Thunder: The Autobiography of a Winnebago Indian.* Edited by Nancy Oestreich Lurie. Ann Arbor: University of Michigan Press, 1981.

Sekaquaptewa, Helen (Hopi). *Me and Mine: The Life Story of Helen Sekaquaptewa as Told to Louise Udall.* Edited by Louise Udall. Tucson: University of Arizona Press, 1969.

Shaw, Anna Moore (Pima). *A Pima Past.* Tucson: University of Arizona Press, 1974.

Stands-in-Timber, John (Cheyenne). *Cheyenne Memories: A Folk History.* Edited by Margot Liberty and Robert M. Utley. 1967. Reprint. Lincoln: University of Nebraska Press, 1972.

Zitkala Sa (Gertrude Bonnin) (Sioux). *American Indian Stories.* 1921. Reprint. Glorietta, N. Mex.: Rio Grande Press, 1976.

Ethnologies, Histories, and Cultural Analyses

Albers, Patricia, and Beatrice Medicine (Lakota). *The Hidden Half: Studies of Plains Indian Women.* Lanham, Md.: University Press of America, 1983. One of the first sociological studies devoted to the life and culture of American Indian women.

Bataille, Gretchen M., and Kathleen Mullen Sands. *American Indian Women: Telling Their Lives.* Lincoln: University of Nebraska Press, 1984.

Bataille, Gretchen M., Kathleen Mullen Sands, and Charles L. P. Silet, eds. *The Pretend Indians: Images of Native Americans in the Movies.* Ames: University of Iowa Press, 1980. A fascinating and outraging compilation of essays on American Indians in film, including some by American Indian scholars.

Benedict, Ruth. *Tales of the Cochiti Indians.* Albuquerque: University of New Mexico Press, 1981. Contains an introduction by San Juan Pueblo anthropologist Alfonso Ortiz.

Boas, Franz. *Keresan Texts.* 2 vols. American Ethnology Society, 1928. Reprint. New York: AMS, 1974.

Brandon, William. *The Last Americans: The Indian in American Culture.* New York: McGraw-Hill, 1974. Still the most complete and intelligent.

Brown, Dee. *Bury My Heart at Wounded Knee: An Indian History of the American West.* New York: Holt, Rinehart and Winston, 1970. Reprint. New York: Washington Square, 1981.

Clark, Ella E., and Margot Edmonds. *Sacagawea of the Lewis and Clark Expedition.* Berkeley and Los Angeles: University of California Press, 1979. One of the best studies of Sacagawea's life and legend.

Deloria, Vine, Jr. (Lakota). *God Is Red.* New York: Grosset and Dunlap, 1973. Paperback reprint. New York: Dell, Laurel Books, 1983.

Etienne, Mona, and Eleanor Leacock, eds. *Women and Colonization: Anthropological Perspectives.* New York: Praeger, 1980. An important collection of articles on the effects of patriarchal colonization of gynocratic systems.

Foreman, Carolyn Thomas. *Indian Women Chiefs.* Washington, D.C.: Zenger Publishing, 1976. Suggests the enormous amount of study needed on women's roles in tribal cultures.

Foreman, Grant. *Indian Removal: The Emigration of the Five Civilized Tribes of Indians.* Norman: University of Oklahoma Press, 1972.

Selected Bibliography

Grahn, Judy. *Another Mother Tongue: Gay Words, Gay Worlds*. Boston: Beacon Press, 1984.

Gunn, John M. *Schat-Chen: History, Traditions, and Narratives of the Queres Indians of Laguna and Acoma*. Albuquerque: Albright and Anderson, 1917. Reprint. New York: AMS, 1977.

Marriott, Alice. *The Ten Grandmothers*. Norman: University of Oklahoma Press, 1945. Concerned with Kiowa culture and belief and the Ten Grandmother bundles that are the ritual center of Kiowa life. The woman's side of Kiowa tradition.

Matthiessen, Peter. *Indian Country*. New York: Viking, 1984.

——. *In the Spirit of Crazy Horse*. New York: Viking, 1981.

McNickle, D'Arcy (Flathead/Kootenai). *Native American Tribalism: Indian Survivals and Renewals*. London: Oxford University Press, 1973.

Mullett, G. M. *Spider Woman Stories: Legends of the Hopi Indians*. Tucson: University of Arizona Press, 1979. This collection provides material for studying Leslie Marmon Silko's *Ceremony*.

Parsons, Elsie Clews. *Pueblo Indian Religion*. Reprint. Chicago: University of Chicago Press, 1974.

Segal, Charles M., and David C. Stineback. *Puritans, Indians and Manifest Destiny*. New York: Putnam's, 1977.

Steiner, Stan. *The New Indians*. New York: Dell, Delta Books, 1968. An exciting and insightful chapter on contemporary American Indian women.

Tyler, Hamilton A. *Pueblo Gods and Myths*. Norman: University of Oklahoma Press, 1964. One of the most inclusive and quixotic studies of Pueblo theological systems.

Vizenor, Gerald (Chippewa). *The People Named the Chippewa: Narrative Histories*. Minneapolis: University of Minnesota Press, 1984. Profound and moving testament to Indian history.

Vogel, Virgil J. *American Indian Medicine*. New York: Ballantine, 1973.

Voices of the People. *Voices from Wounded Knee, 1973*. Mohawk Nation, via Rooseveltown, New York, 1974. Chronicle and photographs of the Wounded Knee protest of 1973.

Walker, James R. *Lakota Belief and Ritual*. Edited by Elaine Jahner and Raymond DeMallie. Lincoln: University of Nebraska Press, 1980.

——. *Lakota Myth*. Edited by Elaine Jahner. Lincoln: University of Nebraska Press, 1983.

——. *Lakota Society*. Edited by Raymond J. DeMallie. Lincoln: University of Nebraska Press, 1982.

Novels and Fiction

Allen, Paula Gunn (Laguna Pueblo/Lakota). *The Woman Who Owned the Shadows*. Spinsters Ink, 1983. 830 De Haro Street, San Francisco, CA 94107.

Bruchac, Joseph (Abnaki). *The Dreams of Jesse Brown*. Austin, Texas: Cold Mountain Press, 1978. 4705 Sinclair Avenue, Austin, TX 78756.

Erdrich, Louise (Chippewa). *Love Medicine*. New York: Holt, Rinehart and Winston, 1984. Paperback edition: Bantam Windstone, 1985.

Mathews, John Joseph (Osage). *Sundown*. New York: Longmans, Green, 1934.

McNickle, D'Arcy (Flathead/Kootenai). *The Surrounded*. New York: Dodd, Mead, 1936. Paperback reprint. Albuquerque: University of New Mexico Press, 1978.

————. *Wind from an Enemy Sky*. San Francisco: Harper and Row, 1978.

Momaday, N. Scott (Kiowa). *House Made of Dawn*. New York: Harper and Row, 1968. Paperback reprint. New York: Signet, 1969. Won a Pulitzer Prize and set off a renaissance of American Indian writing and publishing.

Mourning Dove (Hum-ishu-Ma) (Okonagon). Introduction and notes by Dexter Fisher. *Cogewea, the Half-Blood*. Lincoln: University of Nebraska Press, 1981.

Ortiz, Simon J. *Howbah Indians*. Tucscon: Blue Moon Press, 1977.

Silko, Leslie Marmon (Laguna Pueblo). *Ceremony*. New York: Viking, 1977. Paperback reprint. New York: Signet, 1978.

Ude, Wayne. *Becoming Coyote*. Amherst, Mass.: Lynx House Press, 1981. Box 800, Amherst, MA 01004.

Vizenor, Gerald (Anishinabe). *Darkness in St. Louis Bearheart*. St. Paul, Minn.: Truck Press, 1978. P.O. Box 4544, Industrial Station, St. Paul, MN 55104.

————. *Earthdivers: Tribal Narratives on Mixed Descent*. Minneapolis: University of Minnesota Press, 1981.

————. *Word Arrows: Indians and Whites in the New Fur Trade*. Minneapolis: University of Minnesota Press, 1978.

Welch, James (Blackfeet/Gros Ventre). *The Death of Jim Loney*. New York: Harper and Row, 1979. Paperback reprint. New York: Bantam, 1980.

————. *Winter in the Blood*. New York: Harper and Row, 1974. Paperback reprint. New York: Bantam, 1975; New York: Perennial Library/Harper and Row, 1981.

Poetry

Allen, Paula Gunn (Laguna Pueblo/Lakota). *Coyote's Daylight Trip*. Albuquerque: La Confluencia, 1978. For copies, write Mama Bears, 6536 Telegraph, Oakland, Calif. 94609.

————. *Shadow Country*. Los Angeles: University of California Native American Center, 1982.

————. *Star Child*. Marvin, S.D.: Blue Cloud Quarterly, 1981.

Bruchac, Joseph (Abnaki). *Entering Onondaga*. Austin, Tex.: Cold Mountain, 1976. 4705 Sinclair Avenue, Austin, TX 78756.

Burns, Diane (Anishinabe/Chemehuevi). *Riding the One Eyed Ford*. New York: Contact II Press, 1981.

Cook-Lynn, Elizabeth (Crow Creek Sioux). *Then Badger Said This.* New York: Vantage, 1977. Poetry, narratives, tribal stories, and history.

Erdrich, Louise (Chippewa). *Jacklight.* New York: Holt, Rinehart and Winston, 1984.

Harjo, Joy (Creek). *She Had Some Horses.* New York: Thunders Mouth Press, 1982.

———. *What Moon Drove Me to This?* San Francisco: Reed and Canon, 1980.

Henson, Lance (Cheyenne). *Buffalo Marrow on Black.* Full Count Press, 1981.

Hogan, Linda (Chickasaw). *Calling Myself Home.* Greenfield Center, N.Y.: Greenfield Review Press, 1978.

———. *Seeing Through the Sun.* Amherst: University of Massachusetts Press, 1985.

Kenny, Maurice (Mohawk). *Blackrobe.* Saranac Lake, N.Y.: North Country Community College Press, 1982.

———. *Greyhounding This America.* Chico, Calif.: Heidelberg Graphics, 1985. 1114 Wendy Street, Chicao, CA 95961.

———. *Is Summer This Bear.* Saranac Lake, N.Y.: Chauncy Press, 1985. Turtle Pond Road, Saranac Lake, NY 12933.

Momaday, N. Scott (Kiowa). *The Gourd Dancer.* New York: Harper and Row, 1976.

northSun, nila (Shoshone/Chippewa). *Diet Pepsi and Nacho Cheese.* Fallon, Nev.: Duck Down Press, 1977.

Ortiz, Simon J. (Acoma Pueblo). *From Sand Creek.* New York: Thunders Mouth Press, 1981.

———. *Going for the Rain.* New York: Harper and Row, 1976.

———. *A Good Journey.* Berkeley: Turtle Island Press, 1977.

Rose, Wendy (Hopi/Miwok). *Lost Copper.* Morongo Indian Reservation, Banning, Calif.: Malki Museum Press, 1980.

———. *What Happened When the Hopi Hit New York.* New York: Strawberry Press, 1982.

Sanchez, Carol Lee (Laguna Pueblo/Lakota). *Excerpts from a Mountain Climber's Handbook.* San Francisco: Taurean Horn and Out West Presses, 1985. 920 Leavenworth, #401, San Francisco, CA 94109.

Silko, Leslie Marmon (Laguna Pueblo). *Laguna Woman.* Greenfield Center, N.Y.: Greenfield Review Press, 1974.

TallMountain, Mary (Koyukan). *There Is No Word for Goodbye.* Marvin, S.D.: Blue Cloud Quarterly, 1981.

Topahanso, Luci (Navajo). *Seasonal Woman.* Santa Fe: Tooth of Time Books, 1982.

Vizenor, Gerald (Anishinabe). *Matsushima.* Minneapolis, Minn.: Nodin Press, 1984.

Welch, James (Blackfeet/Gros Ventre). *Riding the Earthboy 40.* New York: Harper and Row, 1975.

Whiteman, Roberta Hill (Oneida, Wisconsin). *Star Quilt.* Minneapolis, Minn.: Holy Cow! Press, 1984. P.O. Box 618, Minneapolis, MN 55440.

Young Bear, Ray A. (Mesquakie). *Winter of the Salamander*. New York: Harper and Row, 1981.

Collections and Anthologies

Astrov, Margot, ed. *American Indian Prose and Poetry: "The Winged Serpent."* New York: Capricorn Books, 1946. Traditional songs and chants in translation. A classic.

Brant, Beth, ed. (Mohawk). *A Gathering of Spirit*. Rockland, Maine: Sinister Wisdom Books, 1984. P.O. Box 1023, Rockland, Maine 04841. Poetry, short fiction, and personal narratives by American Indian women including American Indian lesbians. A groundbreaking collection.

Bruchac III, Joseph, ed. (Abnaki). *Songs from This Earth from Turtle's Back: Contemporary American Indian Poetry*. Greenfield Center, N.Y.: Greenfield Review Press, 1983. RD 1, Box 80, Greenfield Center, NY 12833. Poetry and bio-poetic statements.

Cochran, Jo (Lakota), J. T. Stewart, and Mayumi Tstakawa, eds. *Gathering Ground: New Writing and Art by Northwest Women of Color*. Seattle: Seal Press, 1984.

Cochran, Jo (Lakota), et al. *Bearing Witness/Sobreviviendo: An Anthology of Native American/Latina Art and Literature*. Special issue, *Calyx: A Journal of Art and Literature by Women* 8:2 (Spring 1984). P.O. Box B, Corvallis, OR 97339.

Conlon, Faith, Rachel da Silva, and Barbara Wilson, eds. *The Things That Divide Us: Stories by Women*. Seattle: Seal Press, 1985. Contains new stories by Vickie L. Sears (Cherokee) and Linda Hogan (Chickasaw).

Curtis, Natalie, recorder and editor. *The Indians' Book: Songs and Legends of the American Indians*. New York: Dover, 1950. Traditional songs and stories from a variety of American Indian tribes. Includes some personal memoirs and history. Superb.

Fisher, Dexter, ed. *The Third Woman: Minority Women Writers of the United States*. Boston: Houghton Mifflin, 1980. Fiction, poetry, and personal narrative by American Indian, Chicana, black, and Asian-American women. Still unmatched.

Green, Rayna, ed. (Cherokee). *That's What She Said: Contemporary Poetry and Fiction by Native American Women*. Bloomington: Indiana University Press, 1984. The most recent and complete collection.

Hobsen, Geary, ed. (Cherokee). *The Remembered Earth: An Anthology of Contemporary Native American Literature*. Albuquerque: University of New Mexico Press, 1980. Essays, poetry, fiction, and drama by American Indian writers. One of the earliest and best anthologies.

Marriott, Alice, and Carol K. Rachlin, eds. *Plains Indian Mythology*. New York: New American Library, 1975. Traditional stories in western translation.

Niatun, Duane, ed. (Klallam). *Carriers of the Dream Wheel: Contemporary Native American Poetry*. San Francisco: Harper and Row, 1975.

Ortiz, Simon, ed. (Acoma Pueblo). *Earth Power Coming*. Tsaile, Navajo Nation, Ariz.: Navajo Community College Press, 1984. Short stories by American Indian writers. An exciting collection.

Pacosz, Cristina V., and Susan Oliver, eds. *Digging for Roots: Works by Women of the North Olympic Peninsula*. Port Townsend, Wash.: Empty Bowl, 1945. Box 646, Port Townsend, WA 98368.

Rosen, Kenneth, ed. *The Man to Send Rainclouds*. New York: Seaver Books, 1975. Short stories by American Indian writers.

———. *Voices of the Rainbow: Contemporary Poetry by American Indians*. New York: Seaver Books, 1975.

Silko, Leslie Marmon (Laguna Pueblo). *Storyteller*. New York: Seaver Books, 1981.

Verble, Sedelta, ed. *Words of Today's American Indian Women: Ohoyo Makachi*. Wichita Falls, Tex.: U.S. Department of Education and Ohoyo Resource Center, 1981. 2301 Midwestern Parkway, Suite 214, Wichita Falls, TX 76308.

Critical Studies

Allen, Paula Gunn, ed. (Laguna Pueblo/Lakota). *Studies in American Indian Literature: Critical Essays and Course Designs*. New York: Modern Language Association, 1983. Includes materials for use in American studies, women's studies, and the arts.

Castro, Michael. *Interpreting the Indian: Twentieth-Century Poets and the Native American*. Albuquerque: University of New Mexico Press, 1983.

Chapman, Abraham. *Literature of the American Indians: Views and Interpretations*. New York: New American Library, 1975. Includes a number of essays by American Indian scholars.

Larson, Charles R. *American Indian Fiction*. Albuquerque: University of New Mexico Press, 1978.

Lincoln, Kenneth. *Native American Renaissance*. Berkeley and Los Angeles: University of California Press, 1983. Very useful in reading and teaching contemporary American Indian works.

Swann, Brian, ed. *Smoothing the Ground: Essays on Native American Oral Literature*. Berkeley and Los Angeles: University of California Press, 1983.

Velie, Alan R. *Four American Indian Literary Masters: Scott Momaday, James Welch, Leslie Marmon Silko, and Gerald Vizenor*. Norman: University of Oklahoma Press, 1982.

Permissions
Acknowledgments

Grateful acknowledgment is made to the following for permission to reprint: "Whose Dream Is This Anyway: Remythologizing and Self-Definition in Contemporary American Indian Fiction" by Paula Gunn Allen is reprinted from *Literature and the Visual Arts in Contemporary Society, U.S.A. 20/21: Studies in Recent American History*, No. 2, ed. Suzanne Ferguson and Barbara Groseclose. Copyright © 1985 by Ohio State University Press. All Rights Reserved. Reprinted by permission. For the excerpts from *Black Elk Speaks* by John G. Neihardt. Copyright © John Neihardt, 1932, 1959. Published by Simon & Schuster, Pocket Books, and the University of Nebraska Press. Permission granted by the John G. Neihardt Trust. For the excerpts from *Ceremony* by Leslie Marmon Silko. Copyright © 1977 by Leslie Silko. Reprinted by permission of Viking Penguin Inc. For the lines from "The Way and the Way Things Are," "My Cousin Shadow," and "Moving Camp Too Far" by nila northsun from *Diet Pepsi, Nacho Cheese* (P.O. 1047, Fallon, Nevada: Duck Down Press, 1977), reprinted by permission of the author. The lines from "I Came Far Today" by Jeff Saunders from *Four Indian Poets*, John Milton, ed. (Dakota Press, 1974), reprinted by permission of the publisher. The lines from "Toward Spider Spring" by J. Simon Ortiz from *Going for the Rain* (Harper & Row, 1976), reprinted by permission of the author. The lines from "Vickie Loans Arrow, 1971," and "Vickie Loans Arrow, 1972" by Marnie Walsh from *A Taste of the Knife* (Boise: Ahsahta Press at Boise State University, 1976), reprinted by permission of the author. The lines from "Blackfeet, Blood and Peigan Hunters" by James Welch from *Riding the Earthboy, 40*

(Harper & Row, 1976), by permission of Harper & Row, Publishers, Inc., copyright © 1971, 1976, by James Welch. The lines from "Winter Indian" by James Welch, reprinted by permission of the author. The lines from "Leap in the Dark" by Roberta Hill Whiteman from Star Quilt (Holy Cow! Press, 1984), reprinted by permission of the author and publisher. The lines from "Blessings" by Linda Hogan, from Calling Myself Home (Greenfield Review Press, 1978), reprinted by permission of the author. The lines from "Morning: The World in the Lake" and "The Woman Speaking" by Linda Hogan from Seeing Through the Sun (University of Massachusetts Press, 1985), copyright © 1985 by Linda Hogan, reprinted by permission of the author. "Figure in Clay" and the lines from "The Last Wolf" by Mary TallMountain from There Is No Word for Goodbye (Blue Cloud Quarterly, 1980), reprinted by permission of the author. The lines from "I Expected My Skin and My Blood to Ripen" by Wendy Rose from Lost Copper (Morongo Indian Reservation: Malki Museum Press, 1981), reprinted by permission of the author. "Affirmative Action, Berkeley, 1977" by Wendy Rose, reprinted by permission of the author. The lines from "Toe'osh: A Laguna Coyote Story" by Leslie Marmon Silko from Storyteller (Viking, 1981), reprinted by permission of the author. The lines from "Contradictions" by Elizabeth Cook-Lynn from Then Badger Said This (Fairfield, Washington: Ye Gallem Press, 1983), reprinted by permission of the author. The lines from "3 AM" by Joy Harjo from The Last Song (Puerto del Sol Press, 1975), reprinted by permission of the author. The lines from "Moonlight" by Joy Harjo, from What Moon Drove Me to This (Reed and Cannon, 1979) and She Had Some Horses (Thunder Mouth Press, 1983), reprinted by permission of the author. "The Song, the Dance, the Poem" by Carol Lee Sanchez, reprinted by permission of the author.

INDEX

Abanaki Indians, 23
Abzug, Bella, 214
Acoma Indians, 48, 101, 132, 197, 223, 232; tales about, 158, 226. *See also* Pueblo Indians
Activism, 168, 236; alienation and, 132, 136; tribal society difference from, 2. *See also* Feminism
Adair, John, 32
Albuquerque *Journal*, 31
Alcoholism, 134, 140, 143, 191; and fetal alcohol syndrome, 280n1
Aleut Indians, 197, 198
Algonkian Indians (Mid-Atlantic Coastal), 33, 34, 36, 264
Alienation, 87, 127–46, 162, 169, 170, 210; of "breeds," 129–30, 139, 140, 141, 158; of English-speaking people, 60; of Yellow Woman, 227
Allen, Paula Gunn, 82, 98, 197, 214, 264
All Power, 22
All-Spirit, 56, 57, 60, 68, 70. *See also* Great Spirit; Maheo
American Indian history, 101; Anglo-European/American view of, 49, 151, 211, 214; distortion of, *see* Patriarchy;

women disregarded in, 11, 34, 35–36, 263. *See also* Western/non-Indian thought
American Indian literature, 53–183; alienation as theme in, 127–46; categories of, 4, 71, 72; ceremony and myth as basic forms of, 61–64, 72–75 (*see also* Ceremony; Myth); colonization as theme in, *see* Colonization; critics of, 265–67; distortion of, *see* Patriarchy; egalitarianism reflected in, 59; as "folklore," 54, 67; future trends in, 263–68; humor in, 158–60; importance of, 42; interrelation of forms of, 62; loss of, 55; male tradition in, 86–87; narrative structure of, 240–42; novels/fiction, 76–101, 208; oral nature of, 66 (*see also* Oral tradition); poetry, 149–50, 155–83, 208; simplicity of, 70; stereotypes in, 78, 132, 151, 179; symbolism in, *see* Symbolism; western view of/difference from, 54–55, 62, 67–68, 72, 74, 79–85 *passim*, 109, 180, 235, 237, 241–44; by women, 81–84 *passim*, 95–101, 118–26, 130–41 *passim*, 144–45, 147–83, 187, 208, 243, 264–65

297

Index

American Indian Movement, 200
Andrews, Lynn, 77
Anishinabe Indians, 82, 97
Anthony, Susan B., 213
Apache Indians, 64, 197, 280n1
Apartheid, 190. *See also* Government policy
"Apples," 134, 135. *See also* Alienation
Arapaho Indians, 254
Arrow Youth, 28–29
Astrov, Margot, 64, 66–67, 68
Athabasca Indians, 156, 172
Atseye, Meta, 283n1
Awashonks (Sakonnet sunksquaw), 35
Aztec Indians, 20, 53, 197

Balboa, Vasco Núñez de, 198
Bambara, Toni Cade, 4
Bancroft, Hubert H., 199, 215
Bari Indians, 32, 33
Bear Man, 21
Bear Sings (wise man), 114
Beautyway (ceremonial), 21, 257. *See also* Chantways (healing ceremonies)
Beloved Woman of the Nation, *see* Cherokee Indians
"Berdaches," *see* Homosexuality (gay males and lesbians)
Beverley, Robert, 35
Bias, *see* Cultural bias
Bird Grandparents, 25–26. *See also* Grandmother(s)
Bird Woman, *see* Sacagawea
Black, 114. *See also* Color, significance of
Black Elk: vision of, 107–16, 274n10. *See also* Vision(s)
Black Elk Speaks (Neihardt), 1, 108
Blackfeet Indians, 82, 91, 92
Black Road (medicine man), 113
Blavatsky, Mme. Helena, 69
Blood: and kinship, 251 (*see also* Tribal systems); menstrual or postpartum, 28 (*see also* Menstruation/menstrual blood); in sacrifice, 28
Blue, *see* Color, significance of
Blue Corn (sister of Yellow Woman), 227
Boas, Franz, 116
Brandon, William: quoted, 215
Brant, Beth, 264
Brant, Molly, 263

"Breeds," *see* Alienation
British, the, 35, 37. *See also* Colonization
Broken Prayer Sticks, *see* Remembering Prayer Sticks
Brothers Three (Oskison), 77
Boudinot, Elias, 37, 38
Bundles, *see* Grandmother bundles; Medicine bundles
Burns, Diane, 264

Cacique (Tiamuni Hotchin; "inside," "white," "town," "Mother" chief), 17–22 *passim*, 26, 29, 223n, 232–33, 269n1; Naotsete as prototype for, 20 (*see also* Uretsete and Naotsete); Yellow Woman as, 226. *See also* Hotchin; Sunksquaws
Calendar, *see* Time (ritual)
Canada, 196; Indian situation in, 40, 201
Carpenter, Edward, 197
Castaneda, Carlos, 68, 77, 104
Catholic Church, *see* Christianity
Catlin, George, 199–200
Ceremony: dance and song as elements in, 64, 73, 74 (*see also* Dances; Songs); defined, 61; drum used in, 64, 205; efficacy of, 18; healing, *see* Chantways; holistic/interrelated structure of, 62–63; purpose of, 62–63; repetition in, 63–68; rhythmic form of, 63, 64; secrecy in, 74–75. *See also* Sacred ritual
Ceremony (Silko), 82, 95–97, 118–26, 140–41, 145, 147, 152
Changing Woman (Navajo), 41
Chantways (healing ceremonies), 21, 60, 68, 88, 205; Mountain Chant (Navajo), 64–66, 69; Night Chant (Navajo), 61, 81, 89, 257
Cheani, *see* Medicine men
Cherokee Indians, 25, 40, 41, 76, 108, 206, 220; ceremonial fire of, 19, 80; constitution of, 37–38; Women's Council and Beloved Woman of, 32, 36–38
Cherokee Phoenix (periodical), 38
Cheyenne Indians, 197, 198; creation story of, 57–59; prophet and savior of, *see* Sweet Medicine Man; saying of, on endurance, 212, 267
Chickasaw Indians, 155, 168
Chief: Corn Woman (Naiya Iyatiku) as, 17

298

Index

Cortés, Hernán, 282n7
Coyote tales, 158
Coyote Woman, 45
Crazy Horse (Sioux leader), 115, 263, 266
Creation: Christian vs. non-Christian view of, 15, 56–58; by "Grandmothers," 200–201 (*see also* Grandmother[s]); Keres story regarding, *see* Keres Indians; ongoing, human role in, 57, 67, 73, 206; and women as vitalizers, *see* Childbirth. *See also* Creatrix, the
Creatrix, the, 14, 15–16, 30, 119, 264; and Original or Creation Thinking, 29; replaced by Creator, 41; Thought Woman as, *see* Spider Old Woman/Thought Woman. *See also* Feminine power
Cree Indians, 92, 141–42
Creek Indians, 158, 160, 166, 197
Crow Indians, 32, 158, 197, 198, 252–53
"Crying for pity" (vision quest), *see* Vision(s)
Cultural bias, 67–68, 225; antibackground, 75, 77–78, 96, 244; antipatriarchal (of feminists), 235; European vs. American, 217; homophobic, 198–99, 200, 280n1; male/patriarchal, 4, 216, 222–23, 224, 283–84n6, 250, 266, 268; racist, 77, 191, 192, 198, 235, 280n1, 283n6; Southwestern vs. Plains, 145. *See also* Christianity; Colonization; Male dominance; Media, the; Patriarchy; "Savages"; Western/non-Indian thought
Curtis, Natalie, 116
Custer, George A., 276–77n12

Dances: dream dances, 204; as element in ceremony, 62–63, 64, 115; '49s, 74; Ghost Dance, 115; green-corn, deer, and Feast Day dances, 150, 179; hoop dance, 4; Horse Dance, 112, 114; mask dances (Kochinnenako), 233, 237, 238; rain dances, 63; Sun Dance (wiwanyag wachipi), 61, 62, 205; suppression of (by government, 1920), 199; Zuni dance (Shalako), 73. *See also* Ceremony
Darkness in Saint Louis Bearheart, The (Vizenor), 82, 95, 97–98

Darwinian theory, 68
Death of Jim Loney, The (Welch), 82, 91, 93–94, 141, 142–43, 145, 152
Death ritual, death song, 86, 267. *See also* Sacred ritual; Songs
Decision-making, *see* Feminine power
Deity: as generic concept, 41 (*see also* Great Spirit); Woman as, *see* Woman
Democracy: American concept of, 218, 219; by coercion, 41
Diego, Juan, 26, 45
Direction: orientation to, 110. *See also* West, the (as symbol)
Divorce, *see* Marriage
Dream(s), 22, 204–5, 258; gender designation based on, 196–97; vision equated with, 91, 92, 93, 100, 205, 264, 266 (*see also* Vision[s])
Dream Dances of the Kashia Pomo (film), 204
Dreamer, the (goddess), 98, 204–5, 264, 266, 268. *See also* Spider Old Woman/Thought Woman
Drum, use of, *see* Ceremony
Dumarest, Fr. Noel, 16
Dye, Eva Emery, 215, 220

Eagle Wing Stretches (visionary figure), 111, 112
Earth: as being, 119; femaleness of, 19, 122; -island ("Turtle Island"), 15, 195
Earth Woman, *see* Corn or Earth Woman
Education: enforced, 39, 40, 192, 195; lack of, 42; and miseducation, 216 (*see also* Cultural bias); oral tradition and, 15, 206–7
Egalitarianism, 211, 218, 240–41; contemporary, 33, 217, 220, 223; gynecentric, 33, 40, 195, 223, 266; literature reflecting, 59
Einsteinian energy, 60
Eisenhower administration, 31
Elderly, the: treatment of, 49, 191, 192, 211
Eldest God, 11. *See also* Grandmother(s)
Emma (West German feminist monthly), 201
Endurance, *see* Survival
Energy: Einsteinian vs. Indian view of, 60

Index

Engels, Friedrich, 214, 220
Erdoes, Richard, 258
Eskimo tribes, 197
Esopus Indians, Esopus Confederacy, 35
Evans, Arthur, 197
Extinction, *see* Genocide

Fallacy, "Progressive," "Romantic," 5, 129
Family, *see* Tribal systems
Faulkner, William, 4
Feather Boy medicine bundle, 84–85. *See also* Medicine bundles
Federalist period/federal system, 218–19
"Femaleness": of sun and earth, 19; value of, 212
Feminine power: childbearing as source of, 207, 213, 251, 254, 255 (*see also* Childbirth); creative, 15, 16, 22, 201 (*see also* Creatrix, the); decision-making, 3, 40, 201, 205, 207, 212–13, 219, 220; embodied in Kochinnenako, 233; loss of, 33, 40–42, 48–49; medicine/sacred, legends of, 16, 19, 22–29, 98; political, 31–42, 212–13, 219–20; ritual/tribal, 44, 47–48, 50, 202–7 *passim*, 253, 259–60, 265; ritual imitation of, 255. *See also* Power
Feminism: American/western, 166, 206, 213; history of, 213–16; and Iroquois feminist rebellion (c. 1600), 213; lesbian, 187; modern theories of, 11, 220, 234–37; in "patriarchal trap," 283–84n6; and rejection of tradition, 210; tribal, 213, 220, 222–26, 237–40; West German, 201; white domination of, 224. *See also* Gynecentrism; Gynocracy/gynarchy
"Fertility goddess," 14
Fetal alcohol syndrome, 280n1. *See also* Alcoholism
Finnegans Wake (Joyce), 81
Fire: ceremonial, 80; femaleness of (external/internal), 19
Fire Society goddess, 26. *See also* Corn or Earth Woman (Naiya Iyatiku)
First Mother, First Woman, 3, 23–25, 247. *See also* Mother, Great Mother; Grandmother(s); Woman

Five "Civilized" Tribes, 20
Five Fires (Iroquois Nations), 212. *See also* Iroquois Indians
"Folklore," *see* American Indian literature
Foreman, Carolyn, 32
'49s (dances), 74. *See also* Dances
Four: as sacred number, 72, 276n14
Four Winds (as beings), 16–17
Fox, George, 35
Fox Indians, 197, 198, 199
Frazer, Sir James, 107
French Revolution, 219
Freudian theory, 68, 71

Gay males, *see* Homosexuality (gay males and lesbians)
Gender change in traditional tales, 19–20, 41, 269–70n3
Gender roles, 31, 43; colonization and, 202–3; dual, of supreme Spirit, 15; within gynocracy, 2, 202; homosexuality and, 196–97, 202; and traditional occupations, 243; training for, 206–7; tribal understanding of, 82, 202, 208
Genocide, 3, 5, 6, 11, 36, 129, 190; and belief in imminent extinction, 155–63 *passim*, 193, 267–68; infant mortality and, 189, 191; literature as resistance to, 42; prohibition of ritual and, 195; as theme of novels, 78, 81. *See also* Colonization; Survival
Geronimo (warrior), 56
Ghost Dance, 115. *See also* Dances
Goetz, Delia, 25
Golden Bough, The (Frazer), 107
Goldman, Emma, 214
Gold rush, 76
Government, American, 218–19. *See also* Democracy; Government policy
Government policy: apartheid, 190; tribal, 203; U.S., 31, 32, 37–38, 182–83, 189–93 *passim*, 201, 216. *See also* Colonization
Grahn, Judy, 4, 197, 198, 214
Grandfathers of Powers of the Six Directions, 110–15 *passim*
Grandmother(s), 11, 194, 203, 205, 208, 214, 241, 265, 268; as Creatrix, 200–201; return of, 188; of the sun, 19, 26;

Index

Index

Index

Index

Index

Survival, 2, 101, 158, 189–93, 267–68; Cheyenne saying in regard to, 212, 267; equated with patriarchy, 42; loss of values in, 192; politics of, 168. *See also* Genocide

Susquehanna Indians, 32

Sweet Medicine Man (Cheyenne religious figure), 105, 107, 108, 115, 128, 263

Sword, George, 284n8

Symbolism: in everyday world, 69–71, 75; female, 119, 187; in literary forms, 61, 63, 75, 81; in myth, 108, 112, 114, 115, 116; male, 267; shift of, from war to peace, 265; symbolic childbirth ("rope baby"), 258

Taboos, 28, 47, 75, 197. *See also* Sacred ritual

Talcot, Major (defeats Narragansetts), 33

TallMountain, Mary Randle, 156, 172–73, 175, 264

Tawa, *see* Maseo or Tawa

Thought Woman, *see* Spider Old Woman/Thought Woman

Thunder (god or symbol), 41, 109

Tiamuni Hotchin, *see* Cacique

Tibetan culture, 5

Timberlake, Lt. Henry, 36

Time: perception of, 59, 147–54; ritual, 94, 233, 238, 240

Tinotzin, *see* Guadalupe, Our Lady of/La Virgin de

Tlingit Indians, 108, 197

Tobacco, 24, 25

Tradition: American Indian valuation of, 210–11; and gender change of goddesses, 19–20, 41, 269–70n3; and identity, 210, 224; rejection of, 210, 211 (*see also* Colonization; Cultural bias); women disregarded in, 263. *See also* American Indian history; American Indian literature; Oral tradition

Tribal systems: centrality of relationship in, 59, 60; Christianization effect on, *see* Christianity; "democracy" substituted for, 41; dual/complementary structure within, 18–22, 31–32; family/"household" in, 33, 42, 49–50, 247–52, 256 (*see also* Children; Marriage); gay males

and lesbians within, *see* Homosexuality; kinship within, 23, 212, 251, 278n12; longhouse (or clan), decline in importance of, 33, 201; nuclear family replacing, 33, 42; patriarchal, *see* Patriarchy; ritual centers of, 80; "stasis" of, 56; Western misunderstanding of, 4 (*see also* Western/non-Indian thought); woman-centered, *see* Gynocracy/gynarchy; women's needs disregarded by, 203; worldwide culture shared by, 5–6

Trickster tales, 74, 97–98. *See also* American Indian literature; Oral tradition

Trobriand Islands, 248

Tubman, Harriet, 214

Turkey-Buzzard Spirit, 29

Turner, Frederick III, 56, 59

Turtle Island (New World), 15, 195

Twins, 20, 226, 227. *See also* Little War Twins; Sacred Twins; Uretsete and Naotsete

Tyler, Hamilton, 197

Umane (power), 72

Underhill, Ruth, 116

Unemployment, 42, 189

Universe, the: perception of (Indian vs. Western), 55, 57, 59–61, 75, 80, 165–66, 244; Six Powers of, 112; woman as center of, 22

University of California (Berkeley), 204

University of New Mexico, 1, 154

Urbanization, 31, 96, 192

Uretsete and Naotsete, 13, 16, 19, 28, 98–99, 122; as prototypes for hotchin and cacique, 20 (*see also* Cacique; Hotchin); Uretsete equated with Iyatiku, 20, 99 (*see also* Corn or Earth Woman). *See also* Twins

U.S. government, *see* Government, American; Government policy

Utset (Supernatural Woman), 25, 41

Values, 29, 192, 210. *See also* Cultural bias; Sacred ritual; Tradition

Vietnam War, 21

Villon, François, 214

309

Index

Violence: alienation and, 128, 138–39; child abuse, *see* Children; distaste for, 18, 88, 238; and murder penalty, 32; and survival, 192; against women (wife-abuse, rape, battery, murder), 5, 37, 44–45, 50, 190, 191, 192, 202, 203, 206, 224, 240. *See also* War

Virgin Morena, *see* Guadalupe, Our Lady of/La Virgin de

Vision(s): of Black Elk, 107–16, 274n10; dream equated with, *see* Dream(s); and myth, 107, 108–17; normality of, 168; power conferred by, 109–13; and vision quest (hanblecheya, "crying for pity" ritual), 62, 81, 91, 92, 93, 108, 113, 115

Vizenor, Gerald, 82, 95, 97–98, 101, 264

Voting rights: lack of, for women and blacks, 37; women's suffrage movement and, 215

Wakaŋ Tanka (Life-Bestower), 61, 62

Walotowa Indians, 87, 88, 94

Walsh, Marnie, 133, 136

Wampanoag Confederacy, 34, 35

War: imperialist, 214 (*see also* Colonization); Indian distaste for, 21, 227, 265, 266 (*see also* Pacifism); Iroquois feminist rebellion against, 213; and Little War Twins, 19; undeclared, against Native Americans, 195, 266; and "war captain," "war chief," 18, 19, 29, 212, 271n17 (*see also* Hotchin); and war ceremonies, 21, 63, 271n17, 275n23; and women as warriors, 36. *See also* Violence

War (or Pretty) Woman, 36, 37

Ward, Nancy ("Beloved Woman"), 38, 263

Warrior Priest, 21

Water: significance of, 14, 15, 24–25, 27

Water Fowl (saves Sky Woman), 15, 25

Water of life, 28. *See also* Menstruation/menstrual blood

Waters, Frank, 77

Water Winged Beings, 25

Weetamoo (Pocasset sunksquaw), 35

Welch, James, 81, 82, 86, 90–95 *passim*, 135–45 *passim*, 151–52, 264

West, the (as symbol): color of, 114; Pow-er or Grandfather of, 110, 111; vision of or from, 109–10

Western/non-Indian thought: on Indians as "savages," *see* "Savages"; on literature and tribal narrative, 54–55, 62, 67–68, 71–75, 78–85 *passim*, 109, 180, 235, 237, 241–44; on the supernatural, 59–60; on time and space, 59, 149, 150–51; on tribal systems, 4, 7, 250; on the universe, 55, 60; on women, 149, 202, 243–44, 252, 255, 262–68. *See also* Christianity; Colonization; Cultural bias; Media, the; White men

White, *see* Color, significance of

White Buffalo Cow Woman, *see* Sacred Pipe

White chief, *see* Cacique

White Corn (sister of Yellow Woman), 227

Whiteman, Roberta Hill, 162

White men: culture of, influenced by Indian culture, 217–18; government policies of, *see* Government policy; tribal dealings with, 20, 236; Sioux view of, 69. *See also* Colonization; Western/non-Indian thought

White Roots of Peace, 212. *See also* Iroquois Indians

White towns, 37

White Village, *see* Kush Katret

Whitman, Walt, 4

Wilken, Michael, 197

Williams, Roger, 34

Williams, Walter, 198

Williams, William Carlos, 4

Wilson, Dick, 1

Wind from an Enemy Sky (McNickle), 84–85, 151

Winds, *see* Four Winds (as beings)

Winkte, 258–59. *See also* Homosexuality (gay males and lesbians)

Winnebago Indians, 97, 160, 197, 198

Winnemucca, Sara, 263

Winter in the Blood (Welch), 82, 86, 90–93, 141, 143–44, 145, 152

Winter Spirit, *see* Sh-ah-cock

Witchcraft/witchery: as evil, 61, 87, 89, 96–97, 118–19, 123, 124, 125, 138–39, 141, 152; lesbianism and, 257; respect for, 90. *See also* Supernatural, the

Index

Wiwanyag wachipi (Sun Dance), *see* Dances

Woman: as Creatrix, *see* Creatrix, the; First, *see* First Mother, First Woman; Grandmother(s); as Supreme Spirit, *see* Spirit(s); symbolized, 119, 187; as thought or Deity, 11, 255, 257, 264, 268 (*see also* Spider Old Woman/Thought Woman). *See also* Woman (American Indian)

Woman-centered society, *see* Gynocracy/gynarchy

Woman Who Owned the Shadows, The (Allen), 82, 98–100, 147, 152

Women (American Indian): abstract thinking by, 179; as "chattels," 37; as chiefs, *see* Sunksquaws; colonizers' view and treatment of, *see* Colonization; decision-making by, *see* Feminine power; definitions of, 30, 43; disregarded, devalued, *see* American Indian history; Christianity; Western/non-Indian thought; and gender change of goddesses, *see* Gender change in traditional tales; lesbian, *see* Homosexuality (gay males and lesbians); liberation of, 220; menstruation of, *see* Menstruation/menstrual blood; power of, *see* Feminine power; responsibility of, for oral tradition, 205, 206–7; role models of, 2, 227 (*see also* Gender roles); as shamans, *see* Shamans and shamanism; status of, 30–42, 48–49, 59, 193, 195, 196, 202–3, 211, 224, 232, 235, 243, 252–53, 265; violence against, *see* Violence; as vitalizers, *see* Childbirth; as warriors, 36; as writers, 243, 264 (*see also* American Indian literature). *See also* Woman

Women's Council, *see* Cherokee Indians

World War II, 21, 125

Wovoka (Paiute holy man), 115, 263

Wúwuchim (cosmic cycle), 73

Yaya (religious leader of tribe), 17

Yellow, *see* Color, significance of

Yellow Woman (Kochinnenako), 6, 29, 45, 128; sisters of, 227; stories about, 223, 226–40, 242, 244. *See also* Corn Mother (Irriaku)

Yokut Indians, 198

Young, Fred, 147, 150, 154

Young Bear, Ray, 264

Yuki Indians, 197

Yuma Indians, 196–97, 198

Yurok Indians, 32, 198

Zeisberger, David, 34

Zuñi Indians, 41, 73, 197, 198

3